CONTESTED BOUNDARIES

CONTESTED BOUNDARIES

Itinerancy and the Reshaping

of the Colonial American Religious World

Timothy D. Hall

DUKE UNIVERSITY PRESS Durham & London 1994

Printed in the United States of America on acid-free paper ∞
Typeset in New Baskerville by Tseng Information Systems.
Library of Congress Cataloging-in-Publication Data
appear on the last printed page of this book.

For Sheree,

my love, my soul mate

Contents

ACKNOWLEDGMENTS

AS IN ANY SCHOLARLY endeavor, the author of this work can take only partial credit for its insights while assuming full responsibility for its shortcomings. Among the many friends, colleagues, and family who have offered encouragement along the way, I owe none a greater debt of gratitude than my wife, Sheree. This book is the beneficiary of her excellent editing skills, but my debt to her extends vastly further. She has given me freely her patient, loyal love as we juggled writing, careers, and rearing small children. It is no small mercy that our bond of affection has grown stronger through these years, and we delight in each other's love and friendship now more than ever.

Second only to my debt to Sheree is that to my mentor at Northwestern University, T. H. Breen, without whose early faith in my work this project would never have been initiated. His imaginative scholarship set a high standard to which I continue to aspire, and his acute criticism and steady support prompted me to do my best. He also worked hard to help me obtain the funding necessary to continue my work, and I owe him public thanks for all he has done on my behalf. The other two members of my dissertation committee also deserve my thanks. To valuable scholarly example and professional guidance, James Oakes added personal friendship. I benefited greatly from his keen insight into various strands of critical theory. Karen Halttunen uniquely combined warm personal encouragement with demanding standards of scholarship.

Many others have helped in this project at various stages along the way. Nathan Hatch of the University of Notre Dame and Mark

Noll of Wheaton College each took time out of their busy schedules to read and comment on an early paper that became the basis for the third chapter of this book. Samuel S. Hill of the University of Florida offered valuable encouragement and advice as I was revising the manuscript for publication. Philip Richards of Colgate University likewise offered encouragement during this stage. Barry Shain of Colgate provided the searching, honest criticism of a true friend and the encouragement of a like-minded colleague. Rachel Toor of Duke University Press supplemented valuable editorial assistance with personal encouragement.

I am also grateful to several institutions for providing the financial support that made possible the timely completion of this project. Northwestern University offered the support of a dissertation fellowship. The Society of Colonial Wars in the State of Illinois provided summer research funds, and the Charlotte W. Newcombe Foundation provided a year-long dissertation fellowship. I hope that the finished product in some measure merits this generosity.

Finally, I wish to thank my parents, Wesley and Norma Hall, for their unfailing love and support. Their love for history inspired my own, and their confidence in me prompted me to "finish what I'd started."

Itinerancy - the travelling ministry.

INTRODUCTION

I

IN JUNE 1769, Mary Cooper visited the Quaker meeting in Oyster Bay, Long Island "where a multitude were geathered to here a woman preach that lately came from England." Four days later she noted the presence of "One Indan [*sic*] preacher" in the town. One August Sabbath "some Indans and one Black man came from Montalk" and preached all day. The next week Mary went to "New Light meeten to here a Black man preach." Two days later she and fellow travellers to New England encountered a man whose diatribes against "Mr. Whitefield," the famous English itinerant, proved "as much and something mor than we could well beare to." In late November she again found herself "hurreing to meeten" to hear two Indian preachers who had just arrived in town. They remained for more than a week, holding "very happy meetens" in various places as "greate numbers flocked to here them."[1]

Cooper punctuated her private reflections with reports of visiting preachers from distant places; black and red as well as white, Quaker as well as Baptist and Congregational, female as well as male. Most were "well received" by the people of Cooper's community, and their preaching often left the townspeople's souls "much affected." Cooper and her neighbors were ready to attend any of four different Oyster Bay meetinghouses and a number of private dwellings any time a visiting preacher passed through. She never recorded a firsthand encounter with the preaching of George Whitefield, yet like evangelical Anglo-Americans everywhere she held the "grand itinerant" in high esteem.

The passage of itinerants through Mary Cooper's life suggests how eighteenth-century Anglo-Americans employed religious categories to construe their social world. The freedom with which Cooper and her neighbors welcomed so broad a spectrum of itinerant preachers clashes with the view that evangelical religion constituted a reaction against the forces of change in eighteenth-century life.[2] It implies instead an openness in the religious sphere to an expanding array of choices for belief and behavior in an increasingly mobile, pluralistic world. Situated in its context of dynamic eighteenth-century growth, the exploration of itinerancy as a category of thought as well as a method of preaching illuminates the colonists' creative response to economic, social, and cultural change.

II

Mary Cooper's ready acceptance of itinerant preachers would have appalled ecclesiastical leaders of the 1740s, who construed the flood of New Light itinerancy as something new and threatening.[3] George Whitfield's unprecedented tours through the colonies in 1740 sparked a debate that intensified with the subsequent proliferation of local imitators. Opponents complained that Whitefield and other "stranger ministers" were not content to confine their "roving preachments" to regions lacking a regular settled ministry in the manner of itinerating missionaries. Instead they intruded into settled parishes or pulpits, denounced local ministers, and preached "extempore" sermons that lashed audiences into frenzies of anguish over the state of their souls. The resulting chaos triggered a newspaper and pamphlet war over itinerancy in Boston. Alarmed Connecticut clergymen provoked defenders of the local "Pedlars in Divinity" by persuading the colony's assembly to pass the Act for Regulating Abuses and Correcting Disorders in Ecclesiastical Affairs, which sought to prohibit itinerancy.[4] Many New England clergymen regarded the practice as a threat to the foundations of the social order.[5]

Controversy over itinerant preaching was not confined to New England. It broke out sporadically along the Atlantic coast throughout the remainder of the colonial period.[6] Well before Boston's pamphlet wars had peaked, strife between Log College itinerants and conservative clergy in the Synod of Philadelphia drove the fledgling Presbyterian denomination to open schism. In 1745 the appearance of New Side Presbyterian itinerants in Hanover, Virginia sparked conflict over the practice with the Established church and government officials in that colony. The rise of the Baptists there in the 1760s brought a second wave of controversy over itinerancy that did not subside until the passage of the new state's Act for Establishing Religious Freedom in 1786.

Everywhere the itinerants went, newspaper accounts tracked them, carrying the controversy over itinerancy and "enthusiasm" beyond the confines of parish, denomination, and colony to an intercolonial reading public. Revivalists sought for a time to supplement the newspapers with a periodical containing revival accounts from all over the British Empire.[7] Ministers, government officials, and laymen recorded opinions concerning the phenomenon in diaries as well as in private and official correspondence. Many also chose letters to the editor, pamphlets, or books as weapons in the battle over the revivals. As a result, a huge body of evidence has survived suggesting that this transatlantic event, which contemporaries called a "great awakening" (pace the historian Jon Butler), challenged institutional structures as well as categories of thought and language.[8]

Viewed from the perspective of the debate over itinerancy, the Great Awakening reveals itself as nothing less than a system of meaning that helped participants to construe a particular social world and to situate themselves within it. Social theorists since Max Weber and Emile Durkheim have recognized the inseparability of human action from some overarching interpretive framework, also termed "cosmology" or "worldview," which situates that action within a meaningful, ordered, socially construed reality.[9] This framework is a product of two components: first, the social, historical, economic, environmental, and psychologial elements which constitute the underlying conditions of a society; second, a complex of symbols, concepts, or categories "strategically oriented" to select and interpret those conditions and human activity within them. Those categories, moreover, are oriented toward action and shaped by interaction as well as contemplation.[10]

People living in a stable social and economic environment may experience such a worldview as a set of unexamined assumptions which members of the society hold as too obvious to question.[11] Even as circumstances begin to change, human interpretive activity is capable of gradual accommodations that can preserve underlying assumptions from criticism for long periods of time. Yet persistent change in social conditions may eventually outstrip a given worldview's capacity to adapt, provoking a crisis as the members of a culture probe among a broadened horizon of possibilities to create a more satisfactory model of their new social situation.[12]

The eighteenth-century revivals of religion occurred in just such a context of change: a series of rapid transformations in social reality which Enlightenment theorists such as David Hume and Adam Smith struggled to comprehend. The boundaries of traditional society were weakening, opening avenues whereby the peoples of the English Atlantic could gain a new sense of connection with distant, anonymous, but similar people—an "imagined community," in the historian Benedict Anderson's phrase, which transcended the sphere of immediate experience to embrace a world far beyond local horizons.[13] The vast transatlantic migration of peoples that had begun disrupting Old World communities in the previous century was continuing to augment a bewildering array of ethnic and cultural enclaves along the rim of the Atlantic.[14] Demographic pressures were pushing the children of older settlers to migrate from the communities of their birth to the frontier or the port cities in search of a living.[15]

The rapid growth of a transatlantic consumer economy accompanied migration as a catalyst for economic and social change. Since the later seventeenth century, the development of the British mercantile system had been drawing the colonies into greater dependence on England by securing markets for colonial staples and extending networks of credit to foster production.[16] With the expansion of the market came an explosion of small producers who made available an ever-increasing range of consumer goods. Colonists, in the rush to procure these latest English goods, began to acquire a common set of tastes and experiences that bound them to their fellows throughout the empire.[17] The rapid growth of an intercolonial and transatlantic market for new print commodities such as newspapers and gentlemen's magazines helped to educate the taste of these consumers as well as to draw them into a larger world of letters and great European events.[18] Improvements in transportation and other forms of transatlantic communication likewise worked to shrink the distance between the Old World and the New, drawing colonial inhabitants inexorably nearer their fellows in the British Isles.[19]

The Great Awakening erupted amid this rapidly accelerating revolution in consumption that was thrusting the people of the British Atlantic into a chaotic swirl of new choices and possibilities, possibilities that demanded a corresponding shift in the interpretive categories people employed to make sense of their social world. While the transatlantic scope of the Awakening has become widely recognized, only recently have some historians begun to explore the links between the expansion of the Anglo-American consumer market, with its new communications network, and the emergence of revivalism in the form it took after 1739.[20] The new recognition of this rapidly changing context of consumption raises further questions concerning revivalism's contribution to the transformation of eighteenth-century consciousness from localism to the emergence of an intercolonial and transatlantic "imagined community." From this broad perspective, eighteenth-century perceptions of local awakenings as manifestations of a single, vast transatlantic outpouring of the Spirit take on much greater significance than comparatively insignificant variations among local revivals.[21]

Itinerancy served as a major catalyst for reshaping colonists' categories to accommodate this new world that was opening up before them. Beginning with George Whitefield, itinerants appropriated many of the new possibilities opened up by the consumer revolution, acting in ways that did not fit with existing prescriptions for human behavior. Itinerants' mobility, their disregard of local boundaries or authority, their emotional appeals to the hearts of voluntary listeners, their eagerness to adapt products of the market to spread the gospel—all ran afoul of a well-defined set of expectations concerning the role of minister, church, and laity in community life—indeed, concerning the nature of community itself.

Socially construed boundaries may play a crucial role in the preservation or transformation of a given worldview, and itinerancy's greatest influence on the Anglo-American worldview derived from its intentional transgression of various types of boundaries with which colonists attempted to order the eighteenth-century world.[22] The British anthropologist Mary Douglas has hypothesized that where the boundaries marking off a given social group are well defined and significant, the complex of symbol and ritual its members use to construe their social world will also remain vital. As those boundaries begin to blur, however, the worldview will gradually lose its ability to order the social world in a meaningful way, driving the members of the group to seek a new, more satisfying set of symbols.[23] The action orientation of human categories demands such a shift and can further serve to reinforce or dissolve a set of boundaries by placing values on the human action occurring within them. Where a given worldview has a self-fulfilling character, structuring the social world so that "correct" actions are consistently rewarded and those proscribed are punished, boundaries will tend to persist. Where experience consistently contradicts that worldview, the boundaries associated with it will begin to dissolve.[24]

Most members of the eighteenth-century Anglo-American elite were determined to fashion colonial societies on the model of Augustan England's balanced, stable social order by creating and maintaining a complex system of spatial and social boundaries. Colonial leaders fretted over "leveling" tendencies in society when "the lower orders" clothed themselves in the type of fashionable dress formerly worn only by the more privileged members of society.[25] Participants in the debates over the Massachusetts Land Bank Scheme clashed over the instability and flux the program would wreak, not only on the value of colonial currency but on the social order itself.[26] Political economists debated the best way to set boundaries to political power, whose "restless, aspiring, insatiable" nature conjured up images of the "ocean, not easily admitting limits to be fixed in it."[27]

Itinerants became living metaphors for flux and disorder by violating a wide range of spatial and social boundaries. Ordained Congregational and Presbyterian ministers too often "abandoned" their own "flocks" to travel across neighboring parish boundaries. Dissenting itinerants intruded into Anglican pulpits; itinerant lay exhorters rebuked "unconverted" clergymen; and blacks, Indians, women, and children dared to exhort white males. Itinerants encouraged hearers from various localities, denominations, and ethnic groups to forsake the spatial, social, and confessional bounds that divided them and gather together in great undifferentiated crowds to hear the message of the New Birth. Such actions challenged Americans to thinking of themselves as more than local members of a network of bounded, face-to-face, deferential communities. Through sermons and in print they called on followers to envision the inhabitants of the Atlantic world as one vast company of lost people who needed desperately to hear the message of the New Birth and who could now be reached by new market-generated methods and media on a scale hitherto unimaginable.[28] Itinerant preachers urged individuals to transcend narrower allegiances and to enter into common fellowship through awakening and new birth.[29]

As the number of awakened and reborn grew, a new sense of community began to arise among these widely scattered groups of people which soon took on transatlantic proportions with the help of print commodities and correspondence.[30] Itinerancy's practitioners linked the widely scattered members of the community by providing local assemblies a personal, representative contact with distant, anonymous groups of awakened brethren. In so doing they offered a new model of the church and its surrounding social world: a mobile, dynamic, expansive, potentially unbounded community held together voluntarily by a common spirit among individual members of every locale.[31]

Contemporary critics perceived disastrous social implications in the new method, and this perception compelled them to articulate and defend cherished assumptions concerning traditional spatial and social boundaries and the local, deferential order they implied. At the same time it drove the method's defenders to shape an alternative vision of this new, mobile, market-driven social world—to renegotiate those boundaries in a way that would permit itinerancy to function as a normative enterprise. In the process itinerancy itself became a category: a metaphor for a new type of behavior made possible by market-related changes. At the same time it became the nucleus for a cluster of disputes over community, responsibility, authority, and deference.[32]

III

This study approaches itinerancy less as an activity of unruly persons than as a category of meaning, a contested metaphor for two very different visions of adapting to eighteenth-century change. As such it builds on recent insights into the transatlantic nature of the First Great Awakening by taking fuller account of the conceptual links between that movement and a broader context of dramatic structural change accompanying the century's revolution in communication and consumption.

An explication of these conceptual links is crucial to understanding the Awakening's pivotal role in the transformation of eighteenth-century colonists' self-understanding. This process has recently become obscured by revisionist interpretation of the eighteenth-century revivals but was intuitively grasped in earlier histories which treated the Awakening as a unified movement. This intuition marked interpretations stressing the Awakening as a revival or adaptation of seventeenth-century Puritan and Continental piety. It also underlay older interpretations of the Awakening as an expression of social conflict, a religious adaptation to social change, or an origin of revolutionary impulse. Each perspective has yielded valuable insights and some have complemented others to provide a fuller picture of the phenomenon of the Awakening. Yet the various approaches remain vulnerable to a revisionist critique which denies that a unified intercolonial and transatlantic Awakening ever took place.

The most venerable line of interpretation, originating with colonial revivalists themselves, has presented the Awakening as a resurgence of piety after a long period of religious decline and secularization in the colonies.[33] In this view, itinerancy has played a role first crafted by Gilbert Tennent in his controversial sermon *The Danger of an Unconverted Ministry:* a method that enabled evangelical preachers to bring the warmth of the gospel to cold, dead parishes. In recent years, however, this pietistic interpretation of the Awakening and itinerancy has been modified by historians who have observed that strong devotional traditions persisted throughout the colonial period, bolstered in many regions by periodic local revivals.[34] This modification has strengthened the fundamental contribution of the pietistic interpretation: the recognition of continuity between an older Puritan and Reformed theology of conversion and the revivalist emphasis on the New Birth. Yet the role assigned to itinerancy in this interpretation is problematized by the recognition that many who embraced the older revivalism rejected this "New Light." Indeed, a minister's position on itinerancy indicated much better where he fell within the Old Light/New Light divisions than did his stand on Arminianism. Furthermore, itinerancy suggests the presence of a social dynamic often overlooked in pietistic interpretations. This oversight tends to leave interpreters at a loss, except on supernatural grounds, to explain the timing or scale of a phenomenon contemporaries perceived as a unified, spontaneous "Work" that spanned the empire.

The recent advance of a transatlantic perspective among historians who stress theological, pietistic, or ethnic traditions has enriched this line of inquiry further, yet the picture remains incomplete. Studies that explore the transplantation of various ethnic strands of revivalism from the Old World to the New tend to stress connections between particular regions, often at the expense of the wider imperial context in which midcolonial and Scottish contemporaries self-consciously situated their revival experiences.[35] Michael Crawford's *Seasons of Grace* advances a compelling analysis of how communication among diverse religious and ethnic groups of the British North Atlantic fostered the development of similar revivalistic languages and theological categories, and argues that this shared language provided the basis for the itinerant-led transatlantic Awakening of the 1740s. Yet his consensual approach remains inadequate in itself to explain fully the timing, progress, success, or broader cultural implications of revival in the midst of a commercial revolution.

A relative neglect of the commercial context of controversy over itinerancy in particular weakens Crawford's analysis of divisions among localistic ministers who shared the revivalist language and fervor but understood the revivals of 1740 in very different terms. Attacks on itinerancy brought into focus broader cultural anxieties, while its defenders often constructed continuities between older revivalism and the Awakening by cloaking itinerancy's market-related novelties in the rhetoric of tradition. Ultimately, inattention to the commercial context undermines Crawford's ability to explain why so many ministers in England, Scotland, and New England welcomed in Whitefield's itinerancy a threat to local order far greater than any their fathers had confronted and rejected.[36]

Proponents of the social conflict model of Awakening, while recognizing in general the rise of a transatlantic market, have nevertheless been guided by a class-based mode of analysis which cannot adequately account for the variety of local conditions in which the eighteenth-century revivals throve. At worst, the approach has devolved into reductionism, treating itinerancy and revivalism as manifestations of false consciousness or social pathology masked by professions of religious fervor.[37] The view of the market as a destructive force engendering religiously expressed class conflict fails to explain the appeal of itinerancy and the New Birth across class lines and regional boundaries, in prosperous Philadelphia as well as depressed Boston.[38] The interpretation also founders on the behavior of Whitefield and many itinerant imitators, who, while critical of many market-related cultural changes, did not hesitate to use market-oriented methods to advance religious rather than social goals.[39]

Problems of timing and regional variation have also plagued those who would see in the revivals and itinerancy an early expression of egalitarian ideals and activity that helped to shape the American Revolution. In his study *Religion and the American Mind,* Alan Heimert attempted to trace the origins of popular revolutionary fervor to the Awakening of the 1740s. Yet Heimert's analysis is heavily biased toward New England and flawed by an overly rigid distinction between forward-looking, proto-democratic New Light Calvinists and socially conservative, Arminian Old Light liberals. This contrast oversimplifies both groups' theology, politics, and orientation to the modern world. In addition, it fails to explain the debate outside New England where Calvinism held less sway.[40] Despite its ponderous summarization and analysis of mid-eighteenth-century sources, Heimert's study lacks either a clear sense of chronological development or a demonstration of the relationship between the discourse of revival and its underlying social realities.

Others have attempted to rescue the core of Heimert's thesis by locating the Awakening's significance in new strategies of communication or argumentation which proved adaptable to the subsequent task of political revolt. Harry S. Stout has argued that itinerant, extemporaneous preachers displaced logical, written patterns of thought and discourse with a rhetoric that appealed to a predominantly oral culture, while confronting listeners with an "alternative model of organization and authority" that "disregarded social position and local setting."[41] This interpretation underestimates the role of print in the spread of revival and the degree to which the thought patterns of laymen themselves were shaped by print and writing, a criticism whose validity Stout himself has recently acknowledged.[42] Patricia Bonomi has located the Great Awakening's significance in its very divisiveness, which prompted the revivalists to fashion new forms of argument to defend their minority status.[43] By this interpretation, however, the expansive, all-encompassing vision of the revivalists becomes lost in a torrent of censoriousness, and the Awakening seems to dissolve in hopeless fragmentation and division.

Jon Butler has capitalized on these weaknesses in much of the existing historiography to argue that the concept of a unified, intercolonial Great Awakening has been nothing more than an exercise in "interpretative fiction" on the part of historians. He holds that the variations in time, place, and local setting suggest instead a discrete series of local revivals arising from a plurality of social and ethnic origins. Itinerancy, he argues, was limited in its significance, practiced most often by ordained ministers who jealously guarded their prerogatives against encroachment by unordained laypeople.[44] Yet Butler's model flies in the face of the clear eighteenth-century perceptions of the Awakening as a vast, empirewide movement generated in large measure by an unprecedented form of itinerancy. The antirevival author of "A true and genuine Account of a wonderful Wandering Spirit" pictured the revival as a chaotic, itinerant-led movement engulfing all the colonies along with England and the Continent itself.[45] Revivalists likewise wrote of the revival as a single great movement sweeping across the empire "like a fire set to dried fuel" and sought to situate their local revivals within it.[46]

Several recent lines of investigation show excellent potential for answering Butler's critique of the historiography of the Awakening. The anthropological approach of Rhys Isaac and William G. McLoughlin suggests that the Awakening can be fruitfully analyzed as a system of meaning.[47] Both studies remain vulnerable to criticism, however. McLoughlin's synthetic study rests in part on the older analyses which Butler has so compellingly criticized and in part on a sociopsychological interpretation which is very difficult to verify from existing sources. Isaac's work, in focusing so closely on Virginia, neglects the larger context of Empire in which the Baptist challenge arose. Yet Michael Crawford's recent analysis has shown how the Awakening's meanings could resonate with a transatlantic audience, while recent studies of George Whitefield by Frank Lambert and Harry Stout have shown that the Grand Itinerant's success was inseparable from his skillful exploitation of the emerging transatlantic consumer culture.[48] Taken together, these studies point the way to analyzing the contest over the Awakening as a struggle over meanings, over order, over alternative ways of living, acting, and being in a rapidly expanding social world.

Itinerancy brought this contest of meaning into focus like no other feature of the Awakening, providing in the process an early glimpse into the conceptual transformations entailed in what has come to be called "modernity." My investigation therefore focuses specifically on this feature of the Awakening, seeking to build on the insights of earlier historians by analyzing an eminently accessible record of printed controversy over itinerancy within its context of transatlantic mobility, commerce, and communication. It draws on the insights of the pietistic interpretation by exploring the ways revivalists maintained continuity with the past while creatively reinterpreting and exploiting those elements of their tradition that enabled them to adapt to a new social world. Its analysis of the Awakening's contest over social boundaries builds on the insight of social historians concerning the enormous impact of the market on eighteenth-century life. Yet my approach does not equate revivalism with class conflict or social pathology, and it reveals the rise of a new kind of community from the ruins of a stultifying and oppressive localism. Its implications extend beyond the role of Awakening in revolutionary politics to describe evangelical Christianity's adaptation to the modern world itself. Itinerancy helped eighteenth-century women and men create a freer, more open and expansive world, bound across distance by ties of affection and obligation among an "imagined community."

IV

The full significance of itinerancy within a growing transatlantic commercial society could only emerge as opponents and defenders articulated their alternative assumptions through published debate. This conflict occupied New England presses for nearly five years after Whitefield's first visit and broke out sporadically in other colonies throughout the remainder of the colonial period. This study traces the dialectic of that debate, bearing in mind the crucial role which language itself can play in the social construction of reality.[49] It rests on a fresh reading of familiar writings on both sides of the debate, approaching those sources as artifacts of a particular sociocultural context in which the practice of itinerancy could conjure up powerful images of mobility, dynamism, flux, and disorder. Sociolinguistic theorists have reminded us of the role of language habits themselves in the construction of reality: "We see and hear and otherwise experience very largely as we do because the language habits of our community predispose certain choices of interpretation."[50] Thus the hyperbole which each side employed to advance its views on itinerancy revealed no mere fanaticism or prejudice. Rather, it played a crucial role in exploiting possibilities for human thought and action opened up by the market through interpreting the ways in which this highly meaningful social action of itinerancy challenged existing conceptions of the social world. The interpretation of itinerancy that emerged in the course of debate entailed a concomitant reconceptualization of the world in which itinerants could act.[51]

Thus this study takes as its major task an exploration, through a close textual analysis employing the insights of recent critical theory, of the contrasting interpretations each side placed on itinerancy and the alternative systems of meaning each interpretation reveals.[52] The tropes each side invoked in discussing the practice and its significance, the nuances of their phrases, the creation of new metaphors—comparative analysis of these and other features of the discourse can reveal the alternative frameworks within which each side sought both to make sense of new eighteenth-century sociocultural conditions and to shape social reality itself through the interpretive process.[53]

The conflict was staged on a public battlefield which included not only colonial pulpits and open-air audiences, but a wide range of newspapers, gentlemen's magazines, popular pamphlets, and printed sermons. Concerns that emerged in the debate over itinerancy paralleled and often intersected with transformations wrought by the market in areas often seen as unrelated. Arguments over inflation, market fluctuation, patterns of consumption, social mobility, and political economy raised issues and followed courses similar to the conflict over itinerancy. The wide range of issues opened by market expansion, coupled with the primacy of religion in the minds of colonial revivalists, rendered it unlikely that the interpretive framework they created would transcend the partiality characterizing every worldview. Nevertheless, theirs constituted a powerful alternative that could command a much greater allegiance among a religious populace than could competing models such as republicanism and Enlightenment liberalism. This study of itinerancy as metaphor as well as method can therefore yield insights not only into evangelicalism's ability to adapt to a new social world, but into its role in shaping a new model of that world.

My study's specific focus on controversy over itinerancy as a *category of public discourse* during the Great Awakening leads to some significant departures from most studies of the movement. First, it passes over the traditional beginnings of the Awakening—Theodore Frelinghuysen's revivals of the late 1720s and Jonathan Edwards's Northampton revivals of 1734–35—to focus on the period between 1739 and 1745 when George Whitefield's great tours of the colonies sparked the bulk of the debate over itinerancy. Second, rather than featuring such great revivalists as Jonathan Edwards, it treats defenders of itinerancy as they presented themselves in publications of the period: a long-distance community of "friends of revival" working in concert to promote the "great work." As such, Edwards appears as one exceptionally articulate, highly respected defender of evangelistic itinerancy among a large number of defenders. Third, it provides only brief, suggestive discussion of itinerancy among non-English European, Native-American, and African-American revivalists whose voice is largely absent from the published controversy, and for whom itinerancy's unquestionably central role deserves fuller analysis than possible here.[54]

Chapter 1 surveys the rapid pace of eighteenth-century social, economic, and cultural change of which George Whitefield's itinerancy became so potent a symbol. It reviews the efforts of educated colonial elites to civilize their rapidly changing society by adapting the parochial model of ecclesiastical and social organization to an expanding empire. It goes on to explore the erosion of this localistic, deferential model by rapid growth; long-range mobility; long-distance communication, transportation, and trade; greater social mobility; and greater ethnic and religious diversity. It concludes with an examination of how, in exploiting commerce and mobility to disseminate the Gospel, Whitefield's itinerancy came to embody those changes.

The next two chapters trace the themes of the controversy over itinerancy as it developed between 1740 and 1745. Chapter 2 examines the emerging Old Light discourse of opposition in which itinerancy functioned as an engine of social upheaval, its literal transgression of the parish bound serving as a metaphor for a much more extensive challenge to the traditional place of the social self within a network of deferential social and moral restraints. As itinerancy increased, opponents interpreted its threat as extending beyond spatial boundaries to less tangible but more crucial bounds of behavior, status, class, gender, and race. By 1745, opposition to itinerancy had become an explicit battle for the preservation of a deferential, patriarchal social order brokered by an educated elite.

Chapter 3 traces the New Light defense in which itinerancy became a trope for an alternative conception of the social order by serving as a metaphor of freedom, mobility, and dynamism both of the Spirit of God and of those whom the Spirit touched. In the discourse of defenders, itinerancy came to situate human action and identity in a world of broader spatial, social, and conceptual horizons where greater individual liberty and greater geographic and social mobility could be construed as normative.

Chapter 4 traces the persistence and expansion of itinerancy after 1745, revealing its power as a model for the social ordering of an expanding, mobile world. The persistence of itinerancy also reveals the revivalism it disseminated to be a successful adaptation of evangelical religion to the modern world rather than a retreat to premodern communitarianism. Long after the published debate dwindled, itinerancy continued to challenge the bounded world of deferential, face-to-face relationships with a new model of self situated in a free, dynamic world of permeable boundaries and long-distance, affective relations. Yet the erosion of the parish bound never issued in the unbounded antinomianism which the antirevivalists had feared. Rather, itinerancy provided a means of adapting to a weakly structured, rapidly changing colonial environment by inviting people into close-knit, voluntary local expressions of the transatlantic revival community. The ties of affection that linked members to a long-distance imagined community also bound them to live with one another according to strict standards of internal commitment and moral behavior. Itinerants who planted these local fellowships across the colonial countryside contributed to the emergence of a nationalistic, egalitarian Christianity that was better able to thrive in the mobile, commercial world that America had become.

1

Itinerancy in Historical Perspective

I

On October 30, 1739, George Whitefield disembarked at Lewes, Delaware to commence an itinerant ministry that altered the face of Christianity in the English-speaking world. His itinerancy across the parishes and counties of England and Wales had already "employ'd the Thoughts, Pens and Tongues" of Georgian Englishmen who heard him.[1] The youthful Anglican minister and his entourage ensured that this fame would precede him to America by sending to colonial newspapers third-person accounts describing the tens of thousands who thronged to hear him preach in London.[2] These accounts began appearing in the *Pennsylvania Gazette* early in 1738 and continued until he set foot in America. Within days of his arrival, his preaching was already drawing crowds estimated at six thousand to the Philadelphia courthouse steps.

Within days of his arrival, Whitefield also made the audacious proposal to "preach the Gospel in every province in America," an effort which no regularly ordained minister had yet undertaken.[3] By the end of 1740 he had made good his promise with tours more extensive and personal contacts more numerous than anyone before him. Newspapers reported crowds of thousands "melted by the power of the Word" in nearly every place he preached, and Whitefield and his allies supplemented those reports with a steady stream of pamphlets and correspondence. The Grand Itinerant had successfully introduced a new category of ministry—itinerancy—into the dynamics of Anglo-American religious life.

Whitefield returned to England in January of 1741, leaving behind a contest over itinerancy which reached far beyond doctrinal disputes to include alternative conceptions of religion's role in the maintenance of the social order. In its transgression of local boundaries throughout the colonies, Whitefield's itinerancy challenged a historically sanctioned symbolic system—a deeply rooted conceptual model of Anglo-American society. Colonial Anglican and dissenting elites alike tended to think of this model in terms of the English parochial system, which they had succeeded in replicating throughout much of New England and Virginia. Elsewhere social and religious conditions often rendered a pariochial system difficult if not impossible, yet elites persisted in employing the parish as an important social fiction. In breaching the parish line, Whitefield had assaulted a comprehensive network of mental as well as geographical boundaries—a complex set of assumptions concerning the nature of community and its constituent members, the relationship between community and church, the place of the minister in community life, and the place of the parish and community in the surrounding world.

Colonial revivalists exacerbated this conflict by welcoming Whitefield's itinerancy as God's unexpected means of snatching colonists from the brink of damnation. Where "irreligion had been rushing in like a flood," observed Reverend Josiah Smith of Charleston, God had sent this thundering Anglican to "discharge the artillery of Heaven upon us" through a preaching style Smith imagined similar to that of the Apostle Paul.[4] A New England observer wrote that "*Ministers, Rulers* and *People*" welcomed Whitefield "as an *Angel of God,* or *Elias,* or *John the Baptist* risen from the Dead."[5] Colonial poets lauded the "*crying Voice,*" sent "to bid the World repent," and assured Whitefield that at the final resurrection heaven would rejoice "with Millions thou hast saved."[6] A year after Whitefield's departure Thomas Prince of Boston exulted that Christ's "riding forth in Magnificence and Glory thro' divers Parts of our land," which began during the itinerant's visit, continued in a manner "never seen or heard among us . . . since the Apostles' Days."[7]

The revivalists' hyperbole galled local ministers, who felt beleaguered by itinerancy and who saw in Whitefield's ability to "sway and keep the Affections of the Multitude" an unprecedented threat to "Gospel order."[8] Opponents throughout the colonies defended their ecclesiastical bounds against this man whose "travelling preachments" fomented disorder and error among the "mob," presaging disaster for colonial society. Itinerancy appeared in antirevival rhetoric under metaphors of subversion, flux, disorder, and cataclysm such as comet, "will-with-wisp," "wandring Spirit," and "popish Emissary." Its practitioners disrupted the peace by provoking "Enthusiastick" outcries, fits, and ecstacies among their audiences. The "Mobs and Disorders" attending itinerancy betrayed not the spirit of the apostles but the presence of "*Belial,* taking a Tour in Disguise."[9]

This contest between itinerancy's apostolic power and the local ministry's "gospel order" expressed underlying tensions over sweeping changes taking place in the eighteenth-century social world. The parish had constituted a fundamental unit of European social life for a thousand years but was becoming an increasingly inadequate means of comprehending and ordering new social realities. The parochial model had arisen gradually during the Christianization of Europe as church leaders, government officials, and local communities struggled to impose order on the social and political landscape in the wake of the Roman Empire's collapse. The pattern had become so ingrained that many settlers, churchmen, and magistrates viewed the imposition of parish boundaries on the colonial landscape as an essential part of their effort to recreate a stable European civilization in the New World. Yet the effort to do so was becoming increasingly problematic under the pressure of ongoing migration, expanding commerce, and improving communication. A more mobile, fluid society was emerging to challenge the stable world of the parish—a society for which no clear model yet existed. The itinerancy of Whitefield and his imitators soon came to function as such a model: one that held millennial promise for defenders while threatening anarchy, flux, and chaos for opponents.

II

The eighteenth-century contest over itinerancy tapped an ancient set of tensions between a global apostolic vision and a stable gospel order. These tensions were present in the New Testament itself, whose language and narratives helped structure eighteenth-century perceptions of the social world. The evolution of the parochial system had provided ecclesiastical and civil leaders a particular means of resolving these tensions by balancing a mediated, hierarchical unity within the parishes of Christendom against missionary activity in the "heathen regions beyond." This way of dividing and ordering the social world came to dominate European categories of thought until well into the seventeenth century. The enduring strength of this localistic worldview precluded fundamental renegotiation of the balance between settled and mobile ministry until Whitefield's itinerancy upset it in the late 1730s.

The New Testament language and narratives were eminently susceptible to the constructions which eighteenth-century revivalists placed upon them in defense of itinerancy. The gospel narratives confirmed Thomas Prince, Sr.'s contention that "Our Blessed Saviour was an Itinerant Preacher . . . he preached in no other way."[10] The book of Acts chronicled the itinerant labors of the Apostle Paul in the first-century Roman world.[11] It described Paul's ability to capitalize on the cultural pluralism of the empire by becoming "all things to all men."[12] Paul's epistles offered glimpses of a social vision in which boundaries of place, race, and ethnicity dissolved as faith in Jesus Christ removed the individual from his or her historical community into a transcendent community of believers.[13] These ancient texts revealed a world where links of communication, travel, and mutual support cemented a sense of kinship among those embracing "all those who in every place call on the name of our Lord Jesus Christ."[14]

Yet the Old Lights could counter any inclination to take this expansive vision to extremes by appealing to apostolic resolves against "boasting in another man's line," a fortuitous phrase of scripture which they applied directly to the defense of the parish boundary.[15] Opposers could also point to apostolic injunctions to defend congregations against itinerant false teachers by "setting in order what remains and ordaining elders in every city."[16] Such texts could be construed to suggest that the apostles maintained a careful distinction between the work of resident ministers of established Christian congregations and the labors of itinerant missionaries among the "ungospelized." This construction also enjoyed the support of tradition which since ancient times had structured first the Church and then the entire European social world according to this very distinction.

Defenders of European parochialism traced the origins of the parish to this apostolic method of appointing local teachers to preserve the order and purity of the churches. Very early on, the Church's transcendent unity came to be mediated by a class of literate local bishops who maintained contact with their counterparts in other cities of the empire while devoting themselves to pastoral duties that would later devolve to parish priests.[17] Itinerancy came under strict regulation, falling eventually to a disciplined body of missionary monks and hermits who carried the Gospel to the Roman countryside and barbarian lands from Britain to India.[18]

During the medieval period, bishops and kings cooperated to build a parochial system that would maintain this balance between the ordered, mediated unity among local congregations and missionary travel to the heathen world beyond. In eighth-century Gaul, the Merovingian kings imposed order on their realm by mandating a parochial system as the basic unit of government as well as ecclesiastical life. Merovingian bishops cooperated by restricting roving priests to a single parish.[19] At the same time in Anglo-Saxon England, a parish system emerged through the work of minster churches strategically located in governmental centers. Missionaries used the minster as a base of operations for forays into the surrounding villages, where they conducted services and labored for converts. "Daughter churches," which emerged in these villages and on neighboring estates, would eventually gain a resident priest as the missionary moved on to other areas.[20] By the twelfth century such practices enabled Pope Innocent III to regularize the parish system throughout Christendom.[21]

As the parish system came to organize more and more of the European geographical and social landscape, the day-to-day experience of most Christians could no longer support the apostolic consciousness of the self as direct participant in a spiritual community unbounded by ethnicity or locale. Instead, parish life fostered a sense of self bound within a specific local network of relationships by ties of kinship and obligation. Church gatherings provided spiritual nurture and cultivated a core set of values that parishioners were expected to share. They also constituted important dramaturgical settings in which peasants, artisans, laborers, local gentry, and noble families rehearsed well-defined roles within the local order.[22] The individual now participated in the larger world of kingdom and Christendom only vaguely, through the hierarchical mediation of priest and noble. The cycle of festivals which celebrated that wider unity took on distinctive local character. Festivals and other church-sponsored events, such as fund-raising ales, expressed communal piety and values and further reinforced the local social order. The parish church afforded the prime vehicle for exhibiting local prosperity. The annual rogationtide processions around the parish bounds reminded inhabitants that their identity was inextricably bound up within the community marked by the church building.[23]

This parish-centered localism continued to circumscribe the world of most Europeans well into the seventeenth century while enabling ecclesiastical leaders to maintain the distinction between parish priest and traveling missionary. Itinerant preaching among settled parishes was frowned upon by ecclesiastical authorities and regarded with suspicion by local magistrates and villagers. Itinerants such as the Waldensians in Italy and, later, the Lollards in England were suppressed as heretics. Even the Franciscans and Dominicans, whose poverty and peripatetic style of ministry enjoyed papal sanction, encountered localistic barriers of suspicion and resentment.[24] The strength of medieval hierarchy on the one hand and localism on the other demanded that friars advance carefully, seeking the assistance of powerful patrons and styling their ministry as complementary to the work of bishops and parish clergy. The mendicants' influence came to center on new urban areas where they could reach the greatest numbers, organize new parishes among recent urban migrants, and find resources sufficient for their support.[25] Mendicacy retained a vital role in Church life, yet parochialism remained the hallmark of European society until well after the Reformation.

In the sixteenth century the need for Reformers to cultivate the favor of national and local political leaders, coupled with an anxiety to dissociate themselves from the excesses of radical sects, ensured that the contest between Catholics and Protestants would be one of control over existing parishes rather than battles over the propriety of parish bounds. To be sure, the territorial model of church membership came under attack from radical groups such as Anabaptists, who wished to purify the church by restricting membership to rebaptized adult converts.[26] Yet such views entailed a repudiation of the link between church and community that few were prepared to accept and earned Anabaptists harsh persecution by local officials throughout much of Europe.[27] Protestant leaders allied themselves with sympathetic local and territorial magistrates to carry the Reformation forward, making every effort to preserve and strengthen the parish system in the process.[28] John Calvin refused to recognize anyone as a minister who was not attached to a specific local parish. Protestant missionaries sent out from Geneva labored to establish local ministries as quickly as possible.[29]

English reformers joined Continental brethren in a litany of complaints concerning the quality of the parish clergy yet labored to maintain and strengthen the parochial system. While some followed the earlier Lollard practice of itinerant preaching to spread the new ideas, they viewed it as a temporary expedient that should cease as soon as each parish was supplied a reformed minister.[30] The Henrican Injunctions of 1538 requiring the maintenance of parish registers strengthened the parochial system further by investing the minister with new secular duties that made the parish an instrument of local government.[31] The installation of resident, educated, godly clergymen in every English parish remained a constant Puritan ideal during the years of Elizabeth I.[32] English Reformers regarded the parish as a prize for capture rather than an idol for destruction.

On the eve of English colonization, the parish line still demarcated the conceptual horizons of most Englishmen. Though some local boundaries were beginning to erode, most persons continued to occupy very well-defined stations within local, deferential networks of face-to-face communal relations. The annual perambulation, the one church procession to survive the Reformation, continued to dramatize the limits of local communities by retracing parish boundaries.[33] Older members of the community continued to employ a variety of devices to etch the parish bounds into the minds of their children. The simple concerns of day-to-day life dominated their consciousness. Specific local vocabularies colored their speech. Peculiar festivals and rituals served to forge and reinforce the bonds of kinship and obligation which situated each person firmly within the local social order. Even the larger world was a regional one represented by county communities and regional fairs. The world beyond that was only rarely encountered in the passage of travelers such as friars, peddlers, or migrant laborers. Wider unities ideally remained the province of gentry, noble, and clerical elites.[34]

III

The pattern of English settlement in the New World reveals the enduring power of parochialism both as a system of ecclesiastical organization and as a means of ordering the social world. Settlers, churchmen, and politicians viewed the imposition of local boundaries on the colonial landscape as an essential part of their effort to re-create a stable European civilization in the New World. Yet only in New England and Tidewater Virginia did colonists successfully reproduce the parish-centered localism of European society. In other areas where authorities attempted to establish parishes, the boundaries encompassed a confusing mixture of competing sects and ethnic groups, or stretched across hopelessly vast stretches of territory to draw in the dispersed population. Yet ministers and magistrates continued to cling to the parochial model despite its growing inadequacy for ordering the expanding, mobile, increasingly diverse population of British America.

The Great Migration of Puritans across the Atlantic arose ironically from a localistic response to the intrusive, centralizing reforms of Archbishop William Laud during the 1630s. In that decade thousands of English artisans, yeomen, gentry, and clergy crossed the Atlantic to establish new covenanted communities beyond the reach of Charles I and Laud. Most migrants adhered to a Congregational church polity which ostensibly rejected the parish system in favor of "gathered churches" made up solely of persons who could give a satisfactory account of their conversion experience. Yet Congregationalists, set free in the New World to realize their vision for a pure church and society, chose to replicate the localism they had known at home. Settlers from one English locale generally joined former neighbors to re-create in a New England town the features of the community they had left behind. These localities remained fiercely protective of local rights and resented even the mild governmental control that emanated from Boston.[35]

In their establishment of an ecclesiastical order, the Puritan migrants intensified the bonds between church, minister, and local community. Each town at its founding built one meetinghouse which housed town meetings as well as Sabbath assemblies. Founders restricted full church membership to those who could give a satisfactory account of their conversion but required every member of the community to attend weekly worship conducted by the resident minister. The minister was bound by covenant to the congregation which had elected him. He could claim the title of "pastor" only so long as he remained in covenant with that congregation, and his authority extended no further than the town boundary. Population growth forced one town after another to divide its territory into two or more precincts with separate meetinghouses and eventually forced colonial authorities to resort to a full-blown parochial system.[36] This further reinforced the persistence of a localism that bound minister and people into a close-knit network of deferential, face-to-face relations.[37]

The covenant between the early New England minister and his congregation established a parity unheard of in the Old World, but the minister still retained a large reserve of moral authority in the local community. While local inhabitants sometimes resisted his authority, opposed his leadership, and reserved to themselves the right of independent judgment, they seldom forgot that he was the local "steward of the mysteries of God."[38] The minister's weekly performance before the assembled inhabitants conferred on him special status which was further enhanced by the sacred content of his message.[39] Ministers themselves were conscious of their authority in spiritual matters and did not hesitate to assert it. Over the course of the seventeenth century many worked to enlarge ministerial authority by the formation of ministerial associations, and some strove to remove ordination from congregational control.[40] By the eighteenth century, most had come to regard their sphere of authority within the parish bounds as inviolable and regularly defended their parochial rights in ordination sermons.[41]

Virginia planters likewise ordered the landscape by means of parish as well as county boundaries. Development of these parishes was hampered in the early years by instability, dispersed settlement patterns, and a dearth of qualified clergy.[42] Yet as the colony began to achieve stability and planters to acquire fortunes, ministers and gentry strove to emulate English society by replicating the parish life known to county elites in England. By 1700, inhabitants of the Virginia Tidewater enjoyed easy access to well-built houses of worship supplied with educated clergy.[43] Elsewhere, parsimonious vestrymen who balked at paying their ministers and spending money on churches nevertheless defended their parochial rights as vigorously as did the Congregational leadership of New England towns.[44] The parish constituted a sphere of spiritual authority for which the civil authorities and the Bishop of London's commissaries held clergy responsible. They were expected to preach and administer the sacraments regularly in one of their churches and to insure that prayers and a homily were read in their absence. After the passage of the Toleration Act in 1689, Anglican parish clergy and local gentry kept tabs on the number of those within their parish bounds who adhered to dissenting communions, such as Presbyterians or Baptists. Local vicars regarded any increase that came by Anglican defections to dissent as a violation of parochial rights.[45]

Yet mobility of the Virginia population and territorial expansion of the colony taxed the adaptibility of the parochial system. As settlers continued to fan out into the Virginia Piedmont, officials tried incorporating them into ever larger parishes. By the eighteenth century, frontier clergymen often found themselves in a situation similar to that of Anthony Gavin, minister of the frontier parish of St. James. Gavin rotated regular weekly services among three churches situated in a 25-mile radius of his glebe at Goochland, but his boundaries extended beyond the reach of these. To reach many parishioners, he found it necessary to establish seven "places of service in the mountains," where he assigned the regular reading of prayers to local clerks. In addition, he reported fording rivers nineteen times and traveling a 400-mile annual circuit to preach at least twice per year at twelve other locales in his parish.[46]

The religious and ethnic pluralism that emerged in the Middle Colonies hampered the attempts of religious leaders there to replicate Old World parochial systems, but ethnic and confessional differences often resulted in de facto boundaries that ordered locales in ways similar to the parish line.[47] In New York, Anglicans vied with Lutherans, Dutch Reformed, Presbyterians, and migrant Congregationalists for the allegiance of the colony's apathetic denizens. The policies of toleration pursued by the Calverts in Maryland and William Penn in Pennsylvania permitted a veritable Babel of rival religious and ethnic groups there. The Jerseys also harbored a mixture of ethnic and religious groups. Midcolonial Quakers, German Baptists, Amish, Mennonites, and Schwenkfelders rejected the parochial system, but the tight-knit communities they founded functioned in similar ways by resisting outside intrusion and disruption of local order. Their Anglican, Lutheran, Presbyterian, and

Continental Reformed neighbors all attempted to regulate religious life by organizing overlapping parishes and supplying them with educated, ordained ministers.[48]

Most recognized "founders" of American denominations which had been state churches in the Old World spent themselves traveling throughout the colonial countryside, organizing congregations and parishes in "desolate places." Francis Makemie, for example, left Ulster to travel first to Barbados, then through the mainland colonies from the Carolinas to New York, preaching and establishing congregations, presbyteries, and finally a synod among scattered groups of predominantly Scottish and Scotch-Irish Presbyterians. The irregularity of Makemie's practice attracted the hostility of Lord Cornbury, governor of New York. Cornbury prosecuted Makemie in 1707 for preaching without a license, arguing that the Act of Toleration prohibited "strowling preachers." Makemie defended his ministerial activities on the grounds that the license granted him in Barbados was valid in all British dominions. He also successfully refuted Cornbury's argument by appealing to the example of the Quakers, "who have few or no fixed Teachers, but are chiefly taught by such as Travel . . . and Teach over the Plantations, and are not molested."[49]

Makemie's citation of Quaker practice was a bit disingenuous, for neither he nor New World representatives of any other territorial church wished to emulate Quaker prophets. In their founding years during the mid-seventeenth century, Quaker missionaries earned harsh suppression and even martyrdom for their brazen assaults on parish boundaries throughout the British Atlantic world. Their bravery had won converts to one of the earliest transatlantic sectarian religious movements, but converts in settled areas usually joined this movement at the cost of ostracization from local communities still dominated by adherance to the town or parish church. By the eighteenth century, Quakers themselves had accommodated to localism. The small number of itinerating "Public Friends" traveled about the empire visiting close-knit, sternly disciplined local meetings composed of membership bound by strong kinship ties. Where they were a minority, as in New England, Quakers generally found themselves banished to the fringes of community life. In midcolonial communities where they formed a majority, they defended local bounds as fiercely as their orthodox neighbors.[50]

Francis Makemie and ministers of other confessional churches regarded such voluntary order as insufficient and pressed for an institutionalized local ecclesiastical system. They continued to hold the traditional distinction between settled minister and itinerant missionary, viewing their itinerancy as a temporary expedient to "propagate the interest of religion" in "desolate places where a minister is wanting."[51] Congregations formed in such localities served as the nucleus of a parish whose bounds could encompass a radius of as much as twenty miles in every direction from a church building or meetinghouse. A chronic shortage of ministers throughout the colonial period obliged pastors of neighboring parishes to supply unoccupied pulpits. Once a congregation called its own pastor, however, the job of the missionary or visiting minister was complete and he could leave the parish in the new pastor's care.[52]

Ministers of churches so organized tended to view their parish bounds as inviolable for the members of their own religious confession. Colonial Presbyterian ministers defended the boundaries of impractically large parishes against subdivision, even when this imposed hardship on some parish inhabitants. They regarded unauthorized meetings held anywhere within their parish bounds as "intrusions" and attempted to discourage such activity.[53] Yet Presbyterians often found themselves vying for the allegiance of English-speaking inhabitants with Anglican missionaries sent by the Society for the Propagation of the Gospel (SPG) as well as with preachers of various sects. German Lutheran and Reformed groups likewise competed with sects of German origin. As a consequence of this overlap of religious and ethnic allegiances, midcolonial parishes seldom achieved the integrity of their Old World counterparts. The localism that did emerge in the Middle Colonies centered as much on ethnic as on territorial boundaries.

Even in eighteenth-century New England, the integrity of Congregational parishes was eroding under a steady influx of competing sectarians and Anglican missionaries. The general courts of Massachusetts and Connecticut had extended grudging toleration to Baptists, Quakers, and Anglicans in the late seventeenth century. By 1729 the parish rates for members of those persuasions were being assigned to their own rather than the Congregational ministers. The Bishop of London continued sending itinerant SPG missionaries to organize Anglican congregations in New England parishes despite Congregational protests that none were needed.[54] Though Congregational dominance of the New England countryside necessitated that SPG missionaries travel about competing for voluntary adherents, the Anglicans did not abandon the parochial model. Rather, they hoped to capture the Congregational parochial system for their church by winning New Englanders to their persuasion.[55]

By the 1730s, the inadequacies of parochialism had become glaringly apparent in the face of pluralism, ongoing migration, and difficult frontier conditions. Yet ecclesiastical and political authorities carried on the struggle to impose parochial order on the colonial landscape. Most sects joined territorial church adherents in viewing itinerancy as a temporary necessity to be replaced as soon as possible by a regular local ministry. Ministers and lay leaders of territorial churches exhibited a marked reluctance to abandon systems that for centuries had provided the basis for an orderly religious and communal life. They constantly organized new parishes, tenaciously defended overextended parish bounds, and attempted in many places to exclude members of other persuasions from those bounds. Most colonial governments likewise sought to maintain social order by supporting a parochial system through legal codes and provision for parish rates.

IV

Even as religious change and transatlantic mobility eroded the geographical boundedness of the parish, a revolution in commerce and communication challenged its ability to circumscribe the conceptual worlds of ordinary men and women. At the beginning of the eighteenth century, the localities of the British Empire enjoyed better transportation, new instruments of communication, better access to markets, and a growing availability of manufactured goods. Economic changes were opening new horizons and new possibilities for inhabitants of the empire, creating both exhilaration and anxiety as people groped for ways to comprehend, exploit, and contain the new realities.

The transatlantic mobility of persons uprooted from various Old World locales was itself made possible by improvements in shipping that had been taking place in response to commercial demands since the sixteenth century. Throughout the eighteenth century

English shipping strengthened links among the scattered peoples of the North Atlantic with vessels of trade that continued to increase in size, number, efficiency, and frequency of voyages. Smaller vessels plied the coastline in increasing numbers and penetrated further inland along navigable rivers to facilitate intercolonial trade and travel.[56] These improvements in maritime transportation were augmented by river travel and market roads that reached ever further into the colonial hinterland, enticing formerly isolated agrarian communities to haul commodities to port for sale on an international market.[57]

Migration itself helped to foster a greater awareness of the world beyond the locality. Out-migration from older colonial settlements to the frontier or to port cities combined with ongoing transatlantic migration to increase society's mobility. Migrants linked old localities with new by emotional and familial bonds, maintained by correspondence and occasional visits. News from one community could spread throughout an entire region through the agency of family visitors. Jonathan Edwards, for example, attributed the spread of the Connecticut Valley revivals of 1734–35 to family visitors who reported what they had seen in Northampton to folks back home.[58]

Letters exchanged among distant family members augmented an existing network of intercolonial and transatlantic correspondence and spurred the organization of an empirewide postal system. The increase of commercial shipping aided the growth of this correspondence network and the speed of communication during the eighteenth century. An increase in the number and range of travelers, who often carried letters from one place to another, supplemented the postal system. As the century progressed, these two means of corresponding drew formerly isolated communities steadily closer to one another.[59]

The most important development in communication, however, came with the extension of what the historian Benedict Anderson has termed "print capitalism" across the Atlantic and into an increasing number of locales. The production of books, sermons, pamphlets, broadsides, chapbooks, and almanacs for sale to the empire's literate populace became a vehicle for the dissemination of a common language and set of values.[60] The rise of weekly newspapers multiplied this effect a thousandfold. Under the Licencing Act of 1662 the Crown had restricted publication to only one newspaper, the *London Gazette*. The act's lapse in 1695, however, opened the floodgates to a surfeit of competing periodicals in London, the English provinces, and the colonies.

Boston printers began producing news-sheets as early as 1684 and launched the *Boston Weekly News-letter,* the city's first newspaper with a sustained circulation, in 1704. By 1740 Boston had four newspapers, New York two, Philadelphia two, Williamsburg one, and Charleston one.[61] In these and a number of lesser colonial journals, colonists could read reports from correspondents in other colonies, London, the various English provinces, and the Continent. In addition, colonial publishers regularly reprinted news items, essays, and poetry from other colonial journals, London newspapers, and gentlemen's magazines. This vast increase in the volume and currency of information began to give people in the various locales of the British Atlantic a greater sense of kinship with distant, anonymous people who were now sharing a more standardized language of print and who were beginning to share common assumptions as a result.[62]

Newspapers were both product and agent of an eighteenth-century commercial revolution which they helped foster through advertising. Small manufacturers flooded the market with consumer goods, and merchants learned to use newspapers in sophisticated ways to hawk these "latest English fashions" to inhabitants of the British Atlantic.[63] During the first third of the century the range of cheap imports increased dramatically and penetrated rapidly from the port cities to the remote communities of the colonial hinterland.[64] In the rush to obtain these English goods, colonists began to acquire a common set of tastes and experiences that further intensified a sense of kinship with their British fellows.[65]

The cumulative effect of mobility, communication, and commerce was to expand people's conceptual horizons in profoundly new ways. Participation in the consumer market was enabling people to experience a freedom of choice they had not known before: a freedom that began subtly to challenge old patterns of deference as shopkeepers and artisans donned fashions and purchased goods that had recently been available only to those who styled themselves the "better sort."[66] The surfeit of commodities on the market coupled with a chronic shortage of specie was forcing people to adapt the monetary and credit system in unconventional ways to accommodate increased economic activity. Newspapers, long-range correspondence, and greater intercolonial and transatlantic mobility were all broadening people's horizons to include a world far beyond local bounds. At the same time a wide array of printed media was providing independent access to a world of information and ideas that permitted informed criticism of a political, religious, and social elite who had been accustomed to greater deference.[67]

By the 1730s the boundaries of social life in the British Empire had become unsettled indeed. Controversies of the day reflected the anxiety generated as people attempted to situate themselves in a new world of expanding horizons, unprecedented flux, and precarious order. Colonial elites attempted to arrest social mobility through sumptuary laws. The Massachusetts Land Bank Scheme aroused intense opposition from those who feared the effects of a currency cut adrift from its moorings to sterling. But no controversy better reflected the conflicting hopes and fears of the age than the one that exploded over the new itinerancy of George Whitefield.

V

The inauguration of George Whitefield's itinerancy came at a crucial moment in the transformation of North Atlantic culture. Society had become more fluid, religion and culture more diverse, boundaries more porous than ever before. British Americans, intensely aware of these changes, were eager to exploit the opportunities of this exciting new world. Whitefield's revivals offered not only a setting where colonists could "meet with God" but also a means of participating in an event of transatlantic proportions—a New World replication of the vast responses the newspapers had informed them were taking place in London and the provinces. Colonists who had read of "great numbers impressed" under Whitefield's ministry in London now joined "great numbers" who "flocked" to hear him in America.[68] Settlers who had read of the "visible presence of God" moving Englishmen to tears in open-air meetings now found themselves unable to hold back the tears as they sensed the Spirit's touch under an expansive New World sky.[69] Whitefield's journals assured colonists that their response had in fact surpassed "all I have seen in London" and expressed the belief that God's candle would shortly pass from England to America.

Whitefield's enormous popularity, his unsurpassed eloquence, his skillful manipulation of the press, and his whirlwind tours throughout the empire made him an embodiment of the changes overtaking it. John Willison of Dundee in Scotland declared the youthful Anglican "raised up of God for special Service, and spirited for making new and singular Attempts, for promoting true Christianity in the World, and for reviving it where it is decayed."[70] Indeed, Whitefield's talents coupled with his instinct for exploiting new resources of the market made him "singularly fitted to do the work of an *Evangelist*," an office regarded as defunct since apostolic days.[71] Less sympathetic observers complained that "his motions through the World are so swift, that . . . it is more easy to be informed where he has been, than where he is; and whoever would desire to pursue and overtake him . . . has need of *Mercury*'s Wings for his Assistance."[72]

The secret of Whitefield's success in both England and America depended not only on his personal charisma but also on his skillful exploitation of the press and correspondence.[73] Letters to American correspondents often included third-person reports to be published in newspapers of towns he planned to visit.[74] His correspondents supplemented these with published excerpts of the itinerant's private letters as well as unsolicited endorsements of their own.[75] Whitefield also contracted with Benjamin Franklin and other colonial printers to publish inexpensive editions of his sermons and journals. He provided the press with regular supplements of the journals in which "friends of revival" could track his progress through the colonies. These print commodities accompanied other consumer goods along trade routes, penetrating even remote settlements with the news of revival and whetting the appetites of colonists everywhere for the "sweet refreshings of the Spirit."[76]

Yet Whitefield's role in shaping a translocal consciousness extended well beyond his exploitation of the press. Through itinerancy he also provided personal, representative contact with what was soon to become a vast "imagined community" of saints that transcended geographical and denominational lines through a common experience of the New Birth. The tropes Whitefield employed to describe his ministry emphasized openness, expansiveness, boundlessness, often alluding to the Pauline understanding of the Church as a translocal community composed of "all who call upon the name of our Lord Jesus Christ in every place." He declared "all places equal to me—in America as in England," viewing them "as so many little parts of [God's] great family."[77] He acted on this declaration by exhibiting a studied disregard for geographical or denominational boundaries as he sailed down the American coast and penetrated inland parishes. "Going abroad," he reflected concerning his travels, "cannot but help to enlarge our ideas, and give us exalted thoughts of the greatness and goodness of God."[78]

Whitefield's idea of "exalted thoughts of God's greatness" entailed far more than simple assent to the commonplace that God's presence was not confined to any one place or denomination. It entailed a program of action—a purposive effort to thrust aside the barriers that impeded Christian unity. "Don't tell me you are a Baptist, an Independant, a Presbyterian, a Dissenter," the itinerant urged his hearers, "tell me you are a Christian, that is all I want."[79] Whitefield acted on this exhortation by laying aside the gowns of his Anglican ordination "in point of liberty" to ally himself with Presbyterians in the Middle Colonies, Dissenters in South Carolina, Congregationalists in New England, and Kirkmen in Scotland. His dissenting allies saw his Anglican ordination as an advantage in gaining a hearing among their people and cooperated fully in this blurring of denominational boundaries. Benjamin Coleman of Boston's Brattle Street Church expressed adoration to Providence for "this New Thing in our day," the appearance of a fiery Churchman who honored the liturgy but was "struck with the awful sense of perishing of Truth, with souls from the Earth, through the Earthliness and negligence of [his] clergy brethren."[80] A Scottish clergyman declared that the Lord, by unexpectedly raising up this powerful Calvinist preacher from Anglican ranks, had succeeded in "attracting our Eyes and attention to One, who, had he been formerly of us, would doubtless like others be despised."[81] Such considerations led revivalists throughout the empire to welcome Whitefield into their pulpits, share with him the administration of the Sacrament, join him in the fields, and defend him tirelessly in the press.

The Grand Itinerant dramatized his maxim that "all places are equal to me" by preaching wherever he found an audience, whether in other ministers' churches or in the open fields. While he ordinarily observed the formality of soliciting an invitation to speak from the pulpits of local ministers, he seldom let a refusal prevent his preaching within the parish bounds. One controversy erupted early in Whitefield's career over his unauthorized entry into a pulpit during the local minister's absence.[82] More often, ministers would deny Whitefield the pulpit only to see him take a stand on the churchyard wall, from which he could preach to audiences standing or sitting among the graves.[83] At Moorfields in London, the spectacle of a black-robed clergyman taking his stand to preach near the bear-baiters and jugglers attracted tens of thousands.[84] By 1739 he was drawing crowds that few English churches could accommodate.

Whitefield's field preaching took on great symbolic meaning in the pluralistic environment of colonial North America. From the time he disembarked at Philadelphia in November of 1739, the boundlessness of the open fields permitted the free mingling of Quakers, Baptists, Presbyterians, Lutherans, and Anabaptists, who gathered to receive the Word together in "profound silence."[85] At the end of November Whitefield preached from a balcony in Germantown to the mingled representatives of "at least fifteen denominations," who seemed determined "to agree in one thing, to hold Jesus Christ as their Head, and to worship Him in spirit and in truth."[86] When the commissary of New York denied him the Anglican pulpit there, the itinerant took to the fields rather than become captive to a rival denomination by preaching in the Dutch Reformed pulpit.[87] Upon learning that American ministers of various denominations often shared one another's pulpits, Whitefield preached freely from dissenting pulpits wherever he visited. He nevertheless retained a preference for field preaching, which by the summer of 1740 he had come to view as a symbol of the Gospel's own unboundedness. Reflecting on Philadelphians' desire to build a church large enough to accommodate his crowds, Whitefield mused, "The Lord, I am persuaded, would have His Gospel preached in the fields; and building a church would, I fear, insensibly lead the people into bigotry and make them place the Church again, as they had done for a long time, in the church walls."[88]

This metaphor of the unwalled church, enacted anew with every sermon preached in an open field, presaged a dramatic reconceptualization of the spiritual, physical, and social landscape in which itinerancy was to play a crucial role. Traditional geographical boundaries were dissolving as the Grand Itinerant treated "all places equal" by traveling from locality to locality, preaching here in a Pennsylvania field, there in a Massachusetts meetinghouse, elsewhere in a great London church. Denominational distinctions blurred as people from every imaginable group thronged together to seek the New Birth. The circle of those who had shared a conversion experience under Whitefield's preaching widened as he carried the message to the furthest reaches of the British dominions. His aggressive use of the press further intensified a sense of communion among distant strangers who read reports of other revivals or heard them repeated from pulpits throughout the Empire.

VI

In the midst of this flurry of transatlantic activity, Whitefield was introducing a new category of revivalistic ministry that differed dramatically both from the traveling ministries of missionaries and from the older itinerancy of Reformers and Dissenters. The new itinerancy, unlike its ancient missionary cousin, forsook the old distinction between territories where the Church was established and "ungospelized" regions inhabited only by "heathen." Practitioners of the new itinerancy refused to let any boundary prevent their taking the message of the New Birth to those who had not heard it, whether the potential converts resided in a parish where piety had "woefully decayed" or inhabited a heathen wilderness beyond all parochial bounds. The new itinerancy also regarded all denominations as legitimate "fields of harvest," unlike Quaker Public Friends who roamed the Atlantic world ministering only to "members of their own spiritual house." Whitefield's expansive vision drove him to claim the world as his parish and to press that claim by preaching equally in revivalist strongholds like Jonathan Edwards's Northampton and "ungospelized" regions like the North Carolina frontier. Gilbert Tennent, Whitefield's Presbyterian ally, bolstered this disregard of parish bounds by declaring in his sermon *The Danger of an Unconverted Ministry* that God's "Promises of blessing the Word" were not confined within the "Parish-line."[89]

The most telling indication that Whitefield's itinerancy represented something new came from other traveling missionaries who attacked the evangelist bitterly. Jonathan Arnold, an SPG itinerant from New England, denounced Whitefield in the *Boston Weekly Post-Boy* as "the most irregular Man in Doctrine and Manners, that ever I knew," and warned readers to shun him as "*A Violator of all Rule and Order.*"[90] SPG clergy throughout the colonies complained about the ramblings of the "Noisie Mr. Whitefield," begging the Society to send "tracts levelled against Enthusiasm, to guard the people against this wild man & vile heretick."[91] Commissary Archibald Cummings of Philadelphia could only interpret the "infamous Mr. Whitefield's" indiscriminate ministry among the Dissenters as a "design to set up for the Head of a Sect."[92] John Thomson, a Presbyterian minister who had traversed the Virginia backcountry organizing parishes among Scotch-Irish settlers, also decried Whitefield's "travelling Labours." He complained that the new itinerancy exhibited flagrant disdain for "that Order which not only Presbyterians, but also all other Churches have carefully observed; viz., that every Pastor should stick by his own Flock, unless when sent on the Churches Errand elsewhere." Thomson's own traveling labors had constituted the Church's errand to an unchurched region. By crossing parish lines, however, the new itinerancy flaunted historical efforts to prevent "one Minister's preaching in another's Bounds to the Disturbance of the Peace of the Church."[93]

Whitefield's itinerancy also underlay those features of the revival which his colonial allies regarded as unprecedented. His message of the New Birth—as old, revivalists insisted, as the New Testament itself—had long been proclaimed from evangelical Reformed and Pietist pulpits throughout the Atlantic world. The novelty lay in seeing and hearing an Anglican minister proclaim that doctrine.[94] Revival, an established feature of Reformed church life, had periodically broken out in local congregations of the empire for over 150 years.[95] The novelty lay in the consciousness of the current revival's vast scale, an awareness made possible only as Whitefield published his accomplishments from the Empire's ubiquitous presses and carried revival around the Atlantic rim from one locality to the next. The expansive terms commonly used by revivalists—"great," "general," "momentous"—underscore the element of scale which they regarded as so singular. "It looks as if some happy period were opening, to bless the world with another reformation," Josiah Smith of Charleston declared in 1740. "Some great things seem to be upon the anvil, some big prophecy at the birth: God give it strength to bring forth!"[96]

The novelty of eighteenth-century itinerancy appeared most forcefully in its sudden proliferation after Whitefield's visits. Local pastors who had once been content to minister to their own flocks, departing only occasionally to supply a vacant pulpit or exchange pulpits with a neighboring minister, suddenly began to undertake preaching tours of their own. In the Middle Colonies, Whitefield's visits coincided with and pushed to new levels the practice of itinerancy by various religious groups. Whitefield antagonized many midcolonial ministers by encouraging itinerant Moravian mission activity among midcolonial settlers and urging the Moravian leader Count Nicholaus Ludwig von Zinzendorf to send additional missionaries to America.[97] Among Presbyterians the "Log College men," who had earlier come under censure for unauthorized but otherwise unremarkable preaching in vacant parishes, took up Whitefield's tactics to intrude into parishes occupied by "unconverted" colleagues. The ensuing controversy rent asunder the Presbyterian Synod of Philadelphia. The winter after Whitefield's return to England, Gilbert Tennent took a step unprecedented for an Anglo-American pastor by taking leave of his Presbyterian flock in Neshaminy, Pennsylvania for a three-month preaching tour in the Congregational parishes of neighboring New England.

During the following year, New England ministers like Eleazar Wheelock, Samuel Buell, Jonathan Parsons, Benjamin Pomeroy, the brothers John and Daniel Rogers, James Davenport, and Andrew Croswell were "leaving their own People a long time, to travel about Preaching every Day in the Week . . . to go into other Men's Pulpits or at least into their especial Charge, without their desire or consent."[98] In the Middle Colonies Gilbert Tennent and other New Side Presbyterians continued to draw large crowds by their "travelling preachments."[99] In Charleston, South Carolina, the planter Hugh Bryan startled the local gentry by gathering "frequent assemblies of Negroes" to whom he preached repentance.[100]

"Illiterate *Lay Preachers*" also began traveling the countryside, "delivering themselves with such a peculiar *Pathos,* and Vehemence of Action and Expression, that great Numbers frequently fall down into convulsive *Agitations.*"[101] Not only men, but "Women, Children, Servants, & Negroes" were "strolling about haranguing the admiring vulgar in *extempore* nonsense."[102] The spectacle of such widespread disorder prompted one Boston critic to call for laws regulating the itinerant "Pedlars in Divinity," whose activities he considered "prejudicial to the Commonwealth."[103]

Traveling ministers violated ancient conventions by breaking uninvited into neighboring parish bounds; itinerants from one denomination pursued converts in another; lay exhorters intruded in unprecedented fashion into the right of ordained ministers; blacks and women subverted the "natural" order by exhorting white males. By challenging so broad a range of boundaries, the new itinerancy introduced by Whitefield had broken out of its religious confines to make seemingly irreparable breaches in the local, deferential, patriarchal social order symbolized by the parish. Critics leapt to the defense of that traditional order by attacking itinerancy. In so doing, they elevated it to the status of a conceptual category: a metaphor for a new and unsettling vision of a society whose realization they hoped to prevent at all costs.

2

The Menace of Itinerancy

I

Clerical "opposers" of the revival quickly came to regard itinerancy as a fundamental challenge to their place in the community and their role as guardians of the social order. This perception soon gave rise to a discourse of opposition which represented itinerancy as an engine of social upheaval. Colonial presses began pouring forth a flood of antirevival literature in which doctrine and theology quickly became overshadowed by debates over pulpit rhetoric, the tone of public address, ministerial decorum and authority, and lay deference. Indeed, many who concurred with the itinerants' Calvinist doctrine vigorously opposed their practice.[1] Even those opposed to the Calvinist scheme of grace attacked itinerancy primarily as a theoretical basis for social disorder.

Anglican clergy were the first to recognize evangelical itinerancy's challenge to their self-proclaimed place in the social order. George Whitefield's cavalier disregard for the established hierarchy was played out in his transgression of Anglican parish bounds and his attacks on the clergy who served them. The Grand Itinerant seemed eager to pronounce his Anglican colleagues unconverted bigots who were disobedient to the faith.[2] Anglicans read Whitefield's attack on the Latitudinarian Archbishop John Tillotson as a challenge to the authority of the Established church itself. Clergy responded within weeks of his arrival by shutting him out of church pulpits, preaching sermons against his doctrines, and sending to London for "good books" which they could distribute to counteract his influence.[3] Archibald Cummings, the commissary of Philadelphia, conveyed to the secretary of the SPG his suspicions that the itinerant planned to compete with Anglicanism by "setting up for the Head of a Sect."[4]

Among midcolonial Presbyterians, Whitefield's itinerancy brought to a head a conflict that was already brewing over the meaning and integrity of the local parish bound. To an Old Side faction of Scotch-Irish clergymen, the parish boundary represented both ecclesiastical order and doctrinal purity. This group wielded a bare majority in the fledgling Synod of Philadelphia to defend Presbyterian pulpits and parishes against heretical intruders by imposing stringent requirements for ordination, including university training and strict subscription to the Westminster Confession of Faith. Old Siders also passed Synodical acts designed to seal the local parishes against incursions by unqualified preachers. On the other hand, New Side clergymen, led by graduates of William Tennent's Log College in Neshaminy, Pennsylvania, regarded the parish boundary as a deadly barrier to the advance of the Gospel. Even before George Whitefield's arrival in Pennsylvania, fiery New Side preachers were already flouting the Synod's requirements for ordination and intruding into Old Side parishes without the permission of presbyteries to which the congregations belonged. Whitefield augmented this New Side challenge by forging an alliance with the Tennents and inspiring a host of Presbyterian imitators. New Side itinerancy precipitated a schism in 1741 when the Old Side majority ejected the revivalist Presbytery of New Brunswick from the Synod.[5]

In New England the "settled ministry's" own Calvinism and the ministers' approbation of revival made them slower to recognize itinerancy's challenge to their well-ordered parochial system. When Whitefield visited New England in the autumn of 1740, parish ministers inundated him with letters of invitation not only into individual pulpits but also into the territories of entire ministerial associations. Even those who later became itinerancy's most vitriolic opponents welcomed the Grand Itinerant and imitated his style in their own preaching.[6] Whitefield's whirlwind tour across New England parish bounds aroused little protest. His opposition there consisted mainly of timid exceptions taken to his doctrines in the Boston papers and reprints of bolder attacks by opponents from Philadelphia and Charleston.[7] But opposition grew stronger after December of 1740, when the New Side Presbyterian preacher Gilbert Tennent invaded Congregational territory to "blow up the divine fire lately kindled" in Boston. The proliferation of itinerants after Tennent's departure the following spring fanned this opposition into the most sustained attack on itinerancy of the 1740s.[8]

The opposition literature of antirevival Anglicans, Congregationalists, and Presbyterians drew an explicit link between itinerancy's challenge to the parochial system and its challenge to the entire colonial social order. Critics attacked "roving Strangers" who cut a wide swath across parish and colonial bounds, inviting ordinary laypeople to lay aside their business and congregate with people from other communities and other religious persuasions in one undifferentiated mob. This behavior challenged deeply held assumptions concerning the role of spatial boundaries and of elite brokers in the maintenance of social order. It seemed wildly destructive, threatening to dissolve the order of church and commonwealth into chaos.

Opponents therefore began their critique by explicating the "Language of this going into *other Men's Parishes.*"[9] Itinerancy represented more to them than a mere activity or method of ministry. The action of trespassing willy-nilly across parish bounds also constituted a message, a means of communication susceptible to interpretation.[10] Opponents filled newspapers, essays, pamphlets, and sermons with hostile commentary expounding itinerancy's "language" of destruction. As their critique unfolded, itinerancy developed into a category of social disorder—the harbinger of a growing challenge to the moral and social bounds on which the deferential, elite-brokered order depended. Opponents warned that by attacking these bounds, itinerancy threatened to release individuals from the fabric of traditional constraints which helped situate and preserve each social self within her or his respective place in the community. Critics fretted that by opening new choices and modeling new patterns of behavior, itinerancy would ultimately issue in nothing less than radical social leveling and atomization.

Having expounded itinerancy's destructive message, opponents turned to an explicit defense of their bounded, hierarchical conception of eighteenth-century society. Their discourse constituted far more than the ugly, self-interested clericalism which historians of the Great Awakening have often charged against them.[11] To be sure, their station theoretically established a certain ministerial hegemony over the localities, one that complemented the role of gentry officeholders by upholding moral order within communities and mediating Christian unity among them. Since 1700 an increasing number of clergy had pursued the logic implicit in this social vision. As their gentry counterparts became more Anglicized, they too cultivated the literary tastes, prose style, and pulpit rhetoric which earned them a place among an Anglo-American "public" of "reasonable men," one which excluded the "unlettered" "generality of the people" who fed their minds only on the Bible and almanacs.[12] Yet whether they defended this eighteenth-century version of localism or its simpler, Puritan form, the clergy believed they were acting to preserve their "flocks" from the chaos that would follow if "every man did what was right in his own eyes."[13]

II

Opposers of itinerancy joined battle on a field where their foe already possessed the high ground. Through George Whitefield's skillful use of colonial gazettes, the champions of itinerancy had seemingly already captured the minds of the colonial reading public. Anti-itinerants labored to retrieve this critical public sphere by launching a rhetorical counterattack designed to expose itinerancy as a grave threat to their readers' social world.

The language of anti-itinerant literature played a crucial role in the contest as Old Lights made "itinerancy" a term of opprobrium and described its effects in the most inflammatory phrases. Opposers commonly employed disturbing metaphors of flux, impermanence, and chaos to persuade their readers that itinerancy contained within itself a destructive inner logic, progressing from the breach of the parish bounds to the erosion of colonial society's moral underpinnings. Itinerancy, they warned, was rapidly leading laypeople to abandon the moral injunctions of the minister for the fraudulent pronouncements of "strangers" or capricious inner "Motions," "Impressions," or whims of fancy. Under such conditions community would dissolve into chaos. People would throw off the traditional "bounds of decency and civility" which situated and preserved each person within his or her particular "station" within the local order. As a result, critics warned, the rule of reason would give way to the tyranny of unchecked passion as the mob gained ascendancy over the "better sort."

Several satirical essays adumbrated the nature and extent of itinerancy's threat to the deferential, localistic social order through extended metaphors of motion, instability, transience, and subversion. Although the doctrine of the itinerants played some role in these critiques, their authors devoted far more attention to the destructive social consequences of itinerancy itself.

An Anglican essayist in the *South Carolina Gazette* compared Whitefield's behavior to a comet, or "disorderly kind of a *star* with a *Blaze*." The comet provided a rich metaphor for exploring itinerancy's potential for spatial and social disruption by tapping both its ancient significance as a portent of disaster and contemporary speculation about its disruptive effects in the heavens. Like the track of itinerancy through the parishes, the comet "crosses and interferes with the Paths & Motions of the regular Stars, Planets and other Heavenly Bodies." The novelty of both phenomena drew huge crowds to "stand whole Mornings and Evenings a Gape and a Ghast at the new surprizing Sight!" The comet's rapid motion, like that of itinerancy, betrayed lack of proper deference for the "slow and orderly Planets," which it outstripped "by Ten Millions of Miles in a Day, reproaching their lazy, listless, indolent Course." Its "superior Lustre" increased the comet's arrogant disdain for the "lesser Stars" as it strove to "emulate the Sun himself in dispersing Light and Heat to the cold benighted Regions."[14]

Yet itinerancy and comets both subverted the "regular order of Nature." Like the "wandering, disorderly Comet" whose motion threatened to "disturb and inflame the Order of Nature, and interrupt the regular Influences of the Heavenly Bodies," itinerancy subverted the ministerial guardians of a natural social order. Parish ministers served a function similar to stars by providing steady, reliable points of reference by which the community's members could situate themselves in a bounded, hierarchical, patriarchal social universe. Itinerancy threatened to unleash disruptive influences that would draw away the community's unsteady members by "a kind of sympathetick Power." The consequences could be disastrous for those led "out of their proper course" as well as for the community as a whole.[15]

Critics often invoked this contrast between the deceptive, mobile, unreliable light of itinerancy and the steady light of parish ministers to express both fears of itinerancy's destructive consequences and hopes that such effects would soon fade. Another essayist in the *South Carolina Gazette* preferred the "more ordinary Phaenomenon" of a "*Will-with-Wisp*" which "by a strolling kind of Light, seduces People out of the Way, misguides them into *Boggs* and *Fens,* and there bewildering leaves them."[16] New England ministers such as John Hancock and Isaac Stiles drew a parallel between a comet's irregular motion, which threatened any "Globe, that should happen to come in their way," and itinerancy's "crossing of other men's Spheres," which threatened the churches' "*Peace, Purity* and *Order* exceedingly."[17] Yet the analogy also prompted some colonial critics to take courage from the fact that phenomena such as itinerancy and comets soon passed, losing "most of their Lustre & terror" in the process. They expressed the hope that itinerancy and its New Light, "which has so pestered this part of ye Globe," would soon decline and the "steady lights" regain their customary influence.[18]

The author of "A true and genuine Account of a wonderful Wandering Spirit," which appeared in Benjamin Franklin's *General Magazine* shortly after Whitefield's return to England, detected in itinerancy's disruptive mobility a more pernicious, enduring threat.[19] He warned that this "wandering spirit's" systematic antipathy to rule and order betrayed origins rooted in antinomianism, the belief that salvation released the convert from obligation to any code of conduct, whether human or divine. The essay on the "Wandering Spirit," however, constituted more than a mere theological dispute. It focused instead on the dire social consequences of the antinomian proclivities of itinerancy. The author presented itinerancy's disregard of spatial boundaries as symptomatic of a deeply rooted antipathy to all forms of "bounds and limits," moral and social as well as spatial. The transgression of the parish bound attacked the very foundations of eighteenth-century hierarchical social order.

The author of the "Wandering Spirit" began his diatribe by situating itinerancy within a transatlantic historical context of heterodox, disorderly sectarianism. This spirit, he warned, already possessed a long, troublesome history of antinomian agitation among mobs of sixteenth-century Anabaptists and seventeenth-century Familists, Ranters, and Quakers. Its eighteenth-century manifestations had achieved a transatlantic scope. The spirit was haunting "*Moravia* and many other Places in the *German* Empire" and troubling England even as it made itself "seen, felt and heard by Thousands in *America.*" Its ubiquitous appearance throughout the Protestant world was abetted by a hatred "above all Things" for "Rules and good Order, or bounds and Limits." The spirit possessed a "Protean" ability to "walk gravely in a Quaker dress" at one moment and to "borrow the [Anglican] Gown" the next. At other times it appeared as "the *Arminian,* the *Calvinist,* or *Anabaptist,*" even as "a Fryar or a Monk." In America, however, the spirit's favorite garb was that of a "gifted Brother, or a Lay-holder-forth," and it was readily recognized by its tendency to "ascend the Tribunal that is always at its Elbow" in judgment against reasonable dissidents.[20]

The wandering spirit's appeal to the "mob," a potent term signifying society's disorderly elements, threatened nothing less than moral anarchy. The spirit wielded a dangerous power to make the mob "swell and shake like *Virgil*'s enthusiastick Sybil." At the same time, the spirit weakened the behavioral "bounds and limits" that controlled the mob, teaching that "Say-Soes and Declarations, Wry-Faces and Grimaces, Contortions of the Body and vocal Energy, Faintings and Cryings, delusive Voices and frantick Visions" provided undeniable evidence of conversion while disallowing the testimony of a "holy and pious life." The spirit wrested the Bible, the very source of moral boundaries, from the mob by "persuading its Votaries, that nothing but its Suggestions are GOD's mind in the Scripture." Consequently, some, "while under its Impulses, have wallowed in Lewdness."[21]

The wandering spirit's assault on spatial and institutional "bounds and limits" threatened social leveling as well. Arrogance, impudence, and imposture provided the chief means by which the spirit assaulted social boundaries. It freely dispensed bogus "Warrants and commissions under the broad Seal of an inward Call to all that have Conceit enough to run its Errands." By this device the wandering spirit flooded the countryside with "Lay-holders-forth" who supposed a "sanctified Cobbler" might instantly become "an abler Divine than either *Luther* or *Calvin*." The notion of an authoritative inward call undermined deference to ministers and magistrates whose authority rested on reasoned study and preparation, social recognition, and institutional certification. The spirit's malicious bearing toward these reasonable guardians of social bounds betrayed its fiendish identity as either "*Moloch,* or *Apollyon* the Destroyer."[22]

Other colonial satirists expressed similar fears of social chaos by cloaking itinerancy in the garb of such figures as popish emissaries, Camizar prophets, traveling peddlers, and wandering confidence men. By means of such metaphors, critics articulated their perception of an integral, causative relationship between the practice and a cluster of disturbing moral categories. For persons who conceived of social order as a set of fixed relations anchored by local elites, itinerancy's mobility and popularity wrought fears of subversion, disorder, deception, imposture, impudence, conceit, and moral anarchy. The vivid imagery employed in these metaphors provided powerful tools for expressing the threat opponents detected in itinerancy.[23]

In addition to satire, opposers of itinerancy wielded the newspaper report in tandem with the pamphlet as weapons for recapturing the public sphere. After Whitefield's return to England, the itinerancy which confronted the colonial reading public in newspaper reports was often a representation produced by a hostile pen. Opponents commonly laced accounts of itinerant preaching with inflammatory rhetoric and caustic commentary. As itinerancy increased during 1741 and 1742, they supplemented these newspaper reports with controversial pamphlets which offered fuller expositions of the "language of itinerancy." Both served as devices for exploring more fully the logic of moral and social breakdown inherent in this manifold threat to the colonial social order.

Opposers began by reporting incidents that revealed how this language of itinerancy subverted the collegial deference which had traditionally ordered relations among members of the ministerial elite. An itinerant's very presence in the parish of another constituted a public affront both to the settled minister and the ecclesiastical structure which had ordained him. To a Charleston essayist the itinerant's passage betrayed the arrogant presumption that his gifts were superior to those of the settled clergy.[24] A Boston critic stated the matter plainly during Gilbert Tennent's tour of New England by charging that the "natural Construction" to be placed on the Pennsylvanian's visit was that he considered New England ministers "Insufficient for their Office."[25] Another declared Tennent's itinerancy a "bare-faced Affront to the *generality of the Ministry*."[26] Old Side Presbyterians concurred that the incursions of "new-fangle Preachers" prompted parishioners to "despise their own Pastors . . . as sapless, lifeless Preachers."[27]

Opponents supported their construction of itinerancy's language with quotations from traveling preachers who declared "the body of the Ministry" unconverted and so unfit for their office. Critics constantly reminded their readers that George Whitefield himself had initiated this practice by asserting that most colonial ministers "do not experimentally know Christ" and declaring that unconverted ministers could no more act as agents of salvation than "a dead man could beget a living child."[28] Opposers also targeted Gilbert Tennent for his sermon *The Danger of an Unconverted Ministry,* first preached at Nottingham, Pennsylvania in defiance of Old Side Presbyterian attempts to silence itinerants. In the view of critics, this sermon had done incalculable damage to the colonial parish ministry. The wide scope of its publication alone constituted a public affront to local ministers throughout the colonies who were accustomed to "charitable," or deferential, treatment from their peers. Tennent's sermon further encouraged readers, lay and clerical alike, to withhold deference from unconverted ministers by branding them usurpers of pulpits who held "no Call of GOD to the Ministerial Work under the Gospel-Dispensation." Tennent depicted such men as "Pharisee-Teachers," "crafty as Foxes" and "Cruel as Wolves" in their efforts to gain worldly wealth and preferment through a ministry that neither profited the unconverted nor comforted the converted. Souls confined within an unconverted minister's parish bounds were "truly to be pitied" because of their danger of eternal damnation. Tennent's sermon constituted a proclamation of "Christian Liberty" which declared itinerant laborers free to go forth "into the harvest" and parishioners free to seek spiritual nourishment "out of the Parish-Line."[29]

Opponents read in Tennent's impudent affront to parish ministers a challenge not only to clericalism but to deferential localism itself.[30] Tennent's justification of itinerancy violated a long-standing assumption among ministers that ordained colleagues would defer to one's authority over one's own flock. It also gave parishioners explicit permission to snub the parish minister by seeking spiritual guides outside the parish line. Old Siders therefore moved quickly in the Presbyterian Synod of Philadelphia to enforce this traditional deference among the ministry by acts ensuring that "every Pastor should stick by his own Flock," preventing "one Ministers preaching in anothers Bounds to the Disturbance of the Peace of the Church."[31] Congregational ministers likewise defended the parishes as "flocks" or "*Christ's Inclosures*" over which they had been appointed "shepherds" or "husbandmen."[32]

The tone of hostile news reports grew more strident as Tennent's jeremiad bore its fruit in a proliferation of itinerants. The authority of local pastors over Christ's enclosures seemed to be dissolving as scores of New Light ministers throughout the colonies "pretended to immediate Impressions from the Spirit to leave their own People a long time, and to travel about Preaching." Such persons not only broke with tradition by deserting their own flocks; they compounded their transgression by claiming private "impressions" as "sufficient Warrant to go into other Men's Pulpits, or at least into their especial Charge, without their desire or consent," to declare the settled minister unconverted and usurp his ministerial function.[33]

The career of James Davenport provided opposers such a wealth of useful matter that they made his traveling ministry a paradigm of the chaotic consequences of itinerancy in their hostile reports.[34] Opposers used the Long Island minister's exploits to dramatize how the long-distance, boundary-transgressing character of itinerancy undermined those hierarchical social relations which simultaneously secured the order of the local communities and depended on the security of local bounds. One critic reported that on his itinerary through southern Connecticut, Davenport condemned "almost *all* the Ministers," incited quarrels in every community, and encouraged lay participation in services where reigned "the most amazing confusion that ever was heard."[35] The people in these communities had evidently understood the language of Davenport's itinerancy all too clearly and responded by throwing off the local ministry's social as well as spiritual authority. "What does the man intend," another asked his readers concerning Davenport's attacks on parish ministers, "but to smite the shepherd that the Sheep may be scattered?"[36] Critical reports were fashioned to show how his itinerancy encouraged people to abandon their ministers and cross parish lines to "have their ears tickled" by "such as come from the ends of the Earth."[37]

Critical reports of itinerants who followed Davenport were crafted to show how wide the Long Island preacher had opened the floodgates of outrageous contempt for the settled ministry's parochial rights on the part of parishioners and New Light ministers. A particularly powerful example of such reporting involved the itinerant Philemon Robbins, who preached in southern Connecticut shortly after the Davenport tours of 1741. A correspondent to the *Boston Weekly Post-Boy* reported that in October of that year, this "stranger minister" made bold to baptize a child in Joseph Noyes's New London parish bounds "on the pretense that Mr. Noyes is unconverted and so no Minister." The reporter underscored the invidiousness of this unprecedented act with a quotation from the book of Judges: "And it was so, that all those that saw it, said, There was no such Deed done nor seen from the Day that the Children of *Israel* came up out of the Land of *Egypt* until this Day."[38] Readers would have recognized the quotation as the ancient Israelites' response to the abominable rape and murder of a Levite's concubine by members of the Israeli tribe of Benjamin, and the subsequent dismemberment and distribution of her corpse throughout the land to galvanize the Lord's people into action.

The equation of Philemon Robbins's act with this ancient biblical atrocity exposed the depth and complexity of significance which the violation of parish bounds held for the Old Light ministry. The scriptural allusion invoked the metaphor of marriage, commonly employed to describe the relationship between a pastor and his parish, by identifying the parish with the concubine of a Levite—a figure entrusted with the spiritual training and care of God's people Israel.[39] The allusion made Robbins's administration of the Sacrament within Noyes's parish bounds an abominable act of rape, a violation of the parish as well as the bonds of love between pastor and parishioner. It also carried overtones of betrayal: another minister, a member of Noyes's own brotherhood, was guilty of this outrage.

This metaphor of rape and mayhem was only one dramatic thrust in a larger campaign to depict itinerancy's violation of the parish line as more than simple anticlericalism. Opposers labored to show that itinerancy, by challenging ministerial rights, also assaulted the less tangible but even more crucial "bounds of decency"—those traditional standards of decorum which signified and reinforced the place of each person in the local social order. Itinerancy itself was a violation of decorum in that its practitioners traveled rather than remained settled, preached to strangers rather than their "own People," preached extempore rather than "studied sermons," and disrupted the normal patterns of community life by preaching "every day in the week."[40] Itinerants' "Manner of Diction or Phraseology" likewise constituted a "Disgrace to the sacred Function of the Ministry of the Gospel." Their "Profane Reveries . . . borrowed from *Billinsgate* rather than the Holy Scriptures" terrified audiences into abandoning all standards of public self-presentation as they erupted in a confusion of weeping, outcries, convulsions, and ecstacies.[41] Gatherings thus bereft of decorum qualified as unruly mobs, not civil communal assemblies.

A satirist in the *South Carolina Gazette* illustrated the relationship between itinerancy and the breakdown of public decorum by contrasting the "Exploits and Adventures of the most renowned Fanatic-Itinerant Don Georgio Whitefieldio" with the polite ministry of John Foster, a fashionable London minister. The essay was published nine months after Whitefield had left "the Work" in America to a growing army of colonial itinerants whose "enthusiastic" preaching was raging, according to *Gazette* reports, throughout America.[42] In a passage reminiscent of a Hogarth engraving, the satirist called on his readers to imagine the "mock-St. Paul" mounted on a wagon in London's Kensington Common "surrounded by a Crowd of Porters, Butchers, and Carmen, by the Beggarly and the Idle, the Loose and the Lazy of both sexes . . . pouring forth his dark, mysterious and unintelligible *Jargon* . . . while the ignorant *Rabble* sigh and groan in universal Applause."[43]

Mr. Foster's London church, on the other hand, furnished a model of eighteenth-century decorum. From his proper place in the pulpit, Foster quelled the churnings of the rabble with speech appropriate to a minister: a presentation of "*Truth, Virtue,* and *Religion* with the Force of nervous Sense, clear and manly Reasoning, dress'd in all the Charms of Eloquence, and delivered with the proper Risings and Fallings of a melodious Voice, and a Decorum of Gesture." His meticulous observance of the standards of polite discourse made Foster's church a microcosm of eighteenth-century order, its pews filled with "all the finest Speakers in both Houses of Parliament, the wise and the good among the three *learned* Professions, and a large Circle of Gentlemen and Ladies of distinguished Taste and good Sense."[44] This, in the Charleston satirist's view, was the proper model for American society, and the one which Whitefield's itinerancy was challenging.

If the language of Whitefield's indecorous behavior weakened customary constraints on the public behavior of Englishmen, the itinerancy of his American counterparts posed an even greater challenge to colonial standards of decorum. Old Lights berated the extempore performances of colonial itinerants as poor imitations of Whitefield and worse violations of acceptable public discourse and conduct. The "harangues" seemed calculated to "affright [people's] Imaginations . . . by awful Words and frightful Representations . . . That they are now hanging over the Pit of eternal Destruction . . . and they will often repeat the awful Words *Damn'd Damn'd, Damn'd,* three or four times over."[45] If Whitefield shocked polite sensibilities with "field-preaching," Samuel Buell, James Davenport, and Andrew Croswell added insult to injury by leading people in procession through the streets, exhorting and singing "hymns of human composition."[46] Even when preaching in the meetinghouse, itinerants commonly came out from behind the pulpit to stand in the deacon's seat or even among the congregation.[47] Buell and Croswell transgressed the "bounds of decency" even further by stripping off their shirts as they held forth in the summer heat—an act permissible to a farmer harvesting crops but completely out of character for a harvester of souls.[48]

Opposers perceived itinerancy's challenge to the orderly bounds of public decency, bad though that was, as symptomatic of the much more profound threat to local order posed by antinomian implications of the "inward assurance" that stranger ministers preached. The doctrine that God's Spirit made people instantaneously certain of conversion provoked intense opposition as tending to strip religion of "all good Principles . . . Peace and Order, Humility and Charity, and indeed all Righteousness of our own."[49] The doctrine flatly contradicted the overt Arminianism of people like Commissary Garden of Charleston who saw salvation as the "*gradual co-operative* Work of God's *Holy Spirit,* joining in with our *Understandings,* and leading us on by *Reason* and *Persuasion,* from one Degree to another, of Faith, Good Disposition, Acts, and Habits of Piety."[50] It also ran counter to the subtle New England "Arminianism" descended from Puritan preparationist theology which taught individuals to prepare their hearts for conversion and to base their sense of assurance on observable standards of belief and practice.[51]

Both Arminian and Reformed opposers worried that by appearing to divorce the knowledge of a person's conversion from her or his outward behavior, the doctrine of inward assurance undermined Christianity's role in the preservation of that person's place and the place of every other person within the deferential, elite-brokered social order. Ministers of both persuasions expected the observance of Christian virtues to aid in fixing each member of the community into his or her own place within well-defined local networks of kinship and status. True conversion should actually reinforce and strengthen the bonds of deference and decorum which served to define the individual self by situating it in a particular place in that order. Conversion should prompt more diligent obedience to "them that have Rule over us," greater reverence for one's "betters," more honor for parents, humbler submission of wives to husbands, greater charity among neighbors, and more contentment in one's own calling.[52]

Old Lights warned that itinerancy's doctrine of assurance would loose the bonds of community by rendering conversion a means of releasing individuals from this web of local relationships. James Davenport's dealings with the "distress'd" provided one hostile reporter a concrete example of the disruptive effects on community when strangers presumed to dole out assurance to those they did not know. He reported that Davenport commonly stood in the deacon's seat, took the hands of the distressed, and assured them that "they have received Comfort, tho' he has never seen their faces before, without examining into the Grounds and Reasons of their Hope and Comforts, he acknowledges them true Disciples, welcomes them into the Kingdom of Christ, and sings a Hymn over them: *A Custom that we have not known, nor the Churches of God.*"[53] Davenport not only intruded his own disorderly person into this web of local relationships but also dared to arrogate to himself a right traditionally reserved to members of the local community: that of confirming conversion, a key element in the constitution of an individual's social self. The consequences of such a presumptive break with Congregational tradition became immediately apparent as those who received assurance from Davenport indulged a "bitter, uncharitable, censorious Spirit" that rent the fabric of community life.[54]

Critics presented the complete dissolution of local order as following logically and inevitably from these antinomian claims to assurance. A contributor to the *General Magazine* satirized assurance as a concoction composed of such ingredients as "Pretention, Hypocrisy and Ambition . . . Spirits of Pride . . . Seeds of Discord and Dissention . . . Roots of Obstinacy, Ignorance and Controversy." When the person who quaffed it finished quaking, roaring, and groaning, he could "vaunt like a Pharisee, censure and damn all his Neighbours . . . and then shall he be qualified to delude the People, wound the Church, justify Delusion, foment Rebellion against Authority, and extol Anarchy and Usurpation under the fair Names of the Work of God and Liberty of Conscience."[55]

Antirevivalists reported the conduct of "the mob" in phrases calculated to show that itinerancy was indeed fomenting social anarchy within colonial communities. Critics in the port cities published complaints that Whitefield's preaching "divert[ed] and distract[ed] the Labouring people, who were too much affected by novelties."[56] A Boston correspondent informed readers of the *South Carolina Gazette* that Gilbert Tennent employed his "great Faculty to confound the World" and his unrestrained immodesty and dishonesty to "take us off entirely from all Business, set the Women a gadding about the Streets, and our Chaise and Coach Wheels all in a Flame."[57] Each new wave of itinerancy brought fresh "discoveries" of "Mr. *Whitefield*'s doctrine of *inward Feelings*" as people "*cried out, fell down* and *swooned away,* and, to all appearance, were like persons in *Fits.*"[58] In the view of one Boston wag, only a full-scale invasion by Spanish minions could create more confusion. He accordingly advised itinerants to call on "all able-bodied men from *Grenada* to the *Straits* of *Magellan* to come up and help us in *carrying on the Work.*" He also proposed a building on Boston Common big enough to accommodate the people itinerants were enticing from their traditional stations in community life: "*Teachers, Exhorters,* and *Armor Bearers, Whites* and *Blacks, Young* and *Old,* from the *Shopkeepers,* the *Deacons,* and the *Bakers,* to the *Coblers,* and the People, particularly the *good Women,* who will apply to them."[59]

Critics portrayed itinerancy and the belief in inward assurance as twin assaults on the most basic social categories which members of the community employed to construe one another's social identities. Itinerancy not only eroded the deferential boundaries which subordinated "private persons" to their magistrates and laypersons to their ministers; it also challenged the distinctions of parenthood, gender, and race which eighteenth-century thinkers conceived as establishing a natural hierarchy of authority and status. Itinerants did so both by pronouncing strangers converted and by giving implicit and explicit approval to a variety of public acts traditionally forbidden to community members of lesser status or qualifications.

Opposers depicted itinerant lay exhortation as a primary means by which this social erosion took place. By "endowing" youthful converts "with great Power and Felicity in Speaking in Publick," James Davenport and other itinerants encouraged them to think "they have more of the Spirit of God than their Ministers."[60] Lay exhorters did not confine their effrontery to the ministry. "Swarms" of "*raw, illiterate, weak and conceited young Men, or Lads*" went about declaring that parents, elders, and betters were "dropping into Hell."[61]

Even more disturbing was the transgression of racial decorum that came as black servants began to declaim against their white masters. Many antirevivalists opposed conversion of slaves entirely. Others argued that "poor Negroes have not been vindicated into the glorious Liberty of the Children of God unless their Manners have been altered by becoming better Servants, more faithful, diligent, honest and obedient to their own Masters."[62] New Lights, however, seemed deliberately to be fomenting rebellion. Hugh Bryan's prophecies of the destruction of Charleston by black slaves terrified South Carolina planters, who had crushed the Stono Uprising of slaves only two years before.[63] Bryan abandoned his pretensions after drenching himself in a local river while attempting to emulate the biblical Joshua by parting the waters for the passage of black followers. His humiliation and public confession of delusion delivered a serious blow to "Whitefieldianism" in South Carolina, where the fortunes of evangelical religion did not recover for more than a decade.[64]

In the northern colonies where the African-American population was smaller, the fear of slave revolt was supplemented by warnings that divine order was being violated by the public preaching of blacks. No antirevival text illustrates this more clearly than the brief, probably apocryphal report of a black exhorter from Colchester, Pennsylvania who attempted to exhort in the meetinghouse at the end of Sunday worship. When several white worshipers tried to silence him, he defied them by withdrawing to a nearby orchard. There, according to the reporter, his exhortation to the whites who followed was disrupted by two "large monstrous black Snakes," which "crept up on his Back, and look'd over each of his Shoulders to the great surprise both of himself and his Audience." The significance of this startling portent hardly required explanation for readers steeped in biblical symbolism, and the reporter offered none. Instead, he allowed his reported hearers' response to speak for itself. They quickly killed the serpents and dismissed the black exhorter who had played unwitting host to the very embodiment and color of evil and subversion.[65]

Hostile reporters also represented itinerancy as loosening the bonds of affection and patriarchal authority which located members of the family in hierarchical relationship to one another. They fashioned newspaper and pamphlet accounts showing how itinerancy subverted this fundamental unit of local life. It did so, they argued, by mounting two related challenges to what they conceived as the natural, divinely ordered subordination of women to husbands and fathers. First, itinerancy seduced women's affections from husbands and fathers. Second, it encouraged the overt intrusion of unruly women into public roles traditionally reserved to men. Old Lights took note of Whitefield's facility for "moving the passions of the people, especially the *females.*"[66] The fear of itinerancy's seductiveness underlay the frequent Old Light estimates that a majority of itinerants' converts were women. It also manifested itself in insinuations that itinerants committed fornication and adultery with women who applied to them for "spiritual comfort." Such suspicions occasionally received confirmation, as in the case of a woman who in 1741 swore before a Pennsylvania court that she had been "deflower'd" by a preacher "mentioned by *Whitefield* in his Journal as a holy *Man.*"[67] Itinerancy's seductiveness ultimately undermined patriarchy by the subtle means first employed by the Serpent in the Garden of Eden: by "working themselves into the good esteem" of women, itinerants "soon hook'd in the *Husbands* also."[68]

Critics discovered additional proof of the threat to patriarchy in an increase in public exhortation by women. In Philadelphia an uproar led by a woman broke out in the Baptist meetinghouse against

Ebenezer Kinnersly, a Baptist minister who preached against the revival shortly after Whitefield's visit in the spring of 1740. The woman, who "support[ed] such a Character as Modesty forbids to mention," protested Kinnersly's sermon by running out of the meetinghouse, followed by "a Multitude of Negroes, and other Servants, among whom were some few of higher Stations, but not overburthen'd with Discretion."[69] Andrew Croswell received assistance in Plymouth, Massachusetts from a "big-bellied Woman from an hind Seat" who "straddled into the Pulpit," a sacred space strictly reserved for educated, ordained males. The unfriendly witness to this event reported that she was "inspired with so much useful Matter, as took her up half an Hour to deliver it; which she did as vivaciously as *C——ll,* extending her arms every Way, and not a Muscle of her Body but in Action."[70]

These women and others like them in antirevival literature were depicted as wrenching themselves free of their God-ordained place in the natural order. Detractors asserted that even before itinerancy provided an excuse for their behavior, these women had displayed characteristics that transgressed the bounds of decency, decorum, and morality. The Philadelphia woman allegedly supported an immoral character; the Plymouth woman, indecent obesity and overassertiveness. Itinerancy, however, disrupted the webs of local behavioral constraints which aimed at suppressing or eradicating these unacceptable characteristics of the self. Indeed, it gave women permission to express publicly their scorn for contemporary bounds of decency. In both cases, pandemonium resulted. Black slaves and white servants publicly threw off cultural restraints to follow the reportedly unsavory woman who had taken what was considered a man's place at the head of the procession from the Philadelphia meetinghouse. In Plymouth the public intrusion of the big-bellied woman into the sacred space reserved for educated, ordained males resulted in a total inversion of local order as the parish minister himself "fell in with the Rant." Having already yielded his pulpit to a woman, it was a small matter for him to yield his proper role as spiritual father of his congregation to his exhorting eight-year-old son. A disorderly "singing Procession" around Plymouth ensued in which each participant "delivered the yell he was particularly inspired with, join'd with all the mad Gestures and Actions that *Franticks* show."[71]

What had begun as a violation of the parish bound was quickly progressing, in the antirevivalists' view, to a fundamental dislocation of everyone—women and men, blacks and whites, children and parents, tradesmen and gentlemen, servants and masters—from their God-given place in the natural order. "Sisters, no longer mind old Paul / To Teach we know you have a call," quipped one Old Light bard.[72] His poem went on to express a common conviction among antirevivalists that the subordination of women was the keystone in the arch of familial and communal order, and that the refusal to "mind old Paul" would bring about that order's collapse. In Old Light literature the parishes where women exhorted were commonly portrayed as overcome by a total breakdown of social restraints: craftsmen leaving their callings to exhort, slaves disobeying their masters, children exhorting their parents. "Turn your view," urged the Boston Old Light Charles Chauncy, "into all corners of the Land: Behold the Confusion in Towns; the Contention in Churches; the Alienations and Separations of People from one another and from their Ministers: Behold the Heat of Men's Spirits . . . the Disorders of their Practice."[73]

The general disorder also prompted many who had welcomed Whitefield and the revival to have serious second thoughts. Nathaniel Stone of Harwich, Massachusetts, for example, acknowledged the "Signal Work of the Holy Ghost of late . . . superior to what has been seen in many past Years." Nevertheless, he detected in these manifold disorders "the Work of the Devil, in promoting what tends to blast and ruin that Work."[74] Nathaniel Appleton likewise observed that the itinerancy which "had a plausible appearance at first view" had produced results of "a very dangerous tendency."[75] Others professed themselves "considerably at loss" at the "first appearance of these things . . . and rather inclined to think that God did own such mistaken zeal." The disorders and separations which engulfed the land had disabused them of such weak-minded notions.[76] The gravity of the situation called for aggressive defense of the parish bounds and the deferential order within them.

III

The magnitude of itinerancy's threat made the contest over the parish bound the critical theater of a much larger cultural war. Old Lights did not act merely to defend clericalism. They also advocated a vision of society in which minister and magistrate united to uphold the moral order of the communities and mediate unity among them. Gentry and clergy alike had become more self-consciously Anglicized since 1700, more attuned to the literature, style, and rhetoric of the metropolis. As provincial participants in this literary culture they situated themselves in a transatlantic "public" of "reasonable men" which stood apart from the "private persons" whose views seldom appeared in the press or other organs of public expression. Old Lights therefore championed far more than the spiritual rights of the clergy. They also supported the role of the parish and its ministry in ordering the colonial social world according to eighteenth-century standards of civilization and culture. By restoring the parish bound they not only hoped to restore themselves to the social preeminence traditionally accorded the parish minister; they also sought to restore others—gentry magistrates, "private men," women, youths, children, and servants—to their respective stations within a reasonable, hierarchical social order.

From 1741 to 1745, attempts to repair itinerancy's breaches in the bounds of parish and society focused mainly on New England and the Middle Colonies. Hugh Bryan's escapades in South Carolina had brought discredit to revivalist methods there, and the itinerancy of New Side Presbyterians would not arouse major controversy in Virginia until the later 1740s. Opponents from Pennsylvania to New Hampshire bore the brunt of itinerancy's assault. They began their reconstruction of the social order at the same point itinerants had begun to tear it down: the parish bound itself. Old Siders in the Presbyterian Synod of Philadelphia attempted to stamp out the itinerancy of the Log College men by act of synod; Connecticut Old Lights by act of the General Assembly.[77] Yet both found it necessary to wage the largest part of the battle for the parish bound in the public arena of print.

This published discourse drew upon Scripture, history, tradition, and reason to repair the breaches in the patchwork of local parishes which differentiated the settled landscape from the wild, "ungospelized wilderness" beyond. This attention to the geographical boundary of the parish symbolized a far deeper series of contests over eighteenth-century norms of authority, status, and deference which itinerancy had breached in transgressing the parish. The discourse retraced itinerancy's destructive course through these boundaries.

Anti-itinerants sought to restore mutual deference among ministerial and lay elites to their respective spheres of authority, and humble submission of uneducated "private men" to the superior status and authority of both. They also sought to restore the boundaries of decorum which preserved women, youths, children, and servants within their subordinate spheres. In the process, the system of stationing ministers within "different parts of our Lord's Harvest" emerged as the basic structure of an entire social universe.[78]

Anti-itinerants defended the parish line first and foremost as a metaphor for a deferential relationship between ministerial peers: a mutual respect for exclusive rights to preach, teach, administer the sacraments, and exercise discipline within a given congregation. Itinerants had challenged this conception of ministerial authority and deference not only by uninvited intrusions into Old Light "peculiars" but also by appeals to the New Testament example of Jesus and the apostles, all of whom were traveling preachers.[79] Opponents responded with an alternative explanation of New Testament itinerancy as a temporary necessity arising from the lack of "settled Churches." The apostles remedied this problem as soon as possible by "planting Evangelical Churches" and settling them with pastors and teachers. Moreover, ministers ordained by the apostles provided the true pattern for those in subsequent ages by exemplifying the mutual deference which Old Lights defended. New Testament ministers refused to "neglect their own proper charge, and strole about from Town to Town . . . as the manner of our Travelling Preachers is at this Time." Not even the apostles themselves ever ventured "to subvert and overthrow those settled churches, by telling them their Ministers were Unconverted."[80] Their traveling ministries usually took them to "such as sat in heathenish Darkness, or, if elsewhere, they were constituted Visitors and Inspectors of the Churches."[81]

Far from sanctioning the practice of itinerancy among settled parishes, Old Lights argued, the New Testament pattern indicated that the Holy Ghost called ministers through regular ordination to serve locally over their "respective flocks." This was the "Order of the Gospel" which the Puritan Fathers had instituted in New England. Any minister who invaded the "Peculiar" of another subverted that biblically sanctioned order and the "Peace of the Churches" which it was designed to ensure. Seen in this light, the apostles' example instructed those who found their parishes "too strait for them" to "go abroad among the ungospelized Heathen" rather than intrude into "Another's Line."[82] Faithfulness to the "Gospel Order" demanded that parish ministers do all they could to discountenance itinerants and deny them admission to their pulpits or anywhere else within their parish. It also demanded that laypeople dutifully remain within their own parish line, refusing to attend the preaching of itinerants wherever they might appear.[83]

Anti-itinerants claimed history as a second ally in the battle for the restoration of mutual deference among ministers within their "peculiars." The Old Side Presbyterian John Thomson argued that within historic Presbyterianism, the parish served as the linchpin of the entire Presbyterian system of polity and doctrine. Presbyterian church government was designed to protect and enforce a "sacred and religious Tie" between minister and parishioners, a tie which should never be dissolved without "sufficient Reasons given and proved before a lawful Church-Judicatory." Since the Reformation, he argued, "Our Forefathers . . . both Ministers and People, carried on all their religious Affairs in a regular manner, according to the Rules of Presbyterian Church-Government, every Pastor having his own Flock committed to him to feed, and being also taken Care of by the respective Presbyteries at their solemn visitations."[84] Thomson thus represented itinerancy as a radical break with Presbyterian history as well as a mortal stroke by which "all Order and Government is at once knocked in Pieces, and our Directory exploded as a slavish confining scheme."[85] Thomson knew whereof he spoke. Itinerancy in Ulster had given rise to rogues "unaccountable to any earthly Judge or Judicature," whose challenge pressed beyond the parish bound to the confessions and catechism themselves.[86]

Congregationalists likewise invoked the testimony of history to bolster the ministers' claims to exclusive authority vis-à-vis other ministers within their own "peculiars." By taking special care to bind each resident minister to a single congregation, the "Fathers of these Plantations" had bequeathed an ecclesiastical system that was the "*Strength* as well as *Beauty*" of New England. Charles Chauncy recalled that "*First Fathers* of this Country . . . next to *Faith* . . . esteemed *Order* a Matter of Necessity to the *Well-Being* of these Churches." This esteem prompted them to declare in the Cambridge Platform their "united Judgment" that "*Elders* are appointed to feed, not all *Flocks,* but the *particular* Flock over which the Holy Ghost hath made them Overseers." It was evident from the "whole Scope of the *Platform*" that "our *Fathers* never imagin'd it warrantable, either from *Reason,* or the *Word of God,* for Ministers to *act* in any Church besides their *own,* unless with the *Consent,* not of a Party *only* in the *Church,* but the *Body of the Church;* yea, and with the Concurrence also of the *Elder.*"[87] Others found support for these principles in the writings of later generations of New England ministers and English Dissenters as well. Anti-itinerants read history as a unanimous injunction against itinerancy's break with the Reformed tradition, wherein each minister "stuck by his own charge" and deferred to the parochial rights of colleagues.[88]

Anti-itinerants supplemented this effort to restore deference among ministers with an effort to seal their pulpits against an "unbounded license of publick teaching" by laypersons. Itinerancy had encouraged laymen to "invade the ministerial office" by insisting that the normal qualifications for ministry—an education, a "call" or formal invitation to the ministry of a particular congregation, and ordination by the ministerial association—were all worthless without conversion.[89] Old Lights countered that the Spirit no longer issued direct "calls" as the itinerants claimed, but chose his present-day messengers through "ordinary operations." By these he guided qualified men as they tested the knowledge and gifts of candidates for the ministry, examined their morals, and finally ordained them ministers of local flocks. Laypersons were therefore duty bound to determine that if a minister "prays well, and preaches well, and converses well," they must judge him converted and submit to his God-ordained authority.[90]

Anti-itinerants again drew on Scripture and history to support their closing of the pulpit to uneducated, unordained laypersons. Christ himself had given implicit sanction to education and ordination by training his apostles for three years before furnishing them with "Powers and Credentials sufficient for their Work." The purity of Christianity had depended ever since on the services of its "wise and learned Defenders."[91] The New England churches likewise owed their unparalleled purity to the vigilance of the first generation of educated ministers. They had courageously opposed the Antinomians, "Private Men" (and women) who presumed to need "*no Books* but the *Bible;* and instead of *Learning,* they must *rely on the SPIRIT.*"[92] They had also founded "Seminaries of Learning" in the conviction that "the Interest of *Religion* and *good Literature* have been wont to rise and fall together." Because of the fathers' foresight, the churches of New England and "many other Lands" had long enjoyed the blessings of peace, order, and purity.[93]

This defense of learning represented more than a simple attempt to restore the New England churches to their pristine, seventeenth-century purity. Learning also constituted a bulwark of reason against the social chaos produced by superstition and enthusiasm. It had enabled the fathers to restore the peace of infant towns disrupted by the Antinomian controversy. It was now helping to bring all of New England out of the darkness of seventeenth-century superstition and religious upheaval into the polite, anglicized society which eighteenth-century colonists had begun to enjoy. The authors of the *Testimony and Advice of a Number of Laymen* noted that before Whitefield's arrival an "enlightened spirit" had begun to prevail in the universities and among the people. "Freedom of inquiry" had led New Englanders to reject "Bigotry and Superstition" in favor of the reasonable, tolerant moralism of the "great and good Drs. Tillotson and Clark." As a result, New England had begun to enjoy marks of a virtuous commonwealth: peace and harmony, absence of "Party Zeal and Rage," "Tolerance of differing Opinions," and quiet industry among people who remained within the bounds of their station in the social order.[94]

On this level, restoration of itinerancy's "dreaded Foe and Enemy, Reason" demanded that the defense of ordination and education be supplemented by a restoration of proper pulpit decorum and learned rhetoric which preserved the dominance of an anglicized, cosmopolitan elite. Rhetoric aimed at the passions rather than the reason had breached the bounds of decorum to unleash a torrent of "Uneasiness, Jarring, Divisions, Discontent, uncharitable censuring and judging, and Separations."[95] The Presbyterian John Thomson had called for ministers to remedy a similar situation by adhering to "the form of sound Words contained in the Scriptures."[96] A South Carolinian had noted the orderliness induced by "clear and manly Reasoning, dress'd in all the Charms of Eloquence."[97] Congregational Old Lights voiced their agreement with this solution by calling on ministers to "discountenance itinerants" and labor to restore "a just decorum in speaking in the house of God."[98]

Antirevivalists also fought to restore the rule of reason by lampooning the prose style of itinerancy's supporters. These seemingly pedantic quarrels over style and grammar in fact constituted fierce power struggles for the minds of the reading public. A controversy sparked by the appearance of the Reading, Massachusetts, minister William Hobby's defense of itinerancy provides an excellent example of this struggle. Hobby's *Inquiry into the Itinerancy and the Conduct of the Rev. Mr. George Whitefield* drew a flurry of responses from Old Lights.[99] From opening to conclusion, these pamphlets mingled ad hominem arguments against the New Light author with merciless attacks on Hobby's stylistic foibles. "J. F." castigated the "doughty defender" of "religious Quixotism" who "could not so much as indite a Title-Page, that was *English,* or that express'd what he *intended to defend!*" For J. F., Hobby's errors of grammar and style alone were enough to demonstrate that he had overreached himself by publishing. The New Light should have remained content "to have half the Farmers and Mechanicks in a Country parish, with their Wives and Children, boldly affirm, that *Mr. Hobby* is a great Schollard and a *high-learned Man*" rather than to suppose that "the World would receive his Piece, with the same implicit faith and blind Approbation" as parishioners received his "Sunday Harangues."[100] The anonymous author of *A Twig of Birch for Billy's Breech* took on the role of a schoolmaster to bring Hobby to a sense of his "false Grammar and bad English" with "a little *Birch,* duly apply'd."[101]

Hobby's opponents, by contrast, self-consciously shaped their prose to demonstrate their rightful station in an Anglo-American lettered elite. All strove to emulate the best English style, complete with allusions to Pope and Dean Swift. The Lynn minister Nathaniel Henchman's criticism of Hobby's prose reveals the significance of this anglicized style. Henchman lampooned Hobby's "nervous and conclusive" reasoning, his "natural and instructive" comparisons, his genteel deference to scholarly opponents, and his "acquaintance with the various Parts of valuable Learning and rare Embellishments with rhetorical Flowers." He expressed mock confidence that Hobby's "amiable union . . . of the compleat Gentleman, forcible Reasoner, evangelical Minister, universal Scholar, and illustrious (tho' *late*) Christian" would catapult him to transatlantic fame.[102] Henchman's sarcastic description made Hobby an imposter who, having violated the stylistic canons which authorized participation in the public sphere, was attempting to foist an undeserving piece on "judicious readers."

Henchman joined efforts to protect the boundaries of the public sphere against such impostors by contrasting his own exemplary method of entry into print with that of the presumptuous Hobby. Far from attacking "Gentlemen of the *College*" and pastors of the churches as Hobby had done, Henchman had sought their advice and submitted his prose to their correcting hand. "What I published was approved, before tendered to the View of the World, by several Gentlemen in the Ministry, and by *One* particularly . . . of considerable Note . . . for Learning and Vertue." By deferring to his betters he had avoided the disgrace which Hobby's poor prose had brought upon himself and his cause. Henchman's careful observance of traditional deference and decorum had earned him the public approbation of "Gentlemen in every way our Superiors."[103]

Old Lights complemented these attempts to restore the bounds of spoken or printed public discourse with an effort to restore the "bounds of morality and decency" in community life. They predicated this effort on the proposition that "converting Grace works rather on the Soul and Rational Parts and Powers" than on the body or inward passions and should therefore produce a quiet, humble, moral demeanor in the convert.[104] Charles Chauncy insisted that itinerants had wholly neglected "a great Part of Christ's preaching," which was "taken up in *explaining Morality,* and showing Men their Obligations to it."[105] True conversion issued in submission to these teachings, not in the convulsive displays of conviction or ecstacy, ostentatious claims to superior gifts, or censorious accusations characteristic of itinerancy's converts.

In effect, true conversion should facilitate a mode of self-formation which fixed each individual in a particular station, outfitting each with a particular calling that determined his or her place in a bounded, deferential, patriarchal web of face-to-face relationships. According to Charles Chauncy, the "fruits of the Spirit" produced by conversion worked themselves out in "a faithful Performance of those Duties, which arise from the various Relations [converts] sustain towards each other."[106] Within the family, children should obey and honor parents; parents should "counsel, reprove, warn, restrain and command" their children. Wives should submit to their husbands; husbands should care for their wives. Servants should obey their masters; masters should take paternal care for the physical and spiritual welfare of their servants.[107] Within the community, conversion should make people "*more* honest, and just, and kind, and merciful . . . *better* Neighbors, *better* Relatives," better at "bridling their Tongues . . . more circumspect in their Behavior."[108] Each should remain in her or his own calling, deferring to those of higher station. Each should likewise honor his or her own minister through submission to his authority and dutiful attendance of sermons within the parish bound.[109]

Isaac Stiles of New Haven summarized this social vision in his sermon *A Looking-glass for Changelings,* delivered in support of the Connecticut Assembly's "Act for suppressing Disorders." Stiles founded his bounded, hierarchical model of society, and the place of the person within it, on the basic proposition of contemporary natural law theory that humans were by nature social beings.[110] Persons should be considered not as isolated individuals but as members of various distinct, well-defined, carefully delimited networks of human relationships. Mankind in the natural state was properly conceived as "divided into different and distinct Families, Churches, Towns, Governments, &c." As such, persons were "Members of one another, and thus obliged to be Social." The preservation of harmony within and among these distinct social entities depended on the maintenance of hierarchical authority, for "where there is no King in Israel every one does what is right in his own eyes." Consequently, "it must needs be our bounden duty to Revere, Honour, and Obey them that have the Rule over us."[111]

By arguing that this hierarchy of bounded social groups was a product of human nature itself, Stiles elevated the parish line to the status of a natural boundary. He also identified itinerancy, whose primary characteristic was to transgress the parish bound, as a social pathology in its perversion of the natural order. On this view, the Connecticut Assembly's act to protect the parish bound constituted a justifiable defense against the pathological actions of persons "given to Change" who "invaded the Priests' Office."[112] These individuals, "changeable as the weather & variable as the Wind: mere Weather-cocks," acted "as though they had their Religion to chuse." Attached to good teachers at one time, they suddenly stigmatized them as "*Letter-learned Pharisees*" in favor of "such as come from the Ends of the Earth." Books thought good at one time were burned at another. Congregational polity once regarded as "the only likely Method to promote Religion" was "by & by . . . disliked . . . and superseded by another that is bran-new."[113] This "*Vertigo,* or dizziness in the Head" also extended to civil affairs, where those given to change "raised a Dust" to "Overset the Government; to turn things *topsy turvey* and bring all into Confusion."[114]

Since itinerancy tended to "open a wide and perillous Door for . . . Subversion to all the peaceable Order in a Government," Stiles defended the Connecticut Assembly's attempt to protect the basic boundaries of the social and religious order by statute. He urged readers to support these "Patrons of our Civil and Religious Enjoyments," while refusing to "meddle, mix with or mingle . . . in conversation or activity" with those given to change.[115]

Stiles's sermon, like other polemics against itinerancy, revealed the enormity of the stakes involved in the contest over the parish bound. The patchwork of local parishes at once symbolized and maintained a system of deferential, hierarchical human relationships which ordered the eighteenth-century social world. It signified a whole range of boundaries, some literal and some metaphorical, which helped to order the social life of the community. The pulpit delimited a highly significant space within this social universe: one which only the minister could occupy and which distinguished his calling from those of other community members. Similar boundaries distinguished and ranked other callings, while rules of deference and decorum bounded social behavior within families, churches, towns, and governments. Such fixed, known boundaries enabled people to situate themselves according to "calling" within webs of stable, deferential, harmonious relationships. The polemic against itinerancy constituted an effort to preserve that social world.

IV

By the time of George Whitefield's return to America in the autumn of 1744, opposers had achieved a consensus against itinerancy. Some, like Charles Chauncy, had become fully convinced that the disorders attending itinerancy disclosed the work of quite another spirit than the Holy Ghost.[116] Others, such as Nathaniel Eells of Scituate, Massachusetts, expressed an enduring conviction that "there hath been . . . within a few years past, a great revival of religion" but denied that Whitefield or any other itinerant was a "principle means of reviving it."[117] Whatever their disagreements on the character of "the Work," opponents were united in the opinion that itinerancy had spread throughout the colonies "a perfect *mess-medly* of all kinds of disorder and error, enthusiastic wildness & extravagance."[118] Consequently, George Whitefield became the target of their published attacks, not as a messenger of the Calvinist doctrine of conversion but as the premier symbol of a destructive social force.

Opposers throughout the colonies portrayed Whitefield's itinerancy as the fountainhead of all the errors and disorders that had washed over the colonies in recent years, and urged "sincere lovers of Peace and Order" to close their pulpits against him.[119] Both New England colleges publicly denounced Whitefield's conduct.[120] At least eight New England ministerial associations published tracts declaring him unwelcome in the parishes they represented. Scores of Congregational ministers published tracts opposing Whitefield's practice.[121] Old Side Presbyterians likewise declared him unwelcome in their Middle Colony pulpits until he repented his imposture as "*Vice-Regent of Jesus Christ.*"[122] They reprinted several tracts published against him during his first tour. One defector from the revivalist New Side published a tract attacking Whitefield as "a man under Delusion."[123] Southern opponents likewise censured the "mercenary self-seeking" itinerant in newspaper essays.[124]

A survey of this flood of opposition literature reveals that Whitefield's name had in fact become synonymous with the itinerancy that was destroying the peace of the communities. The Harvard faculty noted that Whitefield had been "first promotor amongst us" of the "itinerant way of preaching." New England had not formerly known a category of minister who "hath no particular charge of his own, but goes about from country to country, or from town to town in any country, and stands ready to preach to any congregation that shall call him into it."[125] Others specified "Mr. Whitefield's itinerancy" as censurable because practiced in well-established parishes where the gospel was already preached rather than in places "where Preachers are *scarce,* and the Inhabitants *Scattered.*"[126]

"Mr. Whitefield's itinerancy," therefore, was the very brand which unruly persons had employed to "thrust themselves into towns and parishes, to the destruction of all peace and order."[127] An association of ministers convened at Weymouth, Massachusetts, lamented the "many sad effects of an enthusiastic, erroneous and divisive Spirit . . . chiefly promoted by Mr. Whitefield's itinerancy, and the other gentlemen who followed." They therefore abjured the "hopeful prospect of an happy state of the Church" which they had entertained during Whitefield's first visit and resolved to close their pulpits to him.[128] Another association, convened at Marlborough, declared the "language" or import of Whitefield's itinerancy and his public denunciations of ministers self-evident. It both signified and produced divisiveness among the laity, disdain of parish ministers, and invasion of the ministry by "illiterate" exhorters. "The devil, with all his cunning," the ministers observed, "could not take a more direct step to overthrow these churches, hurt religion and the souls of men."[129]

A sense of ongoing anxiety underlay this Old Light effort to exclude Whitefield from the pulpit, a fear that the "cockatrice egg" of itinerancy hatched by Whitefield had grown into a monster beyond the power of any to manage. Revivalists were actually encouraging it by countering Old Light opposition in the press and extending Whitefield more than enough invitations for the renewal of his "travelling preachments" in America. With the parish clergy divided, the people would continue to trample the bounds underfoot. Nathaniel Eells expressed the belief that "God, in judgment, and not in mercy to this people, hath sent him again into this country."[130] Another declared in frustration that the "Censorious, uncharitable spirit which had raged with so much Fury was sickning apace and would, in all Probability, have given up the Ghost, had not this second itineration *revived* and *strengthened* it."[131] Reverend William Worthington expressed thanks before the Connecticut General Assembly that a "Merciful God" had lately "put so considerable a Check" to the disorders, but cautioned that "such things have not ordinarily settled down in peace so soon as this comes to." "Alas!" he lamented, "We have taught them to love Strangers, and now after them they will go."[132]

3

Itinerancy and the Evangelical Imagination

I

If opposers interpreted the language of itinerancy in terms that threatened chaos and social disorder, revivalistic defenders construed it as no less than a promise of millennial dawn. Revivalists united in the belief that a "great and general awakening" had issued directly from the "special Labours" of George Whitefield, Gilbert Tennent, and "other itinerant Preachers, animated by their good Example."[1] Glowing reports of Whitefield's travels in England and Scotland testified to itinerancy's vast potential to extend revival abroad.[2] William Cooper of Boston's Brattle Street Church therefore warned that attacks on itinerancy could "*darken the Glory of the divine Power and grace appearing in the Substance of the work,* and beget *Jealousies* and *ill Thoughts* in the Minds of people concerning the whole of it."[3] Joshua Gee of Boston's First Church worried that such attacks would dampen the work not only among New Englanders but also among "many in distant Lands, who are true friends to the Work of God among us."[4]

This willingness to identify itinerancy so thoroughly with the "great revival" imposed an enormous interpretive burden on the revivalist ministers who employed printed literature to represent the movement to a reading public. It required that they develop an alternative reading of the language of going into other men's parishes—one that countered Old Light images of disorder with visions of a newfound openness to receive the Spirit of God wherever and however the Spirit willed to appear. The task also challenged revivalist ministers to explore the new possibilities for human action and identity which itinerancy represented. The freedom with which itinerants traversed the empire, drawing throngs wherever they appeared; the appeal of their message across boundaries of race, class, and gender; the readiness of large numbers everywhere to forsake the parish ministry and hang on a stranger's every word—these novel attitudes and behaviors had afforded a glimpse of possibilities that barely existed in the bounded, deferential, face-to-face world of the parish. Revivalist ministers produced the vast majority of published material in defense of the Awakening. To them fell the task of construing itinerancy and its attendant phenomena as manifestations of God's blessing rather than judgment.

This interpretive effort entailed a fundamental reshaping of revivalists' entire worldview to make sense of the new behavior. The new possibilities for action enabled them to read biblical texts and ecclesiastical history in a new light, finding within them fresh meanings from which to fashion a narrative which situated itinerancy squarely within salvation history and the Protestant tradition as well as in the eighteenth-century world. Such narrative enterprises, Paul Ricoeur has pointed out, carry with them an ontological claim—a description of a world whose structure is delineated as the story unfolds.[5] Itinerancy made possible a world radically open to the free operation of God's Spirit, which could operate unhindered by human boundaries of space, time, custom, class, race, or gender through those who disseminated the gospel freely to all in every place. The defenders of itinerancy proclaimed themselves the true guardians of vital Christianity in this expansive world.

Throughout this process of interpretation, defenders of itinerancy implicitly criticized the Old Lights' strict parochialism while generating a tacit model of the dynamic, expansive world in which itinerancy throve. They made way for this novel activity by pushing back the boundaries of the old localism to transcend traditional, localistic dynamics of community life, forms of self-perception and self-formation. In their place the new model situated human action and identity within a world of broader spatial, social, and conceptual horizons where greater individual liberty and greater geographic and social mobility could be construed as normative.

Revivalists attempted to turn the criticism of itinerancy on its head by casting the practice, despite its attendant disorders, as part of the solution to a much deeper problem of religious decline. Revivalists throughout the empire claimed that the outbreak of revival had arrested the irreligion that was "rushing in, even upon the Protestant world like a flood," prompting pious men to doubt of "the Continuance of Christianity among us."[6] George Whitefield's *Journals* catalogued evidence of the "degeneracy of the times" in every part of the British Empire he visited.[7] Too often, the settled ministry had exacerbated the decline by devoting sermons to "human Politicks, to please the Court;—liberal *Arts* and *Sciences,* to tickle *Scholars'* itching Ears;—*Ethics,* or natural Religion, to gratify the heathen Moralists," all the while neglecting "the important truths and Precepts of the Gospel-Revelation."[8]

Itinerants had reversed the course of this decline by reviving the "searching and awakening preaching" which too many parish ministers had forsaken. God had given George Whitefield a "wonderful *Manner of Entrance*" in every place he visited, drawing "Old and Young, Parents and Children, Masters and Servants, high and low, rich and poor together, gathering and passing as *Clouds* in the *Streets.*"[9] Gilbert Tennent encountered the same response as he traveled in the Middle Colonies and New England, "delivering his Message with Vehemence, Importunity & Thunder."[10] God's Spirit had used the work of these and others who followed their example to catch "Multitudes in the Gospel Net," prompting New Light bards to "honour those (altho' Itinerants) / who have herein been happy Instruments."[11]

In the context of this vast outbreak of revival, the refusal of many parish clergy to admit its "happy Instruments" into their parishes revealed to New Lights the glaring inadequacies in the Old Light conception of the parochial system. Revivalists argued that by claiming such absolute authority over what transpired within their parish bounds, Old Lights not only obstructed the work of "faithful servants of Christ" but also attempted to seal their parish bounds against the Holy Spirit himself.[12] Such naked arrogation of power flaunted the will of God and the laws of man. "Great William," revivalists argued, had by the Act of Toleration "freed his Subjects from the Iron Yoke" that bound people and pastors to a single parish. Parishioners could no longer be restrained from hearing whom they pleased, nor could itinerants be denied permission to preach wherever they could find an audience.[13] The "confusions of the present Day" had not arisen because of itinerancy's intrusiveness but because Old Lights abused the parish bound to quench the Spirit and suppress lawful personal liberty.[14]

Although many revivalist ministers expressed concerns about the disorder caused by itinerants like James Davenport, they recognized that a new world was taking shape in which ministers could no longer hope to maintain their moral and spiritual authority simply by defending parish boundaries. In earlier times orthodox ministers could draw on the localistic sentiments of their parishioners when they asserted their spiritual leadership against figures such as traveling Quaker prophets.[15] Yet now, Davenport's ability to win a following by denouncing parish ministers demonstrated how readily people would abandon local loyalties to entertain a "stranger" within their parish bounds or leave their home parish to hear him elsewhere. Revivalist pastors who permitted the "preaching of the Word of God by Strangers" found that an alliance with itinerants enhanced their status among parishioners.[16] A message from a stranger could now carry more weight than one from the parish clergy. God's Spirit seemed to them to be blessing this novel social reality by using itinerancy to spread revival despite its potential for disorder.

Recognition of this reality led defenders to see the problem posed by itinerancy as one of regulation rather than repression. Where opponents attempted to eliminate disorder by sealing the parishes against a "roving ministry," the "friends of revival" labored to make parish boundaries permeable by evangelical, orthodox "stranger Ministers" and thereby more open to the Holy Spirit's visitation. They wished neither to abandon the parochial system nor to prohibit itinerancy. Rather, they took it upon themselves to defend the legitimacy of both while establishing guidelines for integrating itinerancy with the ongoing work of the settled ministry.

The defense began, therefore, with a definition of itinerancy that minimized its inconsistencies with the Puritan tradition of ministry. Defenders commonly argued that itinerancy should only be practiced, in the Reverend William Hobby's words, by men who "being ordained minister[s] of Christ, and yet not having any particular pastoral Charge of [their] own, make it [their] business to go from Place to Place preaching the Gospel of Jesus Christ."[17] This definition excluded lay exhorters, reserving itinerancy for those who possessed the qualifications for ministry most important in the Puritan tradition: conversion, adequate education, preparation, and calling for ministry certified by ordination. The assumption that the practice of itinerancy belonged exclusively to ordained ministers was present in most discussions of the concept.[18] Apart from James Davenport and Andrew Croswell, few revivalist ministers approved the intrusion of "*illiterate* and *half-learnt*" persons into the gospel ministry. Most also warned that neglect of "*studied Sermons*" would result in loss of "all that the *Fathers* of these Churches have wrought for us."[19]

Having restricted the practice of itinerancy to men who were educated and ordained, revivalists set out to defend it as a legitimate means of bringing the Puritan tradition forward into the eighteenth-century world. They began with a selective reinterpretation of biblical texts and Christian history to recover the kernel of evangelical piety which revivalists believed their critics had lost, while demonstrating that itinerancy was neither so foreign to nor destructive of this core value of Reformed Protestantism as critics had claimed. They labored to show that since apostolic times, traveling preachers had propagated the gospel of conversion through faith in Christ. They argued that the itinerancy of their own age offered an eminently appropriate means of reaching their world with the gospel of grace—indeed, of spreading the apostolic message more widely and more rapidly than anyone before had dared to dream. Itinerancy's effectiveness sparked an effort to render the new category of ministry normative by laying down guidelines for controlling the practice and integrating it into the parochial system.

II

For revivalists as well as opposers the loosening of boundaries formed a central theme of discourse about itinerancy and the Awakening, but the literary defenders of itinerancy celebrated rather than lamented the new openness. Itinerancy had enabled Whitefield and others to break through conventional bounds of space, time, denomination, class, even gender and race in response to the Spirit's leading. An empirewide revival had resulted in "circumstances so wonderful" that William Cooper believed "there has not been the like since the extraordinary pouring out of the Spirit immediately after our Lord's ascension."[20] A poem in the *South Carolina Gazette* exulted in an apostrophe to Whitefield that "all heaven" would rejoice "with Millions thou hast sav'd."[21] A New England bard assured Gilbert Tennent that many souls would eternally bless

God, who "has inclined his Servant for to come / from foreign Lands to drive his Children home."[22] These dramatic results justified continued use of itinerancy despite any disorder that might attend it.

For revivalists, the glorious extent of the work more than compensated for the tendency of itinerancy to weaken traditional patterns of deference and decorum within the localities. Where Old Lights fought to preserve the "station" of each person within a bounded, hierarchical network of face-to-face relationships, revivalists yielded to and often celebrated the erosion of such boundaries as the Spirit's work. They endorsed itinerancy as a "proper Method of promoting and carrying it on."[23] Jonathan Parsons of East Lyme, Connecticut noted that strangers not entangled in the ordinary network of local relationships and behavioral expectations could challenge the townspeople to examine their souls afresh: "*New* Faces, *new* Voices, a *new* Method, all tend to draw the Attention of *hearers;* and hence they were caught by the same Truths that had been offered them divers Times before."[24] Itinerancy possessed the same power to capture people's interest as did the latest London fashions touted in the advertising sections of weekly gazettes.[25] This effectiveness prompted many to follow John Porter of Bridgewater, Connecticut in resolving "like St. John the *Baptist* to *decrease,*" relinquishing the status his position had traditionally accorded him "so that CHRIST may *increase*" by the traveling preacher's message.[26]

Revival narratives from all over the empire further contributed to this erosion of local boundaries both by testifying to the vast reach of the Awakening and by harnessing print to extend the Spirit's work even further. Accounts in newspapers, pamphlets, and periodicals of the 1740s reveal that awakening usually came to communities of the British North Atlantic in the wake of an itinerant's visit.[27] Revivalists celebrated these "refreshings of the Spirit," determined with New Hampshire minister William Shurtleff to look upon such visits as "favourable Providences," notwithstanding "how reproachfully soever any may speak of . . . *itinerancy.*"[28] Others reported that while no itinerants had visited their communities, revival narratives themselves had played the role of itinerant by invading the parish through newspapers, pamphlets, or correspondence to spark local awakenings.[29] Some ministers, to be sure, attempted to avoid allegations of disorder or to stress the supernatural

letters/publications

work of the Spirit by minimizing outside influences and insisting on the spontaneous nature of a local revival. Yet very few were truly spontaneous. From 1734 on, revival generally spread as people heard of revivals elsewhere by printed matter, word of mouth, or firsthand from an itinerant minister.[30]

The reasons that the eighteenth-century Awakening thrived on itinerancy and enjoyed such phenomenal growth can be discerned in these contemporary defenses of revival. The roots of the popular preference for itinerancy over the parish ministry ran far deeper than the mere orality of the itinerant's extemporaneous performance, the feature which some historians have recently cited as the source of itinerancy's popular appeal.[31] Indeed, the role of printed matter and correspondence in propagating empirewide revival suggests that the revival's appeal depended far less on orality than it did on the combined potential of itinerancy and print to break down localism.[32] The preference for strangers over parish ministers disclosed an eagerness to reach beyond the confines of the parish for sources of participatory belonging in a way that paralleled long-distance participation in other areas of social, cultural, and economic life.[33]

Among the varied forces that were eroding local boundaries, itinerancy and print were by far the most visible. Long-distance ties of trade, credit, and consumption also contributed to the opening of local bounds through increased participation in the world beyond the parish. Colonial merchants and planters conducted business and received lines of credit from unseen contacts an ocean away. Ordinary colonists avidly sought an increasing range of imported goods. Yet these links by themselves played at the edge of most people's consciousness, exciting sustained reflection primarily among debt-laden merchants, eighteenth-century political economists, and social theorists.[34] Print, on the other hand, drew readers out of their provincial horizons into conscious participation in a reading, thinking British public that spanned the Atlantic.[35] Itinerancy cut across boundaries to challenge directly the deferential, face-to-face relationships which had traditionally fixed the members of the community in clearly defined roles.[36] For critics itinerancy functioned both as a powerful symbol of a general loosening of eighteenth-century boundaries and as an instrument by which they were further loosened. For converts it modeled an alternative way of situating the self in this open world, a model which the *Christian History* and other prorevival publications encouraged by self-consciously striving to foster the sense of participation in a movement of empirewide scope.

Revivalist ministers eager to promote this great movement of God's Spirit declared that those who would join it must readily open their parish boundaries to a wider world of print and itinerancy, the media through which the Spirit was working. This greater openness entailed a risky alteration in the dynamics of parochial life. Participation in the Awakening demanded that the parish minister gladly accept a diminished role in the religious and social life of the community. He must no longer expect to act as the primary anchor of the parish's moral and spiritual life, or expect to play the role of a spiritual broker mediating unity among the parishes.[37] Instead, revivalist pamphleteers urged him to relinquish a significant measure of his spiritual and moral authority to strangers, and to permit his own conduct and character to be judged by his willingness to cooperate with the movement. It cannot "grieve an holy faithful Pastor," the revivalist bard observed, "If other Workmen drive his Nails yet faster."[38]

Friends of revival also argued that participation in this potentially boundless movement required a willingness to recognize the priority of the New Birth and faith over denominational differences. George Whitefield's itinerancy dramatized this as the Anglican cleric rejected captivity to any single denomination, preached from dissenting pulpits across the empire, held "sweet conversations" with Quakers, and shared the Lord's Supper with Baptist, Presbyterian, and Congregationalist alike.[39] American revivalists followed Whitefield's example with their own evangelical ecumenism. Midcolonial Presbyterians preached from Congregational pulpits; Congregationalists endorsed Baptist revival sermons; all mingled together in open-air meetings. One of the staunchly Presbyterian Tennents urged John Gano, a talented young preacher who adopted Baptist convictions, to preach as a Baptist rather than silence his gift for proclaiming the New Birth.[40] The *Christian History* endorsed the Welsh itinerant Howell Harris's declaration that "it is contrary to the Gospel of Christ, so to join to any party, as not to be free to join with all other Parties of Believers."[41]

Most significant, however, was the effect that participation in this empirewide movement of God exerted on the way in which individual colonists, parishioners and ministers alike, shaped their social identities as the horizons of their world expanded. "Strangers" with little stake in the local community were displacing parish ministers as the "happy instruments of conversion" for an increasing number of people. Itinerants worked primarily to draw these converts into a transatlantic work of God. Some, like Whitefield and Tennent, allied with local ministers and left to them the problem of integrating converts into the bounded, deferential moral world of the parish. Some went much further, denouncing that world and urging converts to reject it.[42] Old Lights complained that itinerants commonly "represent, in every Place where they come, that God is doing extraordinary Things in other Places, & that they are some of the last hardened wretches to hold out."[43] In so doing, itinerants were encouraging people to respond to the example of strangers beyond local bounds in addition or even contrary to the importunity of the parish minister, family, or neighbors.[44] Conversion was beginning to draw people into a worldwide community of imagined strangers bound together by a power transcending local church covenants: a common experience of new birth supplemented by a vast network of itinerancy and print.

The doctrine of inward assurance complemented this reorientation of the self within a long-distance, anonymous community by weakening the networks of deference and obligation which bound persons exclusively to specific local stations within local parishes. The direct "witness of God's Spirit" with the convert's spirit diminished the need to submit one's experience of grace to the approval of one's neighbors or parish minister. Itinerants could help people previously unknown to them find assurance of conversion by helping them to listen for the Spirit's voice. Whitefield pronounced hundreds of American inquirers converted on the strength of evidence such as that of the Roxbury girl who told him that his sermon on "the Lord our Righteousness" had enabled her to say "the Lord *my* righteousness."[45] Critics complained of itinerants pronouncing inquirers converted whose "faces they had not seen before" on the strength of brief interviews concerning "what did they feel? and the Like."[46]

Revivalist ministers further encouraged this reorientation of the self in their eagerness to open their parishes to the Spirit's vast outpouring. They not only entertained itinerants from afar but relaxed or inverted traditional patterns of deference in the quest for souls. Many revivalist ministers encouraged laypersons to exhort congregations publicly on the grounds that "the true Grace of God must not be opposed but encouraged where-ever God was bestowing it."[47] Compassion for tender young souls prompted George Whitefield to bypass ordinary familial deference by urging, "Little children, if your parents will not come to Christ, do you come, and go to Heaven without them!"[48] Several revival accounts described how the Spirit had used to "saving effect" the words of children who threw off customary deference to exhort adults and words of slaves who dared to exhort masters. "We have such Instances every Week from some part of the Country or other," one Bostonian informed a Scottish correspondent.[49]

Revival narratives composed during the Awakening likewise reflect the reorientation of the newborn self within a wider, more open setting than the immediate environment of the local parish. The locus of God's dealings with the individual remained in the heart and soul, and the pastor's ministrations continued to play a role for most. Yet the Spirit brought the light of grace to the hearts of increasing numbers by the mouths of strangers who traveled long distances "like . . . the old apostles." The narrative of the Connecticut farmer Nathan Cole, for example, reveals a poignant awareness that its author's experience was part of a movement of God's Spirit which had already drawn "many thousands" in England, Pennsylvania, New York, and the Jerseys. The mere report of "great numbers converted to Christ" in these places prompted Cole to feel "the Spirit of God drawing me by conviction." The Spirit chose the moment when Cole first saw Whitefield in Middletown, Connecticut to inflict the "heart wound" that would eventuate in his conversion.[50] The youthful David Brainerd, though not converted under the preaching of George Whitefield, declared the news of the Grand Itinerant's passage "through the land" a "great comfort to him" in his spiritual travails.[51] For Samuel Belcher of East Windsor, the moment of truth came by the mouths of two Connecticut itinerants, Eleazar Wheelock and Benjamin Pomeroy.[52] An anonymous convert at Wrentham, Massachusetts experienced awakening under the preaching of John Cotton, who had traveled from Newton to preach.[53] Awakening came to Samuel Blair's congregation in New

Londonderry, Pennsylvania under a visiting minister who was supplying Blair's pulpit while he was itinerant preaching elsewhere.[54]

Narratives prepared or edited by New Light ministers for publication in the prorevival press echo individual testimonies concerning the powerful effects of itinerancy on the self. The echo is often muted by clerical efforts to harmonize the Awakening with earlier communal patterns of revival by stressing ministerial attempts to integrate converts into traditional local religious life while downplaying the role of itinerancy and long-range communication in local awakenings. While such efforts failed in their own day to distract Old Light skeptics from the Awakening's transformation of the relationship between the self and the local community, they have often been more successful with those historians who characterize the revivals as primarily local and unconnected with any larger movement. Yet a close reading of prorevival narratives reveals that the stress on tradition and community formed part of a rhetorical strategy designed to parry Old Light thrusts against the Awakening's tendency to loosen local constraints on individual belief and conduct. The communal rhetoric also aimed to hold within the fragile coalition of New Light ministers a number who perceived the Old Light critique as hitting uncomfortably close to the mark.

The intercolonial, transatlantic context of individual conversions is discernable within even the most cautious ministerial reports of local awakenings. Reverend Oliver Peabody of Natick, for example, declared his conviction that "many more in Proportion have been savingly converted where Ministers and People did not encourage" novel features of the Awakening. He also asserted that some converted during the 1740–43 revival in his parish dated their conversions "before ever Mr. *Whitefield* came hither." Yet Peabody acknowledged the role of revival news from "many Parts of this Land" and expressly set the "hopeful conversions" at Natick in a context of regional revival throughout "my neighbouring Towns."[55] Henry Messinger and Elias Haven, pastors of the two parishes in Wrentham, Massachusetts, insisted that a "general Awakening" there did not arise from "the influence of travelling Ministers." Still they declared themselves "glad to own that *the News of many Conversions* in *Northampton and other Towns . . . some Years before,* and of some remarkable Success of the Gospel in some Parts of *England & America,* were the Means of stirring up *Thoughtfulness* in many, and encouraged godly

Persons to *pray* with the *more Confidence* for the out-pouring of the Holy Ghost also among us."[56] Daniel Putnam omitted mention of either traveling preachers or news from other places in his account of revival at Reading, Massachusetts, yet he concluded with a prayer that "the God of all Grace" would begin revival "where it is not begun; that the *Kingdoms of this World* may become the *Kingdom* of our blessed Lord and Saviour Jesus Christ."[57]

The very caution of such ministers reveals that they, like Old Light critics, perceived itinerancy as the agent of a shift away from a localistic religious orientation among their people. Yet the millennial language of Daniel Putnam reveals the powerful attraction—even for cautious souls like Oliver Peabody—of the dynamic, expansive, potentially global religious orientation that itinerancy was helping to usher in. Where the earlier parochialism had produced only "transient Revivals of Religion in some particular Places," the transatlantic awakening of the 1740s promised nothing less than the advent of the "Redeemer's spreading Empire" which would one day encompass all the earth.[58] Anglo-American friends of revival determined to accommodate in varying degrees to this emerging state of affairs, many by "decreasing" in local status like St. John the Baptist and John Porter of Bridgewater "so that CHRIST may *increase*" through itinerancy.[59] Those who did so claimed to enjoy the benefits of revival with few disorders.

Revivalists concurred in representing any attempt to resist this tide of spiritual renewal as an invitation to disaster in the parishes and as the chief cause of the troubles attending the Awakening. Defenders of itinerancy cautioned that "Opposers" who closed their pulpits to itinerants and prohibited parishioners from hearing them invariably suffered. They charged that "the greatest Errors and Disorders" of the revivals were taking place in parishes where ministers sacrificed their "Respect and Influence" by attempting to silence itinerants.[60] Such efforts were foredoomed to failure, for opposers could not quench the Spirit of God, who impelled the itinerants forward with the message of the New Birth. It was not itinerancy, New Side Presbyterians declared, but "the Methods and Practice of Opposition to the Work of God" which constituted "the Principle true and real Causes of the Breach of the Peace and good order of our Churches."[61]

Revivalists self-consciously labored to increase this awareness among an empirewide community of saints by promoting revival through print and correspondence as well as itinerancy. Written and printed communication paralleled itinerancy in its ability to penetrate local bounds and draw parishioners into the "regenerate World." One defender of itinerancy noted the parallel by declaring it as reasonable to prohibit the reading of books as the preaching of itinerants.[62] When a Philadelphia minister actually did prohibit both, an observer warned that "the next Stroke may probably be the *Liberty of the Press.*"[63] While Old Lights complained of itinerants' touting "God's extraordinary doings" in other places to prompt local awakenings, prorevival ministers and laypersons commonly compensated for the lack of an itinerant by using printed or manuscript accounts to accomplish the same thing.[64] Jonathan Parsons employed both: He sparked awakening in his Lyme, Connecticut parish by preaching a sermon on a "considerable history of the work in many places" which he had compiled; later he invited itinerants and neighboring ministers to further the work in his own parish while he went on preaching tours himself.[65] In Hanover County, Virginia, Whitefield's printed sermons did the work of an itinerant with no minister present at all—only a group of literate laymen who experienced New Birth while reading them.[66]

Prorevival correspondence and publications began flooding across the parishes of the empire, further enhancing the sense of a dynamic movement that knew no bounds. George Whitefield's *Journals* appeared at regular intervals throughout his first American tour, permitting readers to trace the Spirit's path throughout southern England, across the Atlantic, and along the colonial coastline.[67] Newspaper accounts, often submitted by revivalists, reminded all readers that the Spirit was at work simultaneously in the colonies and in places as distant as Edinburgh and Rotterdam. The *Christian History,* which had counterparts in London and Glasgow, labored to expand these conceptual horizons even further by collecting in one publication accounts of revival wherever it occurred. Within its pages a reader could learn that revival had not only swept across New England but had reached Philadelphia, the Jerseys, Charleston, Wales, England, Scotland, and even Egypt.[68]

Revivalist leaders used these bound-breaking media effectively to challenge every "friend of the revival" to expand his or her own horizons even further, calling on readers or hearers to take action themselves to extend this imagined community of the redeemed across the globe. Each minister should recognize that his responsibility to preach the Gospel did not vanish "every time he step[ped] over the Parish-line" but extended over the "whole visible Church."[69] Christ's commission to "go into all the world and preach the Gospel" obliged ministers to preach "wherever they had Opportunity."[70] Ordinary laypersons could pray for the work of revival across the empire, following the example of the monthly "Letter-Meetings" in London. There Whitefield's followers gathered to hear revival accounts "from all Parts of the three kingdoms & *America*" and to "intercede for, mourn with, and rejoyce, according to the State of Christ's Kingdom in general, or the particular Circumstances of societies, private Christians, & especially Ministers."[71] By 1745, no one who had read a revival account, heard a New Light itinerant or parish minister, or joined in prayer for awakening could think of their conversion and religious duties only in terms of their own local parish.

III

While eighteenth-century evangelistic itinerancy promised revival on an unprecedented scale, it also posed an intellectual challenge for the historically conscious religious leaders who advocated it. Its apparent novelty demanded that defenders shape an interpretation of Scripture and the Protestant heritage to accommodate a type of itinerancy which was not restricted to missionary endeavors beyond the parish line but could supplement the work of settled pastors. Critics of itinerancy claimed that both the Bible and the Puritan tradition supported their restriction of each minister to a single parish. Throughout the colonies, Congregational, Presbyterian, and Anglican critics of itinerancy touted the parish ministry as the greatest legacy of their seventeenth-century forbears. The parish constituted the stronghold of an ecclesiastical and social order which the settled pastor anchored. To detach the ministry, educated or not, from the parish would result in social and spiritual chaos.[72]

Defenders of itinerancy responded to these charges by searching for forgotten or suppressed elements of biblical and orthodox experience which could be appropriated into a revised narrative of Protestant history, one in which itinerancy played an honored, essential role. This preoccupation with history represented more than mere nostalgia for the primitive piety of a bygone age. It also represented more than an attempt to retreat into that age from the commercial transformations of the eighteenth centry, much as revivalists deplored their age's preoccupation with "increase Cent per Cent." On the contrary, this New Light interpretative enterprise formed a vital element of a larger effort to bring that older piety forward into a new mobile world of commerce and communication, to adapt the message of New Birth to that world, and to take advantage of new means made available by the commercial revolution for maintaining genuine piety in places already Christianized as well as for proclaiming the message more widely than ever before.

Revivalists throughout the colonies therefore cast the transatlantic awakenings as a fresh outpouring of the first-century Spirit of Pentecost into a world corrupted by sin. Advocates of itinerancy drew parallels between antiquity and the eighteenth century that challenged those drawn by genteel Anglo-Americans.[73] For revivalists, eighteenth-century culture echoed the ancient world's corruption, not its virtue. Both epochs seemed to have slipped almost irretrievably into infidelity, a point Thomas Foxcroft dramatized by employing eighteenth-century categories to describe first-century apostates. Ancient devotion to "human *Politicks* . . . liberal *Arts* & *Sciences* . . . *Ethics* and natural Religion" prompted first-century "heathen Moralists," like their modern counterparts, to "pour contempt on the Doctrine of a *crucify'd Saviour* and a *Kingdom not of this World*."[74] Revivalists compared the "dead formalism" of eighteenth-century religious leaders to the New Testament accounts of first-century Pharisees who had abused their authority to maintain their place within a corrupt social order. It was only natural that such persons should regard a dramatic revival of genuine piety as a threat to their position, especially when it seemed to parallel so closely the apostolic era's spread of the gospel to the farthest reaches of a vast empire.[75]

These elaborate comparisons enabled revivalists to see the openness and dynamism of the New Testament world reflected in their own eighteenth-century context. They also found their new liberty to preach where they wished fully reflected in New Testament practice. The choices which their mobile world had opened to them had also been available to their first-century predecessors. Thomas Prince of Boston declared to the consternation of critics that "our

Blessed Saviour was an Itinerant Preacher; and that he preach'd in no other Way."[76] A Philadelphia poet noted that George Whitefield's transatlantic itinerancy replicated that of the apostles, who "measur'd seas, a life laborious knew / And num'rous converts to the Master drew."[77]

Prorevival pamphlets sought to delegitimate Old Light opposition to itinerancy by casting it as a resurgence of first-century persecution of Jesus and his disciples. Revivalists throughout the colonies drew this comparison, but none more colorfully than Samuel Blair in his response to the *General Magazine*'s "Wonderful Wandering Spirit." The original essay had been written by an Old Side Presbyterian under the sobriquet "Theophilus" or "Lover-of-God," the person to whom the New Testament Acts of the Apostles had been dedicated. In his response Blair published his own version of the "Wandering Spirit," assigning its authorship to a first-century Pharisee with the Hebrew name "Eloheb Soneshed" or "Lover-of-God Malicious One," an oxymoron denoting hypocrisy. Blair peppered his edition of the essay with citations from Acts and other New Testament books showing that first-century opponents could level the same objections against the apostles as those with which "Theophilus" had taxed itinerants. Apostle and itinerant alike censured unconverted ministers. The preaching of both sometimes provoked "violent bodily Convulsions" in repentant hearers. Both relied on "feelings and impressions" from God's Spirit. Both refused to submit to "human Judicatures" who commanded them to cease preaching for the sake of "Rules and good Order."[78]

Indeed, Blair declared, the "wandering Spirits" of Theophilus and Eloheb were "one and the same Spirit" of God, who had blessed the "ministerial Labours" of eighteenth-century itinerant preachers with "happy Success." God's Spirit had prompted those preachers to travel with a message that brought "many slothful secure unconverted People" to the "Experience of a new Spiritual life." Obedience to the Spirit demanded that itinerants ignore those "Schemes and Measures" formed by ecclesiastical assemblies to "bind them up from doing what God requires of them." Blair made it plain that to obstruct revivalistic itinerancy was to stand in the way of God himself and warned that by representing the revivals as "manifest horrid Work of the Devil," the author of the original essay was in grave danger of committing the ancient Pharisees' unforgivable sin of blasphemy against the Holy Spirit.[79]

Essays like Blair's sought to expose Old Light opposition as a replication of New Testament patterns of persecution for the sake of preserving their carefully bounded order. Defenders of itinerancy followed up by casting it as a revival of the apostles' method for flouting such man-made barriers to the "Work." No "precedent Practice" in either Scripture or English law gave ministers the power to prohibit itinerancy, observed a writer to the *Boston Gazette.* Jesus did not "ask Leave of the Jewish Doctors and Teachers to preach and teach in their Temple & Synagogues, much less in the Streets and private Houses." Neither did he direct his apostles to "ask Leave of the Rulers either of Church or State, and to forbear preaching where such Leave could not be obtained." Indeed, their example authorized "every true Minister of Christ to preach in any Place where God shall give him Opportunity."[80] Nowhere in Scripture had either Christ or his apostles "restrictive Bounds defin'd / of Time or Place to preach or hear [God's] Mind."[81]

The revivalist reading of Scripture presented the hopeful vision of a world radically open to the free movement of the Spirit of God through men equipped and poised to go anywhere to preach his gospel at any time.[82] In this vision the Old Lights' "Bounds of time and place" and "Rules and good Order" took on the character of oppressive, illusory structures that secured stability by squeezing the life out of religion, obscuring the light of the Gospel and shutting the meetinghouse door and parish line against the Spirit's visitation. The Pennsylvania itinerant Samuel Finley observed that man-made order so stifled the Spirit that "whenever God would reform his Church he always did something extraordinary," reaching outside ordinary human structures and procedures to "call up eminent Men to warn the World of their Danger." Invariably, the "false priests" of the age betrayed their ecclesiastical system's captivity to the Devil by opposing God's chosen spokesmen.[83]

The conflict of dynamic faith with oppressive ecclesiastical order provided revivalists the theme of a revised Protestant history in which itinerancy played an honored role. This interpretation rested on an argument supported by liberal quotations from Puritan and Reformed divines of the sixteenth and seventeenth centuries. The "best old authors," the revivalists maintained, had always viewed personal conversion through faith in Christ as the core of vital Protestantism. They argued further that ministers in the Puritan tradition had always been ready to disregard any church order which obstructed the free operation of the Spirit in the salvation of souls. In the history of their forebears, revivalists could discern glimpses of the dynamic operations of the Spirit carrying his redemptive work forward into the expansive world that was now bursting into view.

The most sustained historical defense of itinerancy and other revival methods appeared in the *Christian History*. This innovative magazine represented a collaborative effort to situate New England's awakening both within its contemporary context of transatlantic revival and as heir to a historical lineage that reached back through New England's first settlers to the Reformation itself.[84] The magazine boasted an innovative format modeled on newspapers of the day and sought to foster the "Work of God" by reprinting accounts of revival from all over the British North Atlantic, supplemented by selections from Puritan writers of the past.

The *Christian History*'s contributors sought to situate itinerancy within Protestant history by selections of quotations and a use of terms which permitted description of seventeenth-century piety in the language of the eighteenth-century revival. The centerpiece of the magazine's first volume was an interpretive history written by the Reverend Thomas Prince, Sr. for "the less knowing reader" who might be persuaded by the Old Lights' historical arguments against itinerancy. Prince drew on election sermons and revival accounts to demonstrate that the experience of New Birth, not the maintenance of ecclesiastical order, constituted the great legacy of New England's first settlers. He shaped his narrative to show that decline and disorder set in not as people began neglecting the "*form* of godliness" embodied in institutional arrangements and personal behavior but as they began denying its *power* by straying from the central message of the New Birth.

Prince and other contributors advanced three critical points in the evangelical interpretation of New England history: first, that "awakening preaching" accompanied by conversion had formed the core of New England unity; second, that periodic outbreaks of local revival had served to restore New England's pristine unity at critical moments; and third, that Puritan preachers had never allowed ecclesiastical barriers to hinder their propagation of the Gospel. The "FATHERS of these Plantations," Prince asserted, were "bro't up by pious parents under the most *awakening Preachers*" of the English Reformation. The settlers established godly communities on New England shores, aided by the "lively, searching and awakening preaching of the *primitive Ministers*," whose proclamation of the "*absolute Necessity* of the NEW BIRTH" prompted many tearful conversions in local meetinghouses.[85] Only when conversions took place were "the *Colonies* united, and *Courts* united, and *Magistrates* united, and *Ministers* united, and *Churches* united, and *Plantations* united, &c."[86] Subsequent generations neglected conversion in favor of "increase Cent per Cent" through trade, forgetting that "Worldly gain was not the End and Design of the People of New England."[87] This neglect produced a declension in which "Pride, Contention, Worldliness, Covetousness, Luxury, Drunkenness and Uncleanness broke in like a Flood," while those who remained "outwardly conformed to good order . . . *never knew* what the New Birth means."[88]

In Prince's narrative, seventeenth-century ministers affirmed the New Birth as the core of New England's identity by issuing unanimous calls for revival to reverse declension. Prince traced a succession of "transient Revivals of Religion" that had come in response to jeremiads, producing tears and cries of repentance but suppressing sinful disorder by reforming the hearts of sinners.[89] The earthquake of 1727 ushered in a period of "more extensive revival" that grew with the Northampton revivals of 1732–35 and peaked in George Whitefield's tour of 1740.[90] The narrative was crowned with attestations of nearly 140 ministers to the authenticity of the "late revivals" under Whitefield and his successors.[91] New Birth and revival were etched indelibly into New England's history and identity. Without them the fathers had unanimously declared its ecclesiastical order a vain, empty shell.

Testimonies of contributors and extracts from the writings of English divines confirmed that since the dawn of the English Reformation, zeal for the message of the New Birth had often prompted English Protestant itinerants to flout church order in pursuit of souls. In the days of Elizabeth, it had spurred Richard Rothwell to undertake a traveling ministry that earned him the title "Apostle of the North." Godly English preachers ever since had been ready when necessary to ignore parish bounds and church order to disseminate the message of the New Birth.[92] Excerpts from Richard Baxter's writings reminded readers that he and other dissenting ministers had defied ecclesiastical order after the Restoration of Charles II in 1660 to roam the English countryside preaching the Gospel. Baxter even urged English laypersons to ignore parish bounds and "diligently attend" the public preaching and private counsel of a "judicious, faithful, serious, searching, powerful Minister" wherever one could be found.[93] "Outcries attending the work of the Spirit" were "no new Thing"; Baxter and others often encountered and never condemned them.[94] Lengthy excerpts from a tract by the seventeenth-century divine John Wilson defended the "*Fervours* that appear in some in the exercise of Religion."[95]

Revivalists also defended the acceptability of itinerancy in the service of the New Birth from Protestant history in countries other than England. James Robe of Kilsyth in Scotland cited the "Stewarton Sickness" of 1625 to 1630, a revival where Scots from scores of western Lowland parishes gathered in fields to hear the fiery preaching of Presbyterian ministers. The "field-preaching" of the ministers and the "groanings," "bodily distresses," and "sweet consolations" of the laity were the antithesis of order, but the New Birth that resulted was the very core of Presbyterian faith.[96] An excerpted address to Dutchmen by Hugh Kennedy, minister of the Scots Church in Rotterdam, reminded readers that zeal for the New Birth stood at the center of the Dutch Reformed tradition.[97] An account of the Pietist revivals narrated how German Christians had also battled "dead formalism" to return to the vital religion of the Scriptures and the Reformers.[98]

Although these historical examples were chosen to demonstrate that revivalists, not their opponents, held legitimate title to the Reformation tradition, their significance extended far beyond that. The examples showed how God's "Free Spirit" often led faithful ministers to break out of man-made ecclesiastical structures in order to deal with people's souls. Godly people had paid "due respect" to ecclesiastical order whenever possible, but had regarded no boundary of time or place as absolute and no form so inflexible as to hinder proclamation of the New Birth. Biblical and ecclesiastical history consistently supported Samuel Finley's contention that God always did something extraordinary to reform his Church. Itinerancy provided an appropriate—indeed almost literal—model of the Spirit's activity in the expansive eighteenth-century world.

IV

While revivalist ministers worked to expand the conceptual horizons of their congregations and their reading public, few wished to abolish the parish and none to abandon converts to antinomian license. Revivalists detected in the practice of James Davenport, Andrew Croswell, and their unruly followers the echo of the seventeenth-century visionary Anne Hutchinson, whose belief in inward assurance was thought to have led her followers to forsake moral, orderly behavior as mere "works-righteousness." Ministerial friends of the revival responded by employing print media to dissociate themselves from the extremism of Davenport and Croswell. They reaffirmed their regard for the concept of the "settled ministry."[99] They continued to profess esteem for proper training and dismay at the "invasion of the ministerial office" by "illiterate and half-learnt" lay exhorters.[100] Most important, they represented the "essential part" of the transatlantic revival as productive of the enduring peace, order, and harmony which came through the New Birth.

Seen from this angle, the published defense of itinerancy represented a renegotiation of the boundaries of the eighteenth-century religious world—an effort to shape the Awakening into a harmonious movement without restricting the Spirit's freedom. Revivalist ministers proceeded on the one hand to open the parish to God's Spirit by defining itinerancy as a legitimate category of ministry that complemented rather than undermined the settled ministry. They labored on the other to close the parish to demons of disorder by excluding such activities as lay exhortation. In the process, they defined out of the community of the awakened a large number of persons who considered themselves its most fervent participants: the Separates who had departed the Established churches of New England to found "pure Gospel churches" composed exclusively of the converted and free of clerical restrictions on lay leadership, exhortation, and preaching.[101]

Gilbert Tennent made one of the earliest attempts to renegotiate the boundaries of parochial deference in a newspaper essay responding to published criticism of his 1741 tour through New England. Tennent's critic had charged him with abandoning his own flock for months on end to intrude uninvited into New England ministers' parishes in the vain conceit that he could "do more Good" than they.[102] The itinerant's response was a model of humility and cooperation whose themes would be echoed and developed for several years. Tennent assured his readers that he had not left his own flock without a shepherd. Ministers "of whose integrity I have good Assurance" had voluntarily supplied his people. His decision to travel had not been made out of vain conceit but in response to "importunate" invitations from New England ministers and then only after much soul searching and prayer. Through these he overcame reluctance to tax his "mean Qualification of Mind and cold Constitution of Body" and set out to "promote God's kingdom by traveling."[103]

Embedded in Tennent's response were a series of guidelines for reciprocal deference between the itinerant and the parish minister. Others expanded on these as the defense of itinerancy unfolded. Itinerancy was open only to brethren in ministry: men who possessed adequate training and regular ordination.[104] It should be carried on in a spirit of humble service, to "strengthen the hands of those Ministers who deserve to be encouraged" and to avoid bringing the "Standing Ministry" into contempt.[105] It should normally be undertaken at the invitation of parish ministers, unless exceptional circumstances such as the opposition of "dead dry Drones" dictated otherwise.[106]

Defenders of itinerancy also labored to accommodate the behavior of the awakened while preserving order within assemblies and communities. The method's penchant for breaking down social constraints, releasing people to express terrors and joys with unchecked emotion, not only provoked the outrage of foes but also caused discomfort among friends. James Davenport had fueled the fires of controversy by throwing off all restraints, whipping the emotions of his hearers to a fever pitch, leading followers in disorderly procession through the streets of towns with loud singing, even seeming to base the authenticity of conversion on the intensity of emotional release. He had urged people to separate from unconverted ministers, even to shape their conduct exclusively by private impressions and convictions informed by a personal reading of Scripture. Revivalist ministers shared Old Light concerns that such persons were cutting themselves entirely adrift from traditional networks of behavioral constraints.[107]

Revivalist leaders responded by fashioning bounds of decorum which could prevent disruption of communal harmony without denying the validity of emotional religious experience.[108] Jonathan Edwards and Jonathan Dickinson led the way by developing a theology of the Spirit's work in revival that placed strong affections at the very core of true religion. At the same time they reaffirmed the spiritual value of decorous social conduct. Both Edwards and Dickinson rejected the notion that emotional outbursts were necessary features of conversion. Some they acknowledged to be genuine results of the work of God's Spirit on souls. Other outbursts, however, might be mere human emotion aroused in the supercharged atmosphere of a revival meeting. Others might even arise from the prompting of the Devil. The only sure way to determine whether or not the outburst signified the work of God was to measure the convert's subsequent manner of life against scriptural guidelines: love for God and his Word, holiness of life, and humility and charity in conduct toward others.[109]

Revival leaders labored to develop these guidelines for an itinerancy that would open the localities to the Spirit's visitation while remaining subject to the "God of peace." In so doing they also developed more fully their alternative model of the eighteenth-century social world. The *Christian History,* like its counterparts in England and Scotland, provided a ready forum for friends of revival from all over the empire to collaborate in this task. The magazine appeared as controversy over James Davenport's reckless itinerancy was reaching its peak, and its contributors wished to clear both the revivals and itinerancy itself of the obloquy incurred by association with his methods. Guidelines for the orderly practice of itinerancy often emerged in the course of revival narratives as contributors discussed techniques they had found useful for regulating the new methodology and reducing its excesses.

The *Christian History*'s editors highlighted the transatlantic context of this collaborative process at the outset by devoting the first several issues to James Robe's narrative of the revival at his parish in Kilsyth near Glasgow in Scotland. The account described a revival thousands of miles away, yet remarkably similar to American counterparts in the volume of its conversions, its attendant phenomena, and its restoration of a piety that had woefully declined. Its writer went beyond a mere retelling of the main events to shape his narrative into a guidebook, recommending to others the methods he had found most effective for promoting revival while keeping it within acceptable bounds.[110] As such, the narrative offered more than a simple set of suggestions. It provided a tool for interpreting the behavior both of converts and ministers, for judging which elements of their experience were legitimate and which were not. Robe's techniques aimed to foster those elements he and his contemporaries regarded as beneficial to revival while suppressing the more disturbing irrational or disorderly effects. In so doing Robe and those who followed labored to shape the revival itself, fashioning it to fit both its proponents' expectations and its eighteenth-century context, and in the process articulating a vision of the world in which revival occurred.

Robe's narrative developed the model of itinerancy by situating the revivals in a world at once open to the free activity of the Spirit and subject to the "God of order." The effectiveness of evening meetings led by "stranger Ministers" prompted Robe to open both his pulpit and his private counseling sessions to fellow revivalists.[111] When the preaching of "the Terrors of the Law" caused some awakened parishioners to groan, writhe, and cry out, Robe initially maintained order by removing them from the assembly. He soon discovered, however, that intervention interrupted the rhythm of the meeting, thus hindering the Spirit's "convicting work." He therefore recommended leaving distressed persons in the assembly where their cries might awaken others.[112] Robe also opened the doors of his meetings to laypersons from neighboring parishes, but to avoid undermining church order, he urged that lay "strangers" seek counsel from their own ministers concerning the state of their souls.[113] The revival at Kilsyth took place in a world where the Spirit moved freely in the hearts of people and where both laypersons and ministers moved freely across permeable parish lines to participate in the Spirit's work.

More than ninety prorevival ministers from New England complemented Robe's efforts to shape the social world by offering their own set of prescriptions for curbing excesses. Their prorevival "Testimony and Advice" was published separately and reprinted in the

Christian History. Signers sought to distinguish "Antinomian disorders" from the "work of God" and warned readers against falling into this error in their zealous attacks on Arminianism. Laypersons could avoid antinomianism by honoring their pastors, resisting the temptation to "invade the Ministerial Office" by preaching under pretense of exhorting. Ordained itinerants could avoid it by seeking permission from the resident minister to preach in any given parish "in ordinary cases." Parish ministers could prevent the spread of antinomianism by welcoming only itinerants qualified by ministerial training.[114] Proper invitations could avoid much needless misunderstanding, while insertion of the clause "in ordinary cases" deliberately left it to "the serious *Conscience* both of *ministers* and *others* to judge when the Cases are *ordinary* or *not ordinary*."[115] The world of New England revivalist ministers, like Robe's, remained open, mobile—a place of permeable boundaries where the Spirit was at liberty to work through the dictates of conscience.

Revivalist ministers supported this developing model of the world of itinerancy by fashioning narratives in which their experiences of revival conformed to the guidelines of the "Testimony and Advice." Prorevival narratives uniformly set the local experience of itinerancy within an ordered context of openness both to the Spirit's vast outpouring grace and to participation in an expansive community of the awakened. Many recounted how itinerancy had been "wonderfully blessed of God" in bringing revival to their parishes. A number had resorted to itinerancy themselves and described in glowing terms their welcome by ministers and people and the Spirit's attendance on their preaching in every parish. Several pleaded for tolerance among ministerial colleagues who encountered the transient, superficial disorders which accompanied itinerancy. "Bodily agitations," for example, might not necessarily signify the Spirit's presence, but none should judge too harshly when "illiterate Country men and others of small Experience are *ravished* with the Discoveries of *another World* and the *Knowledge of God in Christ*." If the convert's subsequent holiness and humility of conduct displayed the fruits of godliness, then the revival must be regarded a work of God, despite temporary transgression of the "bounds of Decency."[116]

Revivalist ministers crowned their efforts to fashion a model of itinerancy within an open, yet orderly world by securing James Davenport's *Confessions and Retractions.* The repentance of the firebrand who had become the symbol of "enthusiasm" for all parties symbolized for most revival ministers the orderly adaptation of itinerancy to its eighteenth-century environment. They ensured that the document received as much publicity as had Davenport's antics. Davenport's *Confessions* was published as a pamphlet and widely advertized in the newspapers. Several news weeklies reprinted the document in full. It also appeared in the pages of the *Christian History.*[117]

Davenport's *Confessions and Retractions* actually constituted an affirmation of the world his ministerial colleagues were in the process of fashioning. He made this clear at the outset by reaffirming both the authenticity of this empirewide awakening and the validity of the itinerancy by which it had spread. Davenport blessed God for the "*glorious and wonderful Work of his Power and Grace* . . . in *New-England,* in the *neighbouring Governments* and *several other Parts,*" reiterating his belief that "the Lord hath favour'd me, tho' most unworthy . . . in granting special Assistance and Success."[118] Nevertheless, the itinerant repented the "misguided Zeal" and a "false Spirit" which spurred him to promote "Appendages" that blemished the work of God. Davenport then listed five confessions and retractions, each of which supported some aspect of the effort to bring order to itinerancy and revivalism by restoring deference to certain shared behavioral norms. In the first two he repented the breaches he had opened in the social order by pronouncing so many settled ministers unconverted and encouraging parishioners to forsake them. The third repented his renunciation of the scripturally informed wisdom of the religious community and sole reliance on private "Impulses and Impressions" to order his conduct. The fourth retracted his encouragement of unqualified persons to "*a ministerial and authoritative Kind or Method of exhorting,*" while the fifth repented his flouting of communal standards of decorum by frequent singing in the streets.[119]

Davenport's *Confessions and Retractions* thus constituted a key element of the effort to fashion an alternative to the reasonable, anglicized elite-brokered order of the Old Lights. Revivalists continued to support their vision in pamphlets, sermons, gazette essays, and periodicals. The *Christian History* continued to endorse new opportunities opened by eighteenth-century mobility with narratives of ordained itinerants whose cooperation with local ministers was "savingly used of God" to bring revival to the parishes of the North Atlantic world. The clause of the ministerial "Attestation" enjoining itinerants to seek permission "in ordinary cases" preserved Spirit's liberty in extraordinary ones when a minister's obstinacy might threaten his parishioners' eternal well-being. Revival narratives continued to endorse itinerancy by telling how the Almighty had used it to shock hearers out of their complacency, awaken them to their deplorable state, and open their hearts to convicting work of his Spirit. Ministers refused to slight the Spirit by condemning instances of crying, "bodily distresses," or expressions of rapture. They insisted only that "hopeful conversions" be evaluated on the basis of the convert's ability to articulate her or his faith in reasonable, scriptural terms and pursuit of a subsequent manner of life consistent with that faith.

V

By the time George Whitefield returned for his second tour of the colonies late in 1744, revivalist ministers had defined a set of guidelines for the orderly integration of itinerancy and the settled ministry. Itinerancy was to be practiced only by men who had undergone regular ordination. It should not expose the settled ministry to contempt. Rather, itinerancy should strengthen the parish ministry wherever possible. Its practitioners should ordinarily enter parishes only with the consent and coopeation of local ministers and should encourage the awakened to seek spiritual guidance from their own pastors as well. The parish ministry, for its part, should welcome itinerancy as a valuable means of promoting the New Birth while working to confirm its fruits in the souls of the awakened. Laypersons should be free to respond to the Spirit's call whether it came through itinerancy or the settled ministry. The parish line should be permeable, the bounds of decorum elastic.

Whitefield's second tour provided revivalists an opportunity to demonstrate that orderly coordination of itinerancy and a settled ministry was possible. Since 1741 Old Light controversial literature had been tracing the "Errors & Disorders that have prevailed in the Land" to itinerancy and had been portraying Whitefield as the fountainhead of them all. His return in November of 1744 offered a chance to demonstrate that disorders erupting after he took his leave of America had been "no just Consequences from Mr. Whitefield's Principles."[120] Consequently, the Grand Itinerant and evangelical clergy collaborated in a publicity campaign that was much more self-conscious concerning matters of conduct and decorum than publicity surrounding the first tour had been.

Revivalist ministers followed their own guidelines concerning itinerancy by extending Whitefield an eager welcome both in person and from the presses. One hundred thirty-seven colonial ministers placed their own prestige on the line by signing an endorsement of his itinerancy that appeared in Boston and Charleston newspapers.[121] The *Christian History* praised his return in the "same extraordinary Spirit of Meekness, Sweetness and Universal Benevolence as before."[122] Evangelical pastors inundated Whitefield with invitations to preach from their pulpits. One entire revivalist-dominated ministerial association reissued a public invitation first extended to Whitefield in 1740.[123] Another responded to an Old Light association's denunciation of Whitefield by publishing a testimony in his favor.[124]

Congregationalist ministers often dramatized the extent of their cooperation with Whitefield by inviting him to assist in the administration of the Lord's Supper. Other elements of weekly news reports differed little from those which had traced his itinerary through New England five years earlier, but in the matter of Whitefield's administering the Sacrament, the 1745 reports are unique. In principle, Whitefield's Protestant ordination qualified him to administer the Sacrament in New England meetinghouses. In practice, however, his Anglicanism had prevented his dispensing of the Sacrament to Congregationalists during his first American tour.[125] Yet by 1745 Congregational revivalists were prepared to celebrate their unity with the redeemed throughout the empire and their full cooperation with the "happy instrument of Revival" by setting aside such denominational scruples.

Whitefield, for his part, carried on a model itinerancy. Wherever possible he preached by invitation of the local ministers. He never invaded the pulpits of opposers but sometimes found it necessary to preserve liberty of conscience and defy ministerial pretention to "lofty power" by open-air preaching within an Old Light's parish bounds.[126] He encouraged people to seek spiritual guidance from their parish ministers. In New England he rebuked Separate congregations for "rash and unscriptural Separations" from their ministers and regular fellowship.[127] In Hanover County, Virginia where a new dissenting meetinghouse had recently been erected, Whitefield refused to antagonize the Anglican minister of the parish by preaching from the Dissenters' pulpit. Instead he preached in the Anglican church building and in the open air and spoke highly of Anglican ordination. When a Hanover man asked Whitefield to baptize his child, the itinerant made a point of directing him to the parish minister.[128] Wherever he traveled, he avoided arousing unnecessary emotional fervor by "applying himself first to the Understandings of his Hearers, and then to the Affections."[129] By 1746 his exemplary conduct was winning him cordial receptions even from former opponents.[130]

Whitefield's model second tour provided revivalists with evidence that itinerancy could be harnessed into coexistence with a parochial ministry. Old divisions persisted long after 1745, but the relative lack of significant new ruptures satisfied moderate revivalists that no inevitable link existed between itinerancy and disorder. Parish boundaries could be made permeable and the bonds of localism loosened without the social order devolving into chaos. Indeed, in the face of the irresistible movement of the Spirit, such accommodation seemed imperative—both to capture the moment of revival and to avoid the fate of those who tried to suppress it and were crushed in its relentless advance.

Even with these guidelines the new sociocultural orientation entailed in itinerancy represented a radical rethinking of the bounds and dynamics of community. It confirmed opponents' fears concerning the redefinition of a religious self by inward "impulses" rather than outward conformity to communal expectations. It broadened the limits of legitimate human action by recognizing mobility beyond local, provincial, and transatlantic bounds as normative and beneficial in an expanding empire. Moreover, its capacity to penetrate boundaries and to provide long-distance links between people sharing a common inner experience made itinerancy subversive despite its inventors' best efforts to control it. Revivalists had indeed taught their people to "love Strangers," just as William Worthington had warned, and the people were now prepared to "go after" itinerant preachers.[131] The colonial American religious world would never be the same.

4

The Proliferation of Itinerancy

I

The amount of printed material devoted to itinerancy and the Awakening tapered off after 1745, yet the contest between the two visions of the social world persisted. The sporadic reappearance of controversy disclosed itinerancy's persistent push to reorder the Anglo-American world according to the vision developed in revival publications. George Whitefield's three later tours of the colonies reinforced his status as the living symbol of evangelical zeal. They also strengthened his role as the representative link among a transatlantic community of the regenerate drawn from a widening range of religious persuasions and ethnic backgrounds. Revivalists within the denominations labored to extend the transatlantic vision of the Spirit's work developed in the *Christian History* and other prorevival publications. Separate itinerants, paedobaptist and antipaedobaptist alike, aroused controversy as they roved the New England countryside, pushing west to the frontier and south into Virginia and the Carolinas in the later 1740s and 1750s. New Side Presbyterian itinerants also carried the revival west and south.

As itinerancy proliferated throughout the colonies, growing portions of the Anglo-American religious world began reflecting the ordered openness articulated during the 1740s. Itinerancy's disregard of spatial boundaries made it a persistent challenge to parochialism as well as an ideal means of carrying the Gospel to the unbounded frontiers. It continued to push back the boundaries of local life and draw people into a long-distance, affective community linked by networks of print, correspondence, and itinerancy itself. Yet this erosion of the parish bound never issued in the unbounded antinomianism which the partisans of elite-brokered localism had feared. Rather, the model of behavior advanced by itinerancy compensated for the loss of external boundaries by inviting people to enter by faith into a close-knit, voluntary local expression of that wider community. The ties of affection that linked members to a long-distance imagined community also bound them to live with one another according to strict standards of internal commitment and moral behavior.

The religious community fostered by itinerancy was ideally suited to the changing, mobile world of eighteenth-century America. The anthropologist Mary Douglas has argued that when social groups face rapid shifts in their boundaries and composition as did eighteenth-century Anglo-Americans, they tend to forsake highly structured forms of social and religious life. Instead, members adapt to their weakly structured, changing environment by ordering their personal worlds through emotional, internal religious commitments and stringent moral codes.[1]

The pattern of itinerancy's proliferation after 1745 reveals just such a process of adaptation to the eighteenth-century empire's market-driven expansion. George Whitefield's persistence as a living symbol of revival, coupled with efforts to maintain the transatlantic evangelical network, provided long-distance links among the scattered members of the revival community. The Separates of New England developed close-knit, voluntaristic assemblies in tandem with efforts to relax the geographical boundaries of their communities. Presbyterian itinerants extended the revival community southward to Virginia, explicitly defending their efforts as a facet of the Spirit's work within an expanding, mobile world. The 1760s saw the rapid spread of Separate Baptist churches across the Virginia landscape thanks to Baptist leaders' skillful adaptation of itinerancy to this highly mobile environment. By the early 1770s the Established church order in Virginia and the South was facing yet another wave of itinerancy, this time from Methodist lay itinerants commissioned by John Wesley to revive "vital religion" within the Church itself. The readiness of successive waves of revivalists to employ itinerancy successfully in this rapidly changing environment discloses among them an orientation that was the very antithesis of retreat to a premodern world.[2]

II

The contest between the vision of a stable, reasonable, elite-brokered localism and one of an expansive, fluid long-distance voluntary community continued to center on George Whitefield's itinerancy in the years after 1745. Defenders and detractors alike continued to invoke George Whitefield as itinerancy's most potent living symbol. Admirers continued to utilize the transatlantic communications network Whitefield had fostered while extending the consciousness of participation in a vast community of saints through the "concert for prayer," an attempt to unite Christian churches throughout the empire in the activity of prayer. These efforts converged with increasing mobility to intensify colonists' awareness of their place in an open world of permeable boundaries and long-distance, affective ties.

Antirevivalists throughout the colonies attacked everyone who traveled with the message of the New Birth as an odious "Whitefieldian," but itinerants welcomed association with the patriarch of their calling. Revival-minded colonists who disagreed sharply over many issues nevertheless united in upholding George Whitefield as the greatest living spokesman of the Gospel. The Grand Itinerant continued to draw new admirers from among an increasing variety of religious and ethnic groups. In so doing he perpetuated itinerancy's dynamic, mobile model of ministry and the world in which it occurred.

Old Lights continued to regard Whitefield as a grave threat to their model of a settled ministry pursued within a bounded, rational, orderly society. The spectacle of New Englanders "flocking in Crowds" to hear the "*Grand Itinerant*" in 1754 prompted renewed outbreaks of controversy in the Boston press. A satirist in the *Boston Evening Post* predicted that "Things in Church and State will worse proceed" as a result of Whitefield's visit.[3] Opponents sought to counter his influence by reprinting *The Querists,* an anti-Whitefield pamphlet first published in 1740.[4] The Harvard professor Edward Wigglesworth lamented that the lessons of earlier disorders had been lost on New Englanders. An "*Itching Ear,*" he observed, "again despises the threatening of God." He warned that a fresh wave of "Itinerants and Exhorters, who have once and again overrun this, and the neighbouring Provinces and Colonies" would take encouragement from this latest fever to hear George Whitefield. They would again leave their flocks, intrude into neighboring parishes, and attempt to "insinuate themselves into the Affections of other People and Churches."[5]

Whitefield's supporters retorted that such alarmism was wholly unfounded, since "some of the warmest Friends to a settled Ministry, and to the settled ministers, nay, even to some of them who have not tho't so favourably of *Mr. Whitefield,* are to be met with among his greatest admirers."[6] Indeed, revival-minded ministers who remained within the Congregational and Presbyterian fold continued to uphold Whitefield as their generation's premier model of a faithful minister. A rehabilitated James Davenport urged a 1756 gathering of the Presbyterian Synod of New York to bless God for "godly *Mr. Whitefield,* whose *indefatigable and successful* Labours for almost *twenty* Years together, should be improved for the Encouragement and Quickening of all truly engaged in the sacred Work; whose Name is justly very dear to us."[7] Samuel Davies, the Presbyterian "Apostle of Virginia," declared, "I am not ashamed to own that I look upon Mr. Whitefield as a zealous and successful minister of Christ, and as such, do countenance him."[8]

The Awakening under Whitefield also became the new standard by which the friends of revival among regularly ordained colonial ministers measured subsequent "quickenings of the Spirit." Evangelical ministers throughout the colonies cherished the memory of the "very uncommon *Effusion* of divine *Influence,* in the *Conviction,* and *Conversion of Sinners*" ushered in by Whitefield.[9] Samuel Buell, an itinerant of the Awakening who became pastor of the Congregational church in Easthampton on Long Island, appraised Easthampton's revival of 1763 by comparison with the revival of 1740.[10] Forty-eight years after the Awakening, the Presbyterian minister Robert Smith, himself a convert under Whitefield at the age of fifteen, was still evaluating revivals in his son's Virginia congregation by their resemblance to the "power and spiritual glory" he had witnessed in 1740.[11]

The Separates who began departing the New England Congregational churches at the Awakening's peak likewise claimed Whitefield as the exemplar of their brand of ministry. Separate preachers and exhorters pursued aggressive itinerant ministries in the New England countryside during the later 1740s. In the 1750s Baptist itinerants who arose from Separate ranks rapidly extended their influence to other colonies.[12] Separates of both stripes revered George Whitefield as their spiritual father and rejected the parish system in favor of Whitefield's assemblies as the true model for gospel ministry. Separates self-consciously reproduced "the Old Whitefield sound" in meetings which became microcosms of the great revivals of 1740, characterized by vehement extempore preaching to emotional audiences.[13] Thirty years after Whitefield's first tour of the colonies, the Baptist historian Morgan Edwards was still distinguishing Separate Baptists by meetings where the ministers resembled New Lights of 1740 in "tones of voice and actions of body; and the people in crying-out under the ministry, falling-down as in fits, and awaking in extacies."[14]

Veneration for George Whitefield cut across divisions of space, race, social status, ethnicity, and denominational affiliation. The common memory of awakening under his preaching united a scattered host of individuals as diverse as the New England farmer Nathan Cole, the slave poet Phillis Wheatley, and the South Carolina planter Hugh Bryan. The community of those awakened under Whitefield persisted and increased over time as successive tours through the colonies attracted new hearers to "drown in tears" of repentance as the itinerant held forth.[15] A stranger's attitude toward George Whitefield signaled at once his relationship to that invisible community. The Lutheran patriarch Henry Melchior Muhlenberg enjoyed an instant bond of friendship with converts of Whitefield whom he met in his travels—a kindred spirit that enabled him to engage each in an "edifying, heart-to-heart talk" even though he had never before laid eyes on the person.[16] A Virginia Baptist itinerant, on the other hand, recognized opposers of the revival he propagated when they attacked George Whitefield's character.[17]

Leading revivalists labored to strengthen this awareness of long-distance, affective community even further by self-consciously representing their work as a general revival of religion, not as the advance of a particular denomination or "party interest." The "concert for prayer" constituted the most ambitious attempt to foster such a consciousness and transform it into action which would extend the revival worldwide. The concert began in 1744 when a group of Scottish ministers resolved to unite their congregations for two years in a program of "extraordinary prayer" for "an abundant effusion of [God's] Holy Spirit on all the churches, and the whole habitable earth, to revive true religion in all parts of Christendom, and to deliver all nations from their great and manifold spiritual calamities."[18] In 1746 the ministers decided to extend the program for another seven years and to invite like-minded Christians throughout the empire to join with them. Accordingly, they sent five hundred copies of a "Memorial" promoting the project "to be distributed in almost every county in this province of Massachusetts Bay, and also in several parts of Connecticut, New Hampshire, Rhode Island, New York, New Jersey, Pennsylvania, Maryland, Virginia, Carolina, and Georgia."[19]

Jonathan Edwards undertook the task of publicizing the project in America with his *Humble Attempt to Promote Explicit Agreement and Visible Union of God's People in Extraordinary Prayer.* Edwards represented the project to his readers as fraught with the millennial significance which had marked the revival since its inception. The ultimate salvation of the entire world was at stake. The *Humble Attempt* opened with an exposition of Zechariah 8:20–22, a passage which presented the Messiah's kingdom as coming in answer to the united prayers of "great multitudes in different parts of the world" who "shall conspire in this business." Edwards envisioned the fulfillment of this passage as beginning with an express agreement among "God's people in many places" to unite in prayer for revival. The agreement would "gradually spread more and more, and increase to greater degrees . . . till the awakening reaches those that are in the highest stations, and till whole nations be awakened, and there be at length an accession of many of the chief nations of the world to the Church of God."[20]

The concert for prayer provided a means for Christians throughout the empire to labor for that goal by self-consciously exploiting a potential to unite across vast distances in simultaneous activity. Those who joined the concert engaged themselves in a remarkable exercise of imagination: to pray for revival every week on Saturday evening and Sunday morning, and on the first Tuesday of each quarter of the year, as members of one vast prayer meeting that spanned the entire British Empire. Edwards hoped that participants, "knowing that great multitudes of their fellow-Christians, in so many distant places, were at the *same time* (as a token of the union of their hearts with them in this affair) by agreement engaged in the *same holy exercise,* would naturally be enlivened in the duty by such a consideration."[21]

By calling on distant strangers to join self-consciously in simultaneous action, the *Humble Attempt* and the concert for prayer exploited the subtle changes which commerce, communication, and mobility were effecting in eighteenth-century awareness of the world. They explicitly acknowledged the presence of others, beyond the horizon of immediate experience, with whom one did business, corresponded, or read about in the gazette—others whose existence and activity coincided in time. By celebrating and enjoining the conscious practice of this simultaneity among evangelical inhabitants of the empire, the concert surpassed the *Christian History*'s representation of the revival as a unified, transatlantic event. It arguably constituted the century's most explicit attempt to cultivate a transatlantic "imagined community."[22]

Evidence suggests that the concert for prayer continued shaping the thinking of ordinary men and women throughout the colonies and the empire for years. Jonathan Edwards used his own extensive correspondence to promote it in America. The preface to the *Humble Attempt* indicates that ministers of at least four Boston churches were promoting the concert when the pamphlet was published in 1747.[23] The next year an entire Massachusetts association of ministers pledged to "be more especially fervent, in continual Prayer for the advancement of the kingdom of Christ."[24] James Robe of Scotland received letters from several New England clergymen informing him of the "great progress the Concert hath made in these provinces."[25] Ten years later the Synod of New York, which now included churches from the New York and Pennsylvania frontier to the Virginia and Carolina Piedmont, entered an "Agreement for extraordinary Prayer and Endeavours for a Reformation."[26] John Wright of Cumberland, Virginia linked a regional outbreak of revival in 1757 to the entry of several ministers there into the concert.[27] The Separate minister John Cleaveland attributed the 1764 revival in Ipswich to his church's establishment and three-year perseverance in a regular prayer service "agreeable to the Concert for Prayer, first entered to in *Scotland.*"[28]

Revival accounts published after 1750 arose from the correspondence network fostered by the concert for prayer and reveal the persistence of that network into the late 1760s. They supported the concert's expansive vision by informing participants of the Spirit's advancing work in the world and enlisting prayer for even greater outpourings of revival. Samuel Davies, for example, wrote his *State of Religion among the Protestant Dissenters in Virginia* to inform the praying public of the revival's expansion into that colony. He requested the Connecticut minister and concert correspondent Joseph Bellamy to publish it "that it may not only gratify good People, but (as you give me reason to hope) animate their Prayers for us, and also encourage Preachers to come into these Parts." Davies also solicited correspondence from "any Parts of the Church where this narrative may come" so that his own assemblies could pray more intelligently. "Our Acquaintance with the state of the Church in various Parts," he observed, "qualifies us to adapt our Prayers to it."[29] Another pamphlet, *Good News from the Netherlands,* came through the concert's transatlantic correspondence network. Its Scottish sender hoped that news of the revival's expansion onto the Continent would "stir up" readers "more and more to earnest Prayer for the advancement of Christ's Kingdom."[30]

A fresh outbreak of revival that came on the heels of George Whitefield's postwar tour of the colonies in 1763 revealed the persistence of the concert's expansive millennial vision and the continued use of correspondence and print to promote its spread. In that year Samuel Buell of East Hampton on Long Island wrote a friend in Connecticut of a "Work of God" in his congregation which he judged "the most God-like, Christ-like, excellent and glorious, that ever I knew."[31] The friend took the liberty of publishing and distributing Buell's letter without his knowledge to excite revival among other churches, and new editions soon appeared in New York, Boston, and London.[32] Revival spread rapidly to diverse churches in many parts of the colonies, including Separates and Baptists as well as Congregationalists and Presbyterians.[33] Reports of the "Lord's blessing" among people who read the pamphlet from New York to Virginia prompted Buell to write a "more particular account" two years later, hoping that it "may have a happy Effect, by the divine Blessing, for the Revival of Religion in other Places, and the Enlargement of God's Kingdom in the World."[34]

Samuel Buell, like Jonathan Edwards before him, detected nothing less than millennial significance in the fact the "wonder-working

JEHOVAH" had used his pamphlet to awaken sinners and prompt "Godly Ministers and pious People" to "give Glory to God . . . and pray more earnestly for such Effusions of the Blessed Spirit."[35] The extent of the current revival prompted Buell to apply his recent study of the apocalyptic books of Daniel and Revelation to the eighteenth-century world. It signified that "the Days are coming when an immense Plenty of the Lord's spiritual Waters, will be pour'd out upon thirsty Souls, and even Floods upon the dry ground." The millennial flood of revival would spread suddenly and irresistibly over all the earth, so that "the *Pope* in the *West* and *Mahomet* in the *East,* with their Powers, will be utterly ruined."[36]

This persistent determination to see the millennium as a worldwide outpouring of revival reveals that waning public attention to the Awakening after 1745 did not dampen revivalists' consciousness of their place in an expansive work of the Spirit of God. On the contrary, they continued to act and write as though the world's open fields were still ripe for the Spirit's harvest, awaiting laborers bold enough to enter them. They continued utilizing the correspondence network that linked evangelicals across the bounds of parish, colony, and ocean, disseminating news of each fresh revival that extended the work of God begun in 1739. The cherished memory of awakening under George Whitefield continued to unite colonists otherwise divided by ecclesiastical disputes, doctrinal differences, and barriers of race and ethnicity. The regular reappearance of the Grand Itinerant in America over the next three decades reinforced this unity as colonists of divergent beliefs and backgrounds mingled in churches and open fields in a common quest for the New Birth. The evangelical model of a fluid, dynamic, open world in which God's Spirit could move at will to build a long-distance community of saints still throve among the friends of revival.

III

Fired by the vision of fields ripe for harvest, itinerants continued after 1745 to challenge barriers to revival in older communities and impediments to its expansion in new areas. These efforts resulted in further development of their conception of self and community in an alternative vision of the social world. As Separate itinerants battled New England's Standing Order and dissenting itinerants clashed with the southern Establishment, itinerancy's defenders increasingly represented parochialism as a violation of the liberty of conscience as well as an impediment to revival. Where clergy urged laypersons to remain content within their own callings, New Light laypersons demanded liberty to obey the Spirit's call to preach. Where clergy and church leaders sought to preserve order by closing pulpit and parish to strangers, New Lights asserted a right to open their doors to the Lord's servants. Where ecclesiastical authorities required all to receive instruction from their own parish minister, New Lights demanded freedom to cross parish bounds in search of adequate spiritual nurture. Where local bonds of family and deference dissuaded people from embracing the New Birth, New Lights urged the awakened to forsake all and follow Christ.

Through this truculent defense of the liberty of conscience, Separates reinforced a model of the self released from bonds of deference to local custom, family, and society to choose its own community and shape its own identity in a more open, egalitarian world. Yet their passion for liberty did not issue in the antinomian license their opponents so feared. Rather, Separates complemented the relaxation of external boundaries with strict adherence to the rigorous terms of their church covenants. The instability of their outer world prompted them to strengthen the affective bonds of their inner world.[37]

The Separates very quickly came to regard the parish bound as an impediment to the Spirit's free activity in the world. Moreover, the parish bound violated the awakened person's freedom of choice to respond to the Spirit and his or her right of conscience to obey. Separates commonly represented their withdrawal from the parish churches as arising from a desire to keep the bounds of the parish open to the Spirit's visitation through itinerants. The fiery New Light preacher Andrew Croswell defended the formation of Boston's Separate congregation as a means of keeping at least one of the city's pulpits open "to receive Mr. *Whitefield,* and others whom we look upon to be the zealous and faithful Ministers of Jesus Christ."[38] Croswell warned that by excluding itinerants from their pulpits, Boston ministers often excluded the Lord himself. "You cannot reasonably expect *much of the Presence* of Christ in your Assemblies," he warned, "while Mr. *Whitefield* and other godly Ministers, who occasionally come to *Boston,* are industriously kept out."[39] Separates further defended their decision to leave the established congregations as a right of choice to obey conscience, one guaranteed by the Toleration Act.

Ministers and remaining members of the original congregations continued to represent Separate demands for openness and choice as an invitation to disorder. They reiterated the charge that itinerant "*Pretenders* . . . disturbed the Peace of the *Neighbourhood* by their private Intrusions, and their artful Methods to steal away the Hearts of injudicious People from their Pastors."[40] The preachers themselves were disorderly, the anti-itinerants claimed, having already transgressed the bounds of their station by exhorting, claiming ordination by the hands of laymen, or, if regularly ordained, intruding into another's labor. Whoever welcomed such persons betrayed not only utter disregard for order but "Neglect and Contempt of the instituted Worship of GOD." The Separate claim that an "inward motion of the Spirit" gave sufficient warrant to enter the ministry or even to preach in another's parish implied "that there is no standing instituted Ministry in the Christian Church which may be known by the visible Laws of CHRIST'S Kingdom."[41] According to the anti-itinerants, the emergence of Separate congregations compounded the disorder by intruding a plurality of churches and religious choice into a single parish.[42]

The Separates countered that the suppression of openness and choice, not its presence, disrupted parochial life. Disorder arose, they charged, because authorities were forcing tender consciences to obey "the Constitution of the Established and Tolerated Churches under the Supream Government of the Major Vote of the Inhabitants" rather than the "Constitution of the Church of Christ under his supream Government."[43] The Separates withdrew from congregations out of obedience to the Word of God, not out of a spirit of disorder.[44] Separate exhorters "improved" their gifts in assemblies and Separate itinerants preached from place to place out of obedience to the inward call of the Spirit. Refusal to travel about preaching constituted a sinful "quenching of the Spirit" that exacted a heavy toll on the guilty party's mental state, anguish which only obedience and the testimony of a "good Conscience" could relieve.[45]

Separates therefore came to construe the parish bound as an idol for destruction, a symbol of oppression rather than order. A system which confined individuals to parish churches that God had forsaken, prohibited itinerants from preaching where the Spirit led, and seized peoples' goods for refusing to support "dead, formal ministers" was as diabolically anti-Christian as papism itself.[46] Separate leaders like Solomon Paine and Ebenezer Frothingham therefore urged abolition of New England's ecclesiastical constitution and reliance on the civil authority alone to preserve social order.

Frothingham, pastor of the Separate congregation in Middletown, Connecticut, argued that the social order would actually grow stronger if the parish bound were abolished as a tool of coercion. The civil authority would then defend "every one of different sects, in their sacred rights of conscience, not allowing one sect to disturb another while they are peacefully and publickly worshipping God." Frothingham appealed to his own experience of pluralism in Middletown. Despite the existence of "five different worships in the town, within the compass of a mile on the Lord's day," he observed that "no damage accrued to any man's property, or civil interest, any more than if they had all worshipped under one roof."[47]

Yet the implications of the Separate position extended beyond the toleration of proliferating sects within a community still insulated from the outside world. Separates construed the opening of the parish bound as an outreach to the world beyond the locality as well as a toleration of diversity within. The controversy surrounding John Cleaveland in Ipswich, Massachusetts illustrates that even where their challenge to New England's ecclesiastical constitution remained muted, the Separates' zeal for the Gospel led them to open congregations to strangers from other parishes and to seek long-distance, affective ties with "friends of revival" throughout the empire.

The contest over the Chebacco parish bound began in 1742 when Nathaniel Rogers of Ipswich's first parish and his itinerant brother Daniel intruded into pastor Theophilus Pickering's parish with the message of the New Birth. For the next several years Pickering defended the "order of the Gospel and the peace of the Churches" by closing his pulpit to itinerants, discouraging parishioners from traveling elsewhere to hear them, and conducting a public battle against itinerancy in the press.[48] Frustrated New Lights eventually withdrew to form a Separate congregation and issued a call to John Cleaveland in 1747. Nathaniel Rogers and another brother, John, both ministers of the Standing Order, participated in Cleaveland's ordination to the "New-gathered Congregational Church in Chebacco parish."

Pickering's response to this ordination, *A Bad Omen to the Churches of New-England,* represented the violation of his parish bound as an attack on New England's entire ecclesiastical system. The procedure was not only "highly injurious to the Second Church in Ipswich"; it threatened other churches as well by encouraging "unlawful Separations, a disparaging of ecclesiastical Councils, a Breach upon the Fellowship of the Churches and destruction of their Peace and Order." Pickering offered a lengthy account of how the Rogers brothers, who possessed a long history of intruding into his parish, had now delivered the crowning blow by ordaining a rival in his "peculiar." This behavior alone rendered the offensive ordination null and void by violating the minister's authority within his line. The character of the assembly who called Cleaveland likewise invalidated the ordination, composed as it was of people who had thrown off the bonds of local deference embodied in the church covenant. They were no church but a Separation which had "rent themselves off from the Second Church in *Ipswich,* counter to the Covenant Engagement or Church-Relation, and contrary to the Platform of Church-Discipline also."[49]

Cleaveland's response to Pickering laid important theoretical groundwork for loosening the bonds of coercive local deference, freeing the individual Christian to seek edification wherever it might be found. Writing in defense of the "aggrieved brethren," Cleaveland rested his case on an exposition of the church covenant as a contractual instrument that bound the local community of saints to benefit its individual members. He argued that church covenants "suppose two parties, each of which have something to perform as a condition dependent on the other." Individuals who entered the covenant bound themselves to submit to the church's "Watch and Government" so long as the church provided "the Priveleges and Advantages, as the Word, Sacraments, Discipline &c. agreeable to the Gospel." However, when a church neglected "the main thing in Religion, viz. The Edification of the person," it "virtually dissolved" covenant with the individual. In such cases the "Party injured" was set "in Reason and Justice (if not in Form) at Liberty from his Obligation to that Church."[50]

On this interpretation Pickering, not the "aggrieved brethren," had breached the covenant when he denied church members the "Priveleges of the Gospel" by closing the pulpit to itinerants. He subsequently aggravated the injury by using "Arts and Subtilty" to thwart all legitimate attempts to heal the breach or formalize the dissolution. The majority of Pickering's church, which had given "implicit Obedience . . . to his Dictates and Designs," shared the blame. These actions had rendered "extrajudicial" separation the only means for the aggrieved to obtain "edification of the person," to which "all Forms however useful must give Way." Given these circumstances, Pickering's censure of the Separates for breach of covenant amounted to a declaration of "Right to hold those Members only for to abuse them."[51]

The members of Second Church complained that by making "edification of the person" the chief end of religion and obligation of the church, Cleaveland had destroyed the church covenant's hold on individual Christians. They criticized his view of the covenant for excluding God, traditionally the third party who bound each member to seek the other's edification before his or her own, and who enforced the covenant by blessing the faithful and cursing the unfaithful. Even granting what the members regarded as the erroneous primacy of personal edification, Cleaveland's failure to qualify the kind of neglect which justified separation rendered his principles "unsound, and destructive of Order, Peace and Charity." It freed each person to depart one parish and seek edification in another on the flimsiest personal grounds. Cleaveland's principles were already bearing bitter fruit, Second Church complained, in the Separation's admission of "censured persons" from other parishes into its fellowship.[52]

Cleaveland and his church affirmed the very freedom of individual choice and mobility which Pickering's congregation deplored, defending in the process an enhanced, far more centered position for the self in eighteenth-century community life. Cleaveland's congregation welcomed persons from surrounding communities into their fellowship in the belief that the principle of edification gave each individual an "unalienable Right" to cross parish bounds and "seek Edification where he thinks he can best obtain it." A person's use of this right could never constitute a breach of covenant, for "*Edification* is the *Benefit* we ought to have in view in Covenanting," and no church could edify members "against their Judgment or

Choice."[53] The augmentation of the self entailed in Cleaveland's principle of edification was the very consequence of itinerancy which Old Lights such as Isaac Stiles had warned against when people began acting as though they had their "religion to chuse."[54] Cleaveland's principle pushed even beyond the position of revivalists within the Standing Order who had sought to mitigate this effect of itinerancy by continuing to support the parochial ministry.[55]

The principle of edification alone led John Cleaveland to employ the permeability of the parish bound as a metaphor for individual liberty of choice and to embrace a significantly more open, mobile model of the world than that of his rival Theophilus Pickering. Pickering stood tenacious watch over his own limits until his death in 1747, insisting that his parishioners remain "within their line," minding their respective callings and deferring to his authority. Cleaveland, however, defended the right of every person to choose his or her own pastor. He opened his bound to all who chose to come, accepting pastoral responsibility for people beyond Chebacco's line. An ongoing interest in revival extended the boundaries of John Cleaveland's world still further, prompting him and the members of his congregation to take responsibility for much more distant strangers in need. In 1761, his congregation agreed to spend "one Day every Quarter of the Year, in a congregational Fasting and Praying for an Out-pouring of God's Spirit upon us and upon all Nations, agreeable to the Concert for Prayer."[56] When the Lord answered with revival in 1764, Cleaveland cheerfully opened his pulpit to other "instruments of revival," welcomed new members from surrounding parishes, and published a narrative to promote the revival among a wider public.

Cleaveland and other Separates remained alert to the danger of antinomianism posed by this relaxation of the self's external boundaries, and responded by subjecting converts to rigorous internal standards of doctrine, morals, and conduct. They rejected the moralistic "traditions of men" only to clear the way for the Spirit to operate in the consciences of individual men and women, prompting purer obedience to the commands of God. The Separate spokesman Ebenezer Frothingham devoted a lengthy section of his *Articles of Faith and Practice* to principles of church discipline, coupling thorough self-examination according to Scripture with mutual accountability among the members of each local congregation of saints. This mutuality, he argued, worked far more effectively to preserve the order and purity of the churches than the ministry-dominated system of church councils and consociations.[57]

The Separates' readiness to obey the Spirit's voice through conscience opened a wide door for intrusion into the minister's office as well as for transgression of parish bounds in search of edification. Yet though these innovations pressed beyond those of New Lights within the Standing Order, they still constituted a renegotiation, not a repudiation, of the self's boundaries. Separates tempered the freedom of conscience by submitting to the Spirit's words in Scripture and his voice in the exhortations and rebukes of fellow laypersons. Separates covenanted to aid one another in opposing "all sin and Error in our selves as far as in us Lyes and in others allso when Ever they appear." Their list of sinful conduct included "foolish talking and Jesting, Chambring and Wontoness[,] all Vaine disputings . . . that gender strife . . . also vaine Company keeping and spending time Idlelly at Taverns . . . Evil whisperings . . . also Carnal and unnecessary forsaking the Assembling ourselves . . . and all other Sins whatsoever."[58] Separates likewise sought to regulate "publick gifts" such as lay exhortation by encouraging their "improvement" within local assemblies where brethren could evaluate their authenticity. Only those whose preaching the congregation had determined was consistent with Scripture and "blessed of God" would be ordained.[59]

By these means, revivalist groups such as the Separates maintained strict internal constraints on the behavior of converts within an environment of shifting, uncertain external boundaries. They opened the parish bound to any who sought edification. They opened the pulpit to self-taught laypersons. Yet their voluntary bonds of covenantal affection prevented any convert from acting on the strength of an inward call alone. The experience of New Birth, which bound converts into a fluid, expansive, long-distance community of saints, also brought order to their world by binding its members to circumspect, godly behavior.

IV

The New England Separates' battle against the parish bound constituted only one theater of the contest in the years after 1745. As revivalistic itinerancy expanded southward into Virginia, the parish line quickly came to symbolize a similar clash between individual liberty in an expansive, fluid world and deferential conformity within a stable, bounded, ordered society. Virginia's Anglican clergy displayed as much vigor as New England's Old Lights in opposing itinerancy's challenge to their own desire to shape Virginia society according to the balanced, deferential model of Augustan England. The New Side Presbyterian itinerants who made the initial thrust south appealed for liberty of conscience and toleration of dissent in a manner similar to the New England Separates. Yet itinerancy's appearance during a season of rapid migration to the Piedmont and backcountry prompted both sides to set the struggle within a context of expanding empire. As the controversy progressed, itinerancy emerged as more than a symbol of the liberty of conscience. It became a contested metaphor for the flux, mobility, and expansion that confronted all eighteenth-century Anglo-Americans.

Anglican clergy persistently construed revivalistic itinerancy as a breach of every bound for preserving the Establishment and containing dissent. In Anglican correspondence the first New Side Presbyterian itinerants contrast sharply with licensed Presbyterian missionaries who worked among dissenting Scotch-Irish settlers. New Siders "crept into the government" in answer to unauthorized invitations of apostate Hanover County Anglicans. Established clergy complained that such itinerants possessed "no settled place of abode, & no other way of getting their living than by preaching without orders or Licence, & that against the Peace and Amity of the Church." Itinerants threatened to "fragment the established Church" by intruding into well-ordered parishes to preach among Anglican churchmen as well as Dissenters, "telling the People they will all be damned if they go to Church & that they go there to serve the Devil."[60]

Virginia authorities likewise represented New Side itinerancy as a fundamental threat to the peace of "a country hitherto remarkable for uniformity in worship." The colony's ruling elite was determined to preserve a vision of church and social order gleaned from the writings of bishop William Warburton, the eighteenth-century idealogue of the Whig establishment. Warburton taught Virginians that a parochial establishment was essential for "humanizing a savage World, putting the Reins of licentious Appetite into the controuling Hands of conscience, and explaining and inculcating the Duties of social Life; as well as to shew Men the Way of Salvation."[61] The

Virginia elite invoked such views to defend a deferential parochial establishment whose order and stability, especially in the Tidewater counties, was patterned after that of England itself.[62]

This way of thinking about Virginia's establishment led Lieutenant Governor William Gooch to represent the conflict over itinerancy as a struggle between the "rights of society" and "freedom of speech." The former, he declared, compelled his government to "put an immediate stop to the devices and intrigues of these associated schismatics" before they reduced the colony to a "distracted condition." Itinerants' neglect to obtain licenses, coupled with their attempts to draw "weak brethren" from the Church by "railing against our religious establishment," provided sufficient evidence that they did not merely seek liberty to observe their dissenting mode of worship as the Toleration Act allowed. They had breached its provisions, Gooch warned, by prosecuting "not liberty of conscience but freedom of speech," specifically the freedom to shatter the peace of society by slandering the Church. Failure to silence "so dreadful and dangerous a combination," Gooch warned, would constitute a grave injustice "to God, to our king, to our country, to ourselves and to our posterity."[63]

New Lights responded to these initial rumblings by cloaking itinerancy in formal submission to the Toleration Act. Newly formed congregations licensed their meetinghouses, and itinerants such as Gilbert Tennent, Samuel Finley, and Samuel Davies obtained permission from Lieutenant Governor Gooch to preach in them temporarily. However, they continued preaching en route to and from the licensed meetinghouses, sending out "circular letters and Advertisements all over the upper parts of the Colony" to give people ample notice of appointed places and times.[64] When Davies settled as Hanover's dissenting minister in 1748, his license authorized him to itinerate among four locations in the county. The growth of his dissenting flock through unauthorized "missionary journeys" soon necessitated the addition of three new locations.

For a decade Samuel Davies fought a running battle with Establishment clergy, defending as his rightful liberty of conscience the very itinerancy and conversion which the elite branded as unlawful freedom of speech. Anglican clergy near Hanover complained regularly to Virginia Commissary William Dawson of New Light intrusions into their parishes and of the defection of faithful parishioners to dissent.[65] Commissary Dawson and Attorney General Peyton Randolph found it especially galling that Davies's license permitted him to officiate at meetinghouses in several Anglican parishes. Both labored unsuccessfully to make his parish bounds coterminous with those of the establishment.[66] Essayists attacked itinerancy in the *Virginia Gazette*'s pages as a scheme to "turn the World upside down."[67]

Davies countered Anglican "misconstructions" of itinerancy by setting the practice within a context of rapid expansion both of the dissenting population and of God's reviving work. In his *State of Religion among the Protestant Dissenters in Virginia,* written for participants in the concert for prayer, Davies argued that itinerancy did not represent a spirit of factionalism. Instead it reflected the "small numbers of Ministers & Candidates, which was vastly disproportioned to the Vacancies in *Pennsylvania,* and much more to those in *Maryland* and *Virginia.*" New vacancies were multiplying "almost as fast as our Ministers" by the increase of dissenting settlers on the Virginia frontier and "the breaking out of religious Concern in Places where there was little or no Appearances of it before."[68] Davies celebrated revival in both "parts of the harvest" as an expansion of the work God's Spirit had begun in 1740. He assured the ecumenical, transatlantic readership of his *State of Religion in Virginia* that when "I speak of the Increase of Dissenters in these Parts with an air of Satisfaction, I do not boast of them as meer *Captures* from the *Church of England,* but as hopefully *sincere Proselytes to living Religion.*"[69]

Davies invoked the Toleration Act to break open the parochial bounds which maintained Anglican uniformity. He protested that the act neither bound people's consciences to their parish minister nor prohibited dissenting ministers from preaching wherever they received a call. On the contrary, he claimed that the act guaranteed the right to "preach indifferently in any [licensed dissenting] Congregation." Furthermore, the Anglican clergy's "maimed System" of Arminian religion had produced a greater dearth of the Gospel in Established parishes than existed on the frontier, necessitating itinerancy among them. Davies claimed that his itinerancy among a plurality of meetinghouses only followed the Anglican clergy's own practice of itinerating among several "chapels of ease" within a single large parish. A dissenting congregation that was "very much dispersed, and cannot meet at any one place" possessed a similar right "by virtue of said Act [of Toleration] to have a plurality of places licensed for the convenience for the sundry parts of the congregation."[70]

Davies also invoked liberty of conscience to challenge clerical claims on the deference of parishioners. He argued against John Brunskill of St. Margaret's parish that individuals possessed a right to commit themselves into the care of a minister "by their own Consent: & you'll find it hard to prove that others had the right to chuse for them." Just as persons possessed the liberty to commit their own bodies to the doctor, so they were "entitled to the same Liberty in chusing a Physician for their Souls." Davies declared disdain for "that mean and unchristian spirit which chains [a pastor] to his parish, when the most of his Parishioners are weary of him, & would give him no small quantity of Tobacco to get rid of him."[71]

Davies's defense of itinerancy constituted a plea not for abolishing the parish bound but for opening it to pluralism and greater freedom of individual choice. Indeed, he followed the pro-itinerancy arguments of the early 1740s by representing this openness to itinerancy and choice as an openness to the Spirit of God himself. Davies and his Presbyterian colleagues went beyond these earlier arguments in seeking not merely to integrate itinerancy into Virginia's Established parochial system but to organize an alternative system of dissenting parishes that crosshatched the Anglican parish lines. Davies himself claimed a congregation that stretched across at least three different Anglican parishes.[72] Presbyterian ministers who followed likewise claimed congregations that cut across Anglican parish lines.[73]

By invoking Virginia's migratory population in defense of his itinerancy, Davies implicitly acknowledged the grave limitations of the parochial system's adaptability within a context of rapid expansion. Even when conceived as an open system with fluid boundaries, the parochial system could not keep pace with the push of settlements into new areas. Settlers were constantly advancing beyond established parish lines even as the number of educated, ordained ministers to fill existing parishes lagged further and further behind. By 1758, the Presbyterian synods of New York and Philadelphia were openly admitting this. In a statement drawn up to garner British support for a fund for ministerial relief, they complained that the inhabitants of colonial settlements were "inconstant and unsettled . . . always shifting their Habitations, either from a Love of variety, or from the fair Prospect of more commodious Settlements in the Frontiers . . . so that we can have no Certainty of any fixed Number of Parishes or Ministers."[74]

Samuel Davies's ability to link the liberty of conscience with the practical necessities of planting churches among a shifting frontier population reflects his awareness of the revival's place within the expansive, increasingly pluralistic context of empire. An exchange in the *Virginia Gazette* during 1752 over the wisdom of encouraging backcountry settlement reveals that others, too, were recognizing a link between toleration, revival, and mobility and interpreting it in conflicting ways. An expansionist under the pseudonym "Philo Virginia" initiated the exchange by taking up the Dissenters' cause of toleration. He argued that the extension of full toleration, particularly to "*Presbyterians* of the frontier Counties," would "tend to the Advantage of the Colony" by attracting settlers from the northern colonies and Europe. Settlement of the "immense Quantity of Land to the Westward" would increase Virginia's wealth through increased agriculture, trade, and defense. Philo Virginia cited the example of Pennsylvania which, though planted "near a 100 Years after *Virginia,*" was better improved, more "closely inhabited," and boasted a port city which had become the "*Mart of Nations.*" "LIBERTY, charming LIBERTY," the secret of Pennsylvania's success, could enable Virginia to flourish as well.[75] A collaborator, "Bombastia," published an essay two weeks later which concurred with Philo Virginia's claims and seconded his call for toleration "exceeding that allowed by Act of Parliament."[76]

The expansive liberty of conscience which promised prosperity to some conjured demons of disorder for others. "Telltruthia" did not object in principle to Philo Virginia's vision of growth but declared that multitudes provided only the raw materials for building a "strong, handsome Government." "Unanimity of Sentiment and Views" provided the cement necessary to complete the structure, and this the proposed toleration would never supply. Telltruthia therefore professed cordiality for Pennsylvania migrants so long as they left their Presbyterianism behind them. He warned that the sample enthusiast which Pennsylvania had already sent (an oblique reference to Samuel Davies) boded ill for the type of preacher and religion which Philo Virginia's project was apt to encourage. "*Extensive* Toleration," he declared with tongue in cheek, would most likely result in a clash between "Preachers both of the *Church,* and among the *Sectaries,*" who "instead of recommending Virtue and Piety to their Hearers, will get to Daggers drawing among themselves, and mauling one another, while we stand by and cry, *Balloo!* to it Boys! by way of being *edified* with Recreation." He concluded by soberly admonishing his readers to take care "that we have not a Bit more of [Toleration] than is *unfavourably* pinned down upon us by *Act of Parliament.*"[77]

"Peter Limits" attacked the "Root, and Bottom, of the Evil proposed . . . taking away the grand Necessity pretended for bringing in *universal Toleration,*" by showing that "the *widening* of our Settlements to the *Westward* is, itself, no better than a *wide* mistake." Such a project would at best produce a "weak, dissipated, roving People, the mere Skeleton of a Government, without either Nerves or Sinews." At worst, settlement of the backcountry could result in "quickening the march" of the French to Virginia by placing settlers in a position of reliance on French commerce from the Mississippi. The best means of preventing the "Mischief of Sectaries" and promoting Virginia's safety and prosperity lay in encouraging "thick Settlements in narrow Bounds, rather than unnavigated Rivers, unuseful Tracts, *nominal* Estates, and diffused habitations in *unbounded* Countries."[78]

This exchange represented a brief skirmish in the great contest of worldviews which informed eighteenth-century debates over commerce and political economy, situating dissent, toleration, and itinerancy within that larger contest. The participants concurred in identifying Dissenters as primary agents of expansion and their mobility as an outgrowth of their religious belief. Yet their disagreement over the meaning of that religiously motivated mobility paralleled the conflict between advocates of expansive commercial empire and defenders of deferential, homogenous agrarian republics.[79] To the advocates of toleration, the vigorous love of liberty which motivated Dissenters to flee oppressive governments promised to enrich a tolerant Virginia with moral, industrious citizens who would extend the boundaries of empire. To the defenders of uniformity, that restless mobility betrayed a deep-seated instability, inconstancy, and fanaticism that could ruin the colony.

V

The growth of the Separate Baptists in Virginia intensified the contest over the meaning of itinerancy, revivalism, and mobility in Virginia during the 1760s. Separate Baptists first arrived in the colony on the crest of a fresh wave of the northern migration which "Peter Limits" so vigorously opposed. During the 1750s, the push of persecution and the pull of the Spirit's call drove Separate and Separate Baptist itinerants, adherents, and sometimes whole congregations to leave older towns in New England for the "charming Liberty" of the colonial frontier.[80] Shubal Stearns, the patriarch of southern Separate Baptists, emphasized the pull rather than the push, leading his congregation from New England to Sandy Creek, North Carolina in response to the Spirit's call to preach in the southern wilderness.[81] Stearns's Sandy Creek church provided the base from which the Separate Baptist itinerants invaded Virginia parishes.

Separate Baptist itinerancy confronted the Virginia elite with a powerful alternative model of adaptation to the eighteenth-century world in which mobility played a central role. Failure to give mobility its due weight in shaping the perceptions of Baptists' adherents and detractors has impaired otherwise insightful analyses of the Baptist social vision. Historians such as Rhys Isaac have mapped out in detail the contrasting models of the social world advanced by Baptists and their opponents. Virginia clerical and lay elites, like opponents during the first wave of itinerancy in the 1740s, defended a bounded, hierarchical, elite-brokered vision of society against the onslaught of disorderly enthusiasts and social levelers. Separate Baptists, like itinerants of the Awakening, defended their right to carry the Gospel to all against a band of formalists who seemed determined to quench the Spirit for the sake of worldly power and status. Yet the persistent context of mobility suggests that this contest represented more than what Isaac and others have described as a struggle between elite traditionalists and egalitarian communitarians.[82] It represented the continuation of a struggle between alternative methods of accommodating to rapid change and expansion.

The Separate Baptists accomplished their phenomenal growth during the 1760s by adapting a novel form of itinerancy and church formation to reach a migratory population. The Separate Baptist method of planting churches obviated the need for either parishes or college-trained ministers. The churches possessed no definite territorial boundaries but extended as far as itinerancy could take them. They typically began with "great meetings" that drew hundreds of people from the surrounding countryside to hear itinerants. The churches that sprang from these meetings consisted of a "mother church" and several "branches" composed of converts living at a distance. Some branches were established at the church's founding. Others sprang up as laymen within the "mother church" discovered a gift for exhortation and cultivated it by itinerant preaching in new locations. Branches which achieved full standing as "daughter churches" repeated the process, sending out itinerant exhorters who established further branches and daughter churches.[83]

This system situated Baptist converts within an expansive, long-distance community of fluid boundaries. They could think of themselves not simply as members of the local, face-to-face assembly into which they were baptized. They also became participants in a regional network of associations among strangers who lived at a distance but shared a common experience of New Birth and baptism. They shared a common responsibility to propagate their gospel to the world beyond their bounds. The boundaries of their religious world could expand as far as itinerants—indeed as converts themselves—were willing to push them. Expansion was not slowed by the long process of ministerial training and ordination. It could begin as soon as laymen within Baptist ranks discovered a gift and a call to carry the Word abroad. Shubal Stearns's Sandy Creek church exemplified this expansive model. The eighteenth-century Baptist historian Morgan Edwards described it as the "mother of all the Separate Baptists," embracing as daughters every church in Virginia, the Carolinas, and Georgia and extending its reach westward "as far as the great river Mississippi."[84]

The Separate Baptists adapted to their mobile world not only by adopting innovative patterns of church growth but also by developing close-knit, disciplined assemblies. The Baptist obsession with quelling disorder by mutual enforcement of strict codes of moral conduct betrayed a need to order their own rapidly changing environment. Much of the Baptists' explosive growth took place in counties inundated by migrants from the north and east. At least two of the Virginia Baptist churches visited by Morgan Edwards in 1772 were founded by migrants, and most were located in the Piedmont and on the frontier where available land was continuing to draw an influx of migrants.[85] Membership in these churches could also ebb and flow with the tide of in- and out-migration. The membership of Sandy Creek, the "mother of all Separate Baptists," reached a high point in the late 1750s of 606 souls, but by 1772 out-migration had decimated its number to 14.[86]

This context of fluid geographical boundaries and shifting composition of local social groups suggests a more complex motivation for Baptist discipline than the determination to reform Virginia's freewheeling, convivial gentry society.[87] It suggests a more profound effort to compensate for the absence of clearly defined external boundaries by anchoring personal identity and social significance in a set of internal emotional commitments supported by a voluntary community of like-minded brothers and sisters.[88] The Baptists' resolve to bind themselves into a community which would "worship GOD; and rule itself according to his word" reflected an effort to adapt to a world of uncertain external boundaries.[89]

The discourse of elite opposition to Separate Baptist itinerancy provides further evidence that the contest was rooted in alternative ways of adapting to mobility and expansion. Supporters of Virginia's Establishment portrayed the Baptist itinerancy as a movement of flux and disorder and responded by returning once again to the time-honored defense of boundaries. Like Peter Limits in 1752 and the Old Lights of the 1740s, they invoked the transgression of the parish bound as a metaphor for transgressions of law, custom, and station. As early as 1759, Reverend James Craig of Lunenberg County warned Commissary Dawson that "ignorant Enthusiasts" preaching "antipaedobaptist" doctrines threatened "the entire Subversion of true Religion in these Parts." Throughout the 1760s, local elites took steps to fend off the "fatal consequences" of Baptist itinerancy by "apprehend[ing] or otherwise constrain[ing]" the "Principal Persons concerned in this Delusion."[90] Churchmen proposed to shore up the social order by strengthening its "Basis and Cement," the Establishment.

"A Country Gentleman" echoed Samuel Davies's twenty-year-old observations on the inadequacies of the parochial system by setting the Baptist threat in a context of growth that was producing an increasing number of vacancies in Established parishes.

The "Gentleman" proposed to remedy this problem through an American episcopate. The presence of a bishop would "obviate [Dissenters'] Attempts to spread their various tenets" by filling vacant parishes, thus removing the "Temptation of attending on dissenting Teachers, under the Want of any Teacher of [the parishioners'] own Church which they can conveniently attend." An American episcopate would also clarify the extent of Dissenters' privileges under the Toleration Act, preventing them from being "restrained within too narrow Bounds on the one Hand, or carried too far beyond just Limits on the Other."[91]

Even those less supportive of an American episcopate urged containment of the "turbulent sects" through the strengthening of parochial "bounds and limits" by legal means.[92] They detected within Baptist belief and practice a tendency to "push forward with the boldness which prompted [Baptists] to reject established opinions . . . disdain all restraint, and run into wild notions, that often lead to scandalous or immoral conduct."[93] Critics therefore sought to regulate those who "go about publickly preaching and inculcating their Errours" by enforcing the acts which restricted preaching to "qualified Teachers" meeting in "licensed houses." The author of an "Address to the Anabaptists imprisoned in Caroline County" assured his readers that whoever observed those laws would "meet with Protection, and not Interruption, from Magistracy here." He warned, however, that "as often as you break those Limits, and *every One* undertakes to preach *every Where*, you may expect to be proceeded against."[94]

Virginia elites were once again invoking the very metaphors of flux and disorder, bounds and limits, which had marked the contest over itinerancy from 1739 to 1745 and had reappeared sporadically ever since. Like their predecessors of the 1740s, Virginians blamed itinerancy for encouraging invasions of the ministerial office by unqualified persons, insolence toward social betters, and disruption of the fabric of community and family life. Wives were once again being "drawn from their Husbands, Children from the Parents, and Slaves from the Obedience of their Masters. Thus the very Heart-strings of those little Societies which form the greater are torn in sunder, and all their Peace destroyed."[95]

Yet Separate Baptist itinerancy's context of migration and growth helped Virginians to perceive more clearly than their predecessors a structural link between anxiety over itinerancy and anxiety over the vast swirl of eighteenth-century mobility. Virginia and the empire were growing "by Population, and the addition of new Territories." Migration to the hinterland was rending friend from friend and family member from family member far more finally than adult baptism ever could. The neglect of the legislature to order this growth by a sound "civil and religious Policy" seemed only to make matters worse by opening a door for sectaries to foment commotion, turmoil, and division throughout "this poor Colony."[96] Itinerancy drew such vehement hostility from the Virginia elite not only because it threatened their dancing, drinking, gaming, and conspicuous consumption, but because it provided such a visible symptom of the more pervasive problem of uncontrolled growth and mobility.

Virginia Baptists, like others before them, had found in itinerancy a powerful means of adapting to this fluid, expanding world of unprecedented diversity and choice. Their ongoing reverence for George Whitefield linked them with a diverse, transatlantic community of the redeemed that had persisted for more than thirty years. A world of prorevival print still circulated to remind Baptists, as it reminded others, that their experiences of grace fit into a vast, ongoing work of the Spirit of God. The experience of New Birth not only secured Baptist converts a place in heaven and participation in a boundless community of saints; it also initiated them into close-knit local expressions of that wider community where they, like the New England Separates, could find meaning and order in the midst of an uncertain world.

VI

By the time the first shots of the American Revolution rang out at Lexington green, itinerancy had helped effect a dramatic transformation of religion throughout British America. The Grand Itinerant George Whitefield had achieved such esteem that even his former enemies eulogized him at his death in 1770. His name became the symbol of true revival and vital piety among evangelically minded adherents of denominations who could agree on little else. Evangelistic itinerancy had provided a powerful tool for the expansion of Presbyterianism, Separate Congregationalism, and a robust new Baptist movement—to mention only three English-speaking varieties of revivalism—into settled and backcountry areas alike. In the South, Anglican leaders who had been the most intransigent foes of Presbyterian and Baptist itinerancy were now finding themselves compelled to adapt grudgingly to a new wave of Methodist lay itinerancy arising within the Established Church itself. Published controversy over early Methodism was scant, swallowed up by great Revolutionary political issues and further muted as Methodist and non-Methodist Anglicans fell under the common suspicion of loyalism.

Yet despite itinerancy's role in renegotiating the relationship between ecclesiastical boundaries, personal conduct, and communal order, the radical breakdown of community predicted by the Old Lights of 1740 did not occur. In settled areas where itinerancy eroded local geographical and social boundaries, its practitioners encouraged converts to adopt the strong internal codes of belief and behavior which could make them peaceful, productive members of a tolerant community. On the frontier, where few meaningful external boundaries existed, itinerants compensated by propagating revivalism's stringent morality among the awakened and by providing affective links among scattered voluntary communities drawn together by the experience of New Birth.

Conclusion: Itinerancy and the Transformation of the Early American Religious World

In the late 1760s, a cranky Anglican missionary by the name of Charles Woodmason traveled westward on a quest to circumscribe a new parish on the South Carolina frontier. His mission proved much more complicated than those of a generation before. Like his predecessors, he faced arduous travel over treacherous, sometimes impassable trails to reach an ignorant, often indifferent frontier population. Yet where earlier missionaries had usually provided the only religious leadership for frontier settlers, Woodmason found himself competing in a robust environment of religious choice fostered by evangelical itinerancy. The crusty clergyman complained that the absence of parishes in the Carolina backcountry permitted people to be "eaten up by Itinerant Teachers, Preachers, and Impostors from New England and Pennsylvania—Baptists, New Lights, Presbyterians, Independents, and an hundred other Sects." He charged that the "Variety of Taylors who would pretend to know the best fashion in which Christs Coat is to be worn" so bewildered frontier settlers that they neglected religion altogether.

Woodmason thus found himself in the distasteful position of peddler competing in a religious marketplace to sell Christ's coat in its respectable Anglican style. He adapted as best he could by imitating the fashionable extemporaneous delivery of his rivals. He repeated the Liturgy by heart and used "no Book but the Bible, when I read the Lessons." He also boasted that he had the "whole Service and all the Offices at my fingers Ends. I also give an Extempore Prayer before Sermon—but cannot yet venture to give Extempore Discourses, tho' could certainly perform beyond any of these poor Fools. I shall make Trial in a short time."[1]

Charles Woodmason's experience on the Carolina frontier exemplifies the growing dilemma faced by heirs of the Old Lights as they carried the contest over the meaning of itinerancy forward into the revolutionary period and beyond. Large numbers of American religious leaders continued defending a vision of an American church and society civilized by the parochial system: an orderly world of fixed, known boundaries—some literal and some metaphorical—wherein people could situate themselves according to "calling" or "station" within webs of stable, deferential, harmonious, reasonable relationships. This vision represented not an anachronistic urge to revert to premodern society but a desire to fashion eighteenth-century America after the stable, hierarchical, enlightened English model of the latest gentlemen's magazines.

Revivalists continued to propagate in varying degrees a much different model of the social world, one that their civilized opponents persisted in reading as chaos approaching barbarism. Through itinerancy, the remarkable work of the Spirit of God burst all bounds to spread like a "moor-burn" throughout the empire. The openness of parish bounds and pulpits to itinerants came to symbolize an openness to the work of God's free Spirit in a mobile, expansive world. Those converted under itinerants' preaching transcended the parish bound to enter a free, mobile community of anonymous people linked across vast distances by a shared experience of awakening strengthened by a great network of print and correspondence.

The parish bound so strenuously defended by the Old Lights and their heirs continued to mark many parts of the American landscape well into the nineteenth century. Thomas Jefferson still described Virginia as divided into parishes in the late 1780s even though Anglicanism had been disestablished by the Virginia assembly's Act for Establishing Religious Freedom.[2] In Connecticut, Congregationalism and its parochial system remained established until 1818, in Massachusetts until 1833.

Nevertheless, by the revolutionary period itinerancy had made great headway in transforming the Anglo-American religious world. Separate Baptists itinerants were traversing the New England countryside, intruding greater religious choice and pluralism into Congregational parishes. Baptist itinerants were steadily gaining ground throughout the South, planting new daughter churches in every direction. A wave of Wesleyan Methodists were bringing new order to itinerancy by organizing preachers into regular mobile circuits which the founding bishop Francis Asbury came to regard as the very life of the church. Asbury set forth a vision of mobility diametrically opposed to that of Anglican satirists who in 1740 had compared Whitefield to a comet and execrated mobility as the bane of church and society. "Everything is kept moving as far as possible," Asbury boasted of his circuit riders, "and we will be bold to say, that, next to the grace of God, there is nothing *like this* for keeping the whole body alive from the centre to the circumference, and for the continual extension of that circumference on every hand."[3]

Asbury's vision of a vital religious world in motion may have clashed with that of his Anglican colleagues, but it formed a remarkable parallel to the dynamic metaphors employed by bards of British American commerce who celebrated the constant circulation of colonial "rivulets" of trade into "the Great *British* Stream."[4] In addition, it comports well with the historian Bernard Bailyn's description of the North Atlantic as "worlds in motion."[5] The parallels underscore the close relationship between the new evangelical itinerancy of the Great Awakening, the explosion of the century's revolution in commerce, and the unprecedented human mobility throughout the empire. George Whitefield had adapted the consumer revolution's advertising methods to pioneer this novel practice of supplementing the regular parish ministry with the preaching of traveling evangelists. The same routes that brought first settlers, then merchants and peddlers with imports from afar also brought Whitefield and his successors with the message of the New Birth. Newspapers carried accounts of the latest revivals as well as news of the latest imports to an ever-increasing audience, and shrewd publishers like Benjamin Franklin used revival news to increase their papers' circulation even faster.[6] The extension of conceptual horizons already being engendered by these various commercial activities was enhanced by a transatlantic network of revivalists who created new print commodities with the express purpose of forging a transatlantic revival community.

Itinerancy thus paralleled commerce and embodied mobility, working hand in glove with both to challenge not only boundaries of space but those of society and self as well. The partnership with commerce was tinged with irony for preachers, including Whitefield himself, who often preached against the ostentatious use of consumer goods like "jewels, patches and gay apparel."[7] The mobility of itinerancy likewise clashed with religious leaders' traditional expectations, and even clergy who were already forced to ride wide circuits in vast parishes sought to soften the effects of the breach in their "line." Indeed, itinerancy's challenge was rife with unintended consequences which spilled out in the practice of Whitefield's followers. In the contest that ensued, friends and foes alike poured out reams of printed copy in an effort to explicate, contain, or renegotiate the boundaries of place, station, and decorum which itinerancy had disrupted.

The preceding chapters outline three major responses to the unintended challenges which itinerancy posed for the boundaries of eighteenth-century life. No response was exclusively either reactionary or progressive. All represented ways of bringing cherished traditions forward and adapting them to a world of new possibilities, shaping that social world in the process. Opponents of itinerancy explored its challenges most fully in the course of interpreting the "language of entering other men's parishes." Their interpretive enterprise also resulted in an articulation and defense of a bounded, deferential worldview which prior to Whitefield's advent had been largely assumed. The opposition literature revealed how geographical boundaries were regarded as crucial to the whole structure of eighteenth-century society, dividing the landscape into ordered localities within which each inhabitant was situated in graded stations known to themselves and all their neighbors. Opponents therefore shaped critiques showing how itinerancy's breach in the local boundary was producing a breakdown of other, less tangible bounds that held society together, and sought to stem the social breakdown by shoring up the parish line. While appeals to the Bible and Protestant tradition formed a portion of this enterprise, so did a determination to ensure colonial society's progress toward the polite standards of civilization that governed Augustan England.

Revivalists who remained within the churches of their ancestors embraced the open, mobile world of itinerancy while negotiating flexible boundaries that would enable them to preserve cherished features of a locally covenanted religious and social life. They welcomed itinerants into their parishes, labored to ensure that the awakenings occurring during those visits would issue in "hopeful conversions," and celebrated the place of local revivals—and individual conversions—within a transatlantic outpouring of God's free Spirit. In the process they exposed parishioners to a wider world of choice and situated them within a long-distance, affective community parallel to that being forged by commerce and print. At the same time revivalists worked to temper the "excesses" threatened by this relaxation of spatial and social boundaries, establishing guidelines for the practice of itinerancy and employing tools such as covenant renewals to remind converts of their place in local as well as transatlantic communities of saints. Like their opponents they sought to adapt by forging links between past and present, appealing to elements of Scripture and Protestant tradition which supported their efforts to seize new opportunities by employing new methods to advance revival on an unprecedented scale.

Separates, Separate Baptists, and Methodists embraced itinerancy most fully and with it a radically unbounded vision of their world. In the early years of the Awakening, Separates provided fodder for Old Light jeremiads concerning the interrelated dissolution of bounds to parish, society, and self by renouncing all at once. Itinerancy encouraged Separates to reject their unconverted ministers and ignore their parish lines. It also provided a means for individuals to opt out of the station fixed for them by social convention, opening an avenue for "disorderly, unqualified" women, children, and men of African and Native-American as well as European descent to assert for themselves exalted identities as messengers of God's judgment to their unconverted "betters."

Yet even in renouncing traditional cultural constraints on the self, virtually no revivalist group of the colonial era permitted its adherents to abandon themselves wholly to the antinomian extremes their opponents dreaded. Instead, Separates and other radical New Lights compensated for the lack of external boundaries with a set of internal constraints on the self, which they persisted in viewing as the seat of depravity. Separates appealed to the authority of the New Testament and primitive Congregationalism in rejecting parish boundaries by opening meetings to all comers and welcoming any itinerant whose preaching evidenced the Spirit's anointing. They looked to the same sources to restrict membership solely to converts, while conducting comparatively egalitarian meetings open to participation by laymen—and often laywomen—regardless of age or race. New Light Baptist meetings followed a similar pattern as did the earliest Methodist classes. Despite their backward glance at primitive Christianity, all three employed itinerancy to adapt their religion thoroughly to the shifting, mobile, weakly bounded environment of eighteenth-century America. All compensated for the lack of structure in their outer world by ordering their inner worlds through stringent moral codes enforced by mutual discipline in close-knit, voluntary communions.

The contest summarized above brought to light some startling new possibilities for human action and left several enduring legacies. Most of its sensational aspects proved short-lived but nevertheless permitted new voices to make themselves heard in American religious discourse. At the height of the Awakening, itinerancy's challenge to traditional bounds of behavior extended to the sphere of laywomen as well as men. Women were prominent in the numerous praying societies that sprang up during the Awakening, a number of women joined men in exhorting, a few preached in colonial pulpits, and some took leading roles in local revivals. Few even among the most enthusiastic New Lights were prepared to support a breach in the bounds of gender and moved to dampen women's newfound assertiveness in the quest to temper itinerancy's effects.

Nevertheless, the heightened role accorded to the converted self in the traveling preacher's wake endured, and many remained willing to hear the Spirit's voice in the exhortations of their spiritual sisters.[8] Ebenezer Frothingham defended the Separates' ongoing practice of female exhortation, though he accorded it a lesser status than preaching.[9] Sarah Townshend exercised a leading role in the New Light meeting at Oyster Bay on Long Island in the early 1770s.[10] Shubal Stearns's sister Martha Marshall exhorted by her husband Daniel's side as they itinerated through Virginia in the 1760s and 1770s establishing Separate Baptist congregations.[11] Even the New Divinity minister Samuel Hopkins celebrated the leading role taken by a female parishioner, Sarah Osborne, in the Newport, Rhode Island revival of 1766–67.[12] The modest gains made by female exhorters in the late colonial period paved the way for a much larger role in nineteenth-century evangelical life.

By breaching the bounds of race as well as gender, itinerancy also opened a way for voices of African descent to make themselves heard and played an integral role in the Christianizing of the African-American population. Scattered references to black itinerants in late colonial records reveal their rising presence and influence especially in the South. At least four slave itinerants in prerevolutionary Virginia used their preaching skills as a means of fleeing bondage.[13] African Methodist Episcopal Church founder Richard Allen and the Georgia Baptist missionary George Liele won manumission as a result of their exemplary conduct as itinerant preachers.[14] To be sure, white leaders took measures to shore up the boundaries of race in the later eighteenth century, working to limit the activity of black itinerants and to relegate black converts to an inferior place in white congregations. Nevertheless black itinerant preaching provided the means for spreading the vibrant slave religion that formed a powerful source of dignity, comfort, and enduring resistance for those in bondage.[15]

Evangelical itinerancy's role in eroding the bounds of gender and race, limited though it was, provides concrete evidence of its powerful place in the great cultural transformation that swept the eighteenth-century Atlantic world. As part and parcel of that vast transformation, it was far from benign, disrupting families and communities in a variety of ways. The mobility of itinerancy symbolized for many critics a loss of cohesiveness and control brought about by other forms of mobility across boundaries: the exchange of paper currency whose value varied widely from colony to colony; the traveling confidence man who could forge his identity in a commercial world increasingly more reliant on paper transactions than on face-to-face relations; the migration which pulled apart families and scattered a lawless population across a savage landscape. In addition to augmenting such external forces of dissolution, itinerancy worked insidiously to disrupt communities from within. Like peddlers whose wares cut into local merchants' clientele, itinerant preachers offered alternatives to the local minister's variety of religion. They invited individuals to choose their religion for themselves, seizing that choice from ecclesiastical leaders, civil authorities, even from "the Supream Government of the Major Vote of the Inhabitants."[16] As religious choice expanded in the later eighteenth century, communities became less uniform, and the bonds between religion, self, and society weakened.

Yet itinerancy's very disruptions, like those of the broader transformation of which it was a part, often benefited ordinary colonists. By infusing a new element of religious choice into the communities, itinerancy became a direct cause of the growing demand for religious freedom. Indeed, itinerancy's defenders consistently placed themselves on the cutting edge of this conflict. In 1744 Elisha Williams, a judge of Connecticut's Superior Court, entered the lists on the side of itinerants against the colony's repressive Act for Regulating Abuses. Williams grounded his stand for the itinerants on the right of private judgment protected by the Act of Toleration, which empowered "*any Number* of Christians, greater or less, [to] hear *any Protestant Minister* they desire, without controul from the Will of others, or Authority of the civil State."[17] Samuel Davies likewise defended his itinerancy across Virginia parish lines on the basis of the Toleration Act's guarantee of liberty of conscience.[18] Itinerancy figured prominently in the pleas of Separate leaders for total disestablishment and religious liberty.[19] Similarly, the itinerancy for which Virginia Baptists suffered most became the catalyst of their campaign for religious freedom during the revolutionary era.[20]

The element of choice in religious life highlights another enduring effect of the vast cultural transformation in which itinerancy played a role: the relaxation of cultural constraints which had fixed the self in a particular station within a deferential, bounded community. Here too itinerancy complemented other forces: the alternate push and pull of land scarcity and frontier abundance which forced individuals to make for themselves new places in new communities; and new opportunities for entrepreneurship and consumption which could enable a shrewd apprentice like Benjamin Franklin to read, write, publish, dress, house, and furnish himself into the person of a philosophe. Itinerancy could likewise provide an avenue for a tradesman to become a preacher, and the same Spirit which elevated lay preachers above unconverted ministers could similarly imbue their hearers with superior spiritual insight. The itinerancy of the First Great Awakening established the egalitarian foundation for what the historian Nathan Hatch has termed the Second Awakening's "democratization" of American Christianity.[21]

Historians have alternately hailed and lamented the individualizing effects of these modernizing forces without recognizing how itinerancy, like commerce and print, mitigated individualism by opening the way for commitment to new forms of community.

Anglo-Americans realized this potential in the realm of literature and publication by forging what communications historian Michael Warner has termed a transatlantic "republic of letters."[22] T. H. Breen has recently shown how intercolonial consumption of British imports enabled prerevolutionary Americans to launch successful boycott movements by constructing "interpretive communities around a temporary withdrawal from an Atlantic marketplace."[23] Likewise, the common experience of New Birth, propagated by itinerancy and communicated through print, enabled revivalists to forge the transatlantic movement known to posterity as the Great Awakening.

Seen in this light, the transatlantic movement delineated in the published contest over revival was anything but the "interpretative fiction" of later historians as Jon Butler has charged.[24] Instead, it was a historical phenomenon consciously forged across barriers of distance to embrace all who responded to the message of New Birth. To be sure, the Awakening was a product of an interpretive community whose hermeneutic was driven in part by the need to defend itinerancy as a legitimate category of ministry. The revival community did so by representing itinerancy as a valuable tool employed by the Spirit of God to accomplish a unified, meaningful, transatlantic work of revival.

The foregoing analysis has shown that the act of interpreting local revivals as manifestations of this great transatlantic movement in no way reflected fictive rhetorical play. Rather, accounts disclosed a genuine interconnectedness among local revivals as visits or news from one part of the empire sparked awakening in another. Those who published expressly did so to extend the web of divine influence even further. This act alone transformed the consciousness of participants since it entailed both recognition of place within a larger world and the performance of a specific action to influence events far beyond local horizons.

An eagerness to identify local revivals with the "great Work" further transformed the way in which converts conceived of the local event and their experience within it. The act of identification led persons whose conversions incorporated diverse traditions or circumstances to claim for their experiences a significance that transcended local revival customs or histories. To do so, they sometimes deemphasized local idiosyncracies, subordinating them to common experience of New Birth. Other peculiarities found their way into standard revival practice, as for example the Scottish communion seasons which gave rise to American camp meetings.[25] The result was a gradual homogenization of the main features of the revival experience, enabling each convert to imagine herself in a universe of unseen fellows similarly touched by awakening preaching in the "old Whitefield style."

By such means the Awakening became a reality as enduring as the category of evangelistic itinerancy itself, attending traveling evangelists as they pushed across new boundaries to transform the religious world of new groups of people. The persistent growth of itinerant preaching through the revolutionary period belies the common assumption that itinerancy went dormant for thirty years after a short burst of uncoordinated activity in the early 1740s.[26] Whitefield's repeated tours of the colonies until his death in 1770, the constant push of Samuel Davies, Charles Beatty, and other Presbyterian itinerants west and south, the dogged perseverance of Separate itinerants such as Solomon Paine in the face of Congregational persecution, the proliferation of Separate Baptist itinerancy throughout the colonies under the leadership of men like Isaac Backus and Shubal Stearns—all indicate that itinerancy flourished rather than languished in the late colonial period. All self-consciously represented their ministries as the continuation and extension of the Awakening first begun in 1740. The great swarm of traveling preachers that traversed the American landscape after 1783 learned itinerancy and the language of the Awakening directly from their parents' and grandparents' example.

Wherever itinerants traveled, they carried with them the vision of an expansive, potentially worldwide revival first forged in the early 1740s. The vision endured in the literature supporting the trans-atlantic concert for prayer. It reappeared in every fresh revival account of the colonial period. It survived in the rhetoric of hundreds of itinerant preachers who represented themselves as the heirs of Whitefield and their ministries as the continuation of the outpouring that first appeared in 1740. This consistent representation of local revivals as a small part of a much larger whole continued to encourage people to think of themselves as local participants in a vast, flowing, expansive movement of the Spirit of God. In so doing, the successive waves of revival in the late colonial period forged a continuous, unbroken link between the Awakening of the eighteenth century and that at the turn of the nineteenth.[27] In the passage from one to the other, itinerancy not only adapted Christianity to its modern American environment but played a decisive role in shaping that mobile, expansive environment itself.

Notes

Introduction

1 Mary Cooper, *The Diary of Mary Cooper: Life on a Long Island Farm 1768–1773*, ed. Field Horne (Oyster Bay, N.Y., 1981), 13, 19, 23–24.

2 This view is taken in, for example, John C. Miller, "Religion, Finance and Democracy in Massachusetts," *New England Quarterly* 6 (1933): 29–58; Gary B. Nash, *The Urban Crucible: Social Change, Political Consciousness, and the Origins of the American Revolution* (Cambridge, Mass., 1979), 161–263; and Elizabeth I. Nybakken, "New Light on the Old Side: Irish Influences on Colonial Presbyterianism," *Journal of American History* 68 (1981–82): 813–32.

3 Itinerancy, of course, was an old problem whose history is discussed in chapter 1 below. Yet historians of the Awakening from Joseph Tracy forward have recognized that it took on new prominence in controversial literature of the Awakening after 1740. See, for example, Joseph Tracy, *The Great Awakening: A History of the Revival of Religion in the Time of Edwards and Whitefield* (Boston, 1845), 75–119, 230–54; Alan Heimert, *Religion and the American Mind: From the Great Awakening to the Revolution* (Cambridge, Mass., 1966), 36, 118–22, 161–64, and passim; Alan Heimert and Perry Miller, eds., *The Great Awakening: Documents Illustrating the Crisis and Its Consequences* (Indianapolis and New York, 1967), 147–51, 228–364 passim; Richard L. Bushman, *The Great Awakening: Documents on the Revival of Religion, 1740–1745* (New York, 1970), 19–65; Harry S. Stout, "Religion, Communication, and the Ideological Origins of the American Revolution," *William and Mary Quarterly*, 3d ser., 34 (1977): 519–41.

4 Bushman, *The Great Awakening*, 58–60.

5 See, for example, Charles Chauncy, *Enthusiasm describ'd and caution'd against* (Boston, 1742), ii–iv.

6 Jon Butler has argued that these sporadic outbreaks were largely unrelated; see his "Enthusiasm Described and Decried: The Great Awakening as Interpretive Fiction," *The Journal of American History* 69 (1982–83): 305–25; and his *Awash in a Sea of Faith: Christianizing the American People* (Cambridge, Mass., 1990), 164–93. I will argue in contrast that after 1739, colonists themselves perceived revivals throughout the colonies to be integrally related as they read about dis-

tant "outpourings of the Spirit" and self-consciously sought by itinerancy and other means to reproduce those revivals in their own locales. See chapter 3.

7 Thomas Prince, ed., *The Christian History, Containing Accounts of the Revival and Propagation of Religion in Great Britain and America,* 2 vols. (Boston, 1744–45); hereafter cited as *Christian History.*

8 Jon Butler, in his criticism of the historiography of the eighteenth-century Great Awakening as an "interpretative fiction," argues that even the term itself was an invention of the nineteenth-century historian Joseph Tracy. However, a survey of prorevival literature on both sides of the Atlantic reveals that the term was used frequently by contemporaries. Moreover, as I will argue at greater length hereafter, eighteenth-century revivalists were keenly aware of their place in a great transatlantic movement. Compare Butler, "Enthusiasm Described," 305–25; Tracy, *The Great Awakening,* 14, 400–401, and passim; Michael J. Crawford, *Seasons of Grace: Colonial New England's Revival Tradition in Its British Context* (New York, 1991), 149; and Josiah Smith, *A Sermon, on the Character, Preaching &c. of the Rev. Mr. Whitefield,* excerpted in Heimert and Miller, eds., *The Great Awakening,* 62–69.

9 The terms "cosmology" and "worldview" are notoriously imprecise, taking on varied nuances according to the contexts in which they appear. The former usually appears in the parlance of symbolic anthropologists, mythologists, and historians of religion, while sociologists and philosophers use the latter to describe distinct but overlapping phenomena. Further, one term or usage may be defined so strictly as to exclude the other. Nevertheless, enough overlap exists both in the interpretive frameworks the terms describe and in the communicative devices humans use to construct such frameworks that, for purposes of this study, I think myself justified in using the terms interchangeably.

10 This discussion of human systems of meaning draws on the theory of several anthropologists, notably Clifford Geertz, *The Interpretation of Cultures* (New York, 1973), 10–13; Sherry B. Ortner, *Sherpas Through Their Rituals* (Cambridge, 1978), 8; Mary Douglas, *Natural Symbols: Explorations in Cosmology* (New York, 1970), 144; idem, "The Effects of Modernization on Religious Change," in *Religion and America: Spirituality in a Secular Age,* ed. Mary Douglas and Stephen M. Tipton (Boston, 1982), 25–43; and Fredrik Barth, *Ethnic Groups and Boundaries: The Social Organization of Culture Difference* (Boston, 1969), 29. The philosopher Paul Ricoeur's analysis of the process of meaning creation in response to shifts in the horizon of possibilities for human action has also been very helpful, as has the social theorist Jürgen Habermas's analysis of communicative action. See Paul Ricoeur, *Time and Narrative,* 3 vols. (Chicago, 1984), 1:52–87; and Jürgen Habermas, *The Theory of Communicative Action,* vol. 1, *Reason and the Rationalization of Society,* trans. Thomas McCarthy (Boston, 1984), 70. Habermas recognizes that a particular worldview most often becomes "decentered" as changes in social experience outstrip the worldview's ability to adapt, but he predicates his work on the conviction that such decentering is also possible through rational communicative action.

11 On such assumptions see Stanley Fish, "Normal Circumstances, Literal Language, Direct Speech Acts, the Ordinary, the Everyday, the Obvious, What

Goes Without Saying, and Other Special Cases," in *Interpretive Social Science: A Reader,* ed. Paul Rabinow and William M. Sullivan (Berkeley, 1979), 243–65. Although I do not accept Fish's conclusions concerning language and human (ir)rationality, this article provides a lucid and entertaining exploration of the role of cultural assumptions in the formation and interpretation of meaning.

12 Douglas, *Natural Symbols,* 144; Ricoeur, *Time and Narrative,* 3:247–56.

13 Benedict Anderson, *Imagined Communities: Reflections on the Origin and Spread of Nationalism* (London, 1983), 41–49.

14 Bernard Bailyn, *The Peopling of British North America: An Introduction* (New York, 1985); J. G. A. Pocock, "British History: A Plea for a New Subject," *Journal of Modern History* 47 (1975): 601–28.

15 David Grayson Allen, *In English Ways: The Movement of Societies and the Transferal of English Local Law and Custom to Massachusetts Bay in the Seventeenth Century* (New York, 1981); T. H. Breen, *Puritans and Adventurers: Change and Persistence in Early America* (New York, 1980), 3–23; Stephen Innes, "Land Tenancy and Social Order in Springfield, Massachusetts, 1652 to 1702," *William and Mary Quarterly,* 3d ser., 35 (1978): 33–56; Philip J. Greven, *Four Generations: Population, Land and Family in Colonial Andover, Massachusetts* (Ithaca, N.Y., 1970), 220–58; James A. Henretta, "Families and Farms: *Mentalité* in Pre-industrial America," *William and Mary Quarterly,* 3d ser., 35 (1978): 3–32; Nash, *Urban Crucible,* 161–263.

16 Ralph Davis, *The Rise of the Atlantic Economies* (Ithaca, 1973), 231–300; Nash, *Urban Crucible,* 129–57.

17 T. H. Breen, "'Baubles of Britain': The American and Consumer Revolutions of the Eighteenth Century," *Past and Present* 119 (May 1988): 73–104; idem, "An Empire of Goods: The Anglicization of Colonial America, 1690–1776," *Journal of British Studies* 25 (1986), 467–99; idem, "The Meaning of Things: Interpreting the Consumer Economy in the Eighteenth Century," in *Consumption and the World of Goods,* ed. John Brewer and Roy Porter (London, 1993), 249–59; Gloria L. Main, "The Standard of Living in Colonial Massachusetts," *Journal of Economic History* 43 (1983), 101–8; Lorena S. Walsh, "Urban Amenities and Rural Sufficiency: Living Standards and Consumer Behavior in the Colonial Chesapeake, 1643–1777," *Journal of Economic History* 43 (1983): 109–15; Carole Shammas, "How Self-Sufficient Was Early America?" *Journal of Interdisciplinary History* 13 (1982): 247–72; Greg Nobles, "The Rise of Merchants in Rural Market Towns: A Case Study of Eighteenth-Century Northampton, Massachusetts," *Journal of Social History* 24 (1990): 5–23.

18 Michael Warner, *The Letters of the Republic: Publication and the Public Sphere in Eighteenth-Century America* (Cambridge, Mass., 1990), 19–30; Anderson, *Imagined Communities,* 41–49.

19 Ian K. Steele, *The English Atlantic, 1675–1740: An Exploration of Communication and Community* (New York and Oxford, 1986), 78–93, 132–88, 251–78.

20 On the transatlantic context of the Awakening, see Susan O'Brien, "A Transatlantic Community of Saints: The Great Awakening and the First Evangelical Network, 1735–1755," *American Historical Review* 91 (1986): 811–32; Marilyn J. Westerkamp, *The Triumph of the Laity: Scots-Irish Piety and the Great Awakening,*

1625–1760 (New York, 1988); Leigh Eric Schmidt, *Holy Fairs: Scottish Communions and American Revivals in the Early Modern Period* (Princeton, 1989); Michael J. Crawford, *Seasons of Grace: Colonial New England's Revival Tradition in Its British Context* (New York, 1991). On the relationship of the Awakening to the consumer revolution, see Frank Lambert, "'Pedlar in Divinity': George Whitefield and the Great Awakening, 1737–1745," *Journal of American History* 77 (1990–91); 812–37; idem, *Pedlar in Divinity: George Whitefield and the Transatlantic Revivals, 1737–1770* (Princeton, 1993); Harry Stout, *The Divine Dramatist: George Whitefield and the Rise of Modern Evangelicalism* (Grand Rapids, Mich., 1991). See parts III and IV of this chapter for a historiographical discussion of these studies.

21 On the interpretative stance of Jon Butler, who stresses local variations to argue a fragmentary view of eighteenth-century revivalism, see above, n. 7, and part III of this chapter.

22 Barth, *Ethnic Groups and Boundaries*, 29. Barth points out that even ethnic boundaries are socially construed and maintained, but seeks to establish the uniqueness of ethnic boundaries by arguing that their criteria for membership are more stringent than those of other types of social differentiation such as stratification. This distinction based on graded criteria, not wholly convincing even in the twentieth century, is even less so in an age where many still held that orders of men were fixed by nature, sought to enforce boundaries between those orders by such devices as sumptuary laws, and marked passage from one stratum into another by rituals such as knighthood or elevation to the peerage.

23 Douglas, *Natural Symbols*, 14.

24 Barth, *Ethnic Groups and Boundaries*, 29.

25 Breen, "Meaning of Things," 255.

26 Rosalind Remer, "Old Lights and New Money: A Note on Religion, Economics and the Social Order in 1740 Boston," *William and Mary Quarterly*, 3d ser., 47 (1990): 571–73.

27 Alexander Martin, *America, A Poem, by Alexander Martin . . . to Which Is Added, Liberty. A Poem. By Rusticus. . . .* (Philadelphia, 1769), quoted in Bernard Bailyn, *The Ideological Origins of the American Revolution* (Cambridge, Mass., 1967), 56.

28 See Thomas L. Haskell, "Capitalism and the Origins of the Humanitarian Sensibility," *American Historical Review* 90 (1985): 339–61, 547–67, on the role of the market in the emergence of new forms of "recipe knowledge" involving consciousness of personal responsibility for the well-being of ever-expanding groups of distant, anonymous people.

29 This is the ultimate significance of the tolerance cultivated by George Whitefield and his followers. See, for example, Whitefield's declaration that "all places and persons [are] so many little parts of [God's] great family," in *George Whitefield's Journals: A New Edition Containing Fuller Material than Any Hitherto Published*, ed. William Wayle et al. (Edinburgh, 1960), 338.

30 O'Brien, "Transatlantic Community of Saints," 811–32.

31 The egalitarian impulse of the revivals, though never fully realized, was nonetheless genuine. The itinerants' use of persuasive appeals implicitly acknowledged the right of individual judgment, a point which Virginia Baptists later

made the foundation of their appeals for disestablishment there. Contemporaries regarded Whitefield's argument for evangelizing black slaves as a threat to the ideological foundations of chattel slavery. Indeed, some Virginia Baptists may have accorded blacks a remarkable degree of equality within their congregations. On Long Island, men listened while women stood and exhorted at New Light meetings, and white listeners sometimes sat under the preaching of black or Indian itinerants. See Rhys Isaac, *The Transformation of Virginia, 1740–1790* (Chapel Hill, 1982), 285–97; George Whitefield, *Three Letters from the Reverend Mr. G. Whitefield: viz. Letter I. To a friend in London, concerning Archbishop Tillotson. Letter II. To the same, on the same subject. Letter III. To the inhabitants of Maryland, Virginia, North and South-Carolina, concerning their Negroes* (Philadelphia, 1740); Mechal Sobel, *The World They Made Together: Black and White Values in Eighteenth-century Virginia* (Princeton, 1987); Cooper, *Diary*, x, 37.

32 For the ability of human action to open new horizons of meaning, see Paul Ricoeur, "The Model of the Text: Meaningful Action Considered as a Text," in *Interpretive Social Science*, ed. Rabinow and Sullivan, 73–102.

33 For the declension model of revival, see Jonathan Edwards, *Some Thoughts Concerning the present Revival of Religion in New-England, and the Way in which it ought to be acknowledged and promoted, Humbly offered to the Publick, in a Treatise on that Subject*, in *The Works of Jonathan Edwards*, gen. ed. John E. Smith, vol. 5, *The Great Awakening*, ed. C. C. Goen (New Haven and London, 1972), 293–347; Tracy, *The Great Awakening;* Perry Miller, *Errand into the Wilderness*, (Cambridge, Mass., 1956), 153–66; Charles Hartshorn Maxon, *The Great Awakening in the Middle Colonies* (Chicago, 1920); Edwin Scott Gaustad, *The Great Awakening in New England* (New York, 1957).

34 Charles E. Hambrick-Stowe, *The Practice of Piety: Puritan Devotional Disciplines in Seventeenth-Century New England* (Chapel Hill, 1982); David D. Hall, "Religion and Society: Problems and Considerations," in *Colonial British America: Essays in the New History of the Early Modern Era*, ed. Jack P. Greene and J. R. Pole (Baltimore, 1984), 326–27; Crawford, *Seasons of Grace*, 104–23 and passim.

35 Westerkamp, *Triumph of the Laity;* Schmidt, *Holy Fairs*.

36 The jealousy of New England ministers for their parish boundaries has been noted in a number of studies and is treated extensively below. Crawford himself notes the decline of the English Societies for the Reformation of Manners when parish ministers opposed them on the grounds that they invaded the ministerial office. See Crawford, *Seasons of Grace*, 40, 141–66.

37 For examples of the social conflict model, see John C. Miller, "Religion, Finance and Democracy," 29–58; Nash, *Urban Crucible*, 161–263; Richard L. Bushman, *From Puritan to Yankee: Character and the Social Order in Connecticut, 1690–1765* (Cambridge, Mass., 1967).

38 Butler, "Enthusiasm Described and Decried," 317. Tax lists which could be used to categorize the Awakening's converts are not extant for the period. Yet non-quantitative evidence such as the social composition of various Boston converts suggests that social class may not have been a decisive factor. Rosalind Remer has recently attempted to skirt this issue by identifying revivalists with new-money Land Bankers and their opponents with old-money Silver Schemers.

Her argument, however, fails to recognize that the revivalists themselves were divided over the propriety of the Land Bank. Compare Remer, "Old Lights and New Money," 571–73 and Heimert, *Religion and the American Mind,* 56.

39 Lambert, "Pedlar in Divinity"; Stout, *Divine Dramatist,* 205–7.

40 For examples of Calvinism among the Old Lights see *The Querists: Or an Extract of Mr. Whitefield's Sermons & c. with Scruples by Presbyterians,* (Philadelphia, 1740); Theophilus Pickering, *Mr. Pickering's Letter to Mr. Whitefield: Touching his Relation to the Church of England; his Impulses and Impressions; and the present unhappy state of Things & c. Offered in Excuse of Mr. Pickering's Disinclination to open his pulpit to him in his Late Visit to Ipswich & c.* (Boston, 1745). For the complex political stance of both groups, compare Heimert's treatment of the Old Light Jonathan Mayhew's support of resistance to the Stamp Act with his interpretation of the New Light Joseph Bellamy's submission to the Act (Heimert, *Religion and the American Mind,* 259–60, cf. 347).

41 Harry S. Stout, "Religion, Communications, and the Ideological Origins of the American Revolution," *William and Mary Quarterly,* 3d ser., 34 (1977): 519–41. Idem, *The New England Soul: Preaching and Religious Culture in Colonial New England* (New York and London, 1986), 194–211.

42 See Lambert, "Pedlar in Divinity," 812–37; Richard D. Brown, *Knowledge is Power: The Diffusion of Information in Early America, 1700–1865* (New York, 1989), 132–59; Warner, *Letters of the Republic,* 21–22, 182, n. 40; compare Stout, *Divine Dramatist,* xxii, 90–91.

43 Patricia Bonomi, *Under the Cope of Heaven: Religion, Society and Politics in Colonial America* (New York, 1986), 132.

44 Butler, "Enthusiasm Described and Decried," 305–25; idem, *Awash in a Sea of Faith,* 164–93.

45 "A true and genuine Account of a wonderful Wandering Spirit, raised of late (as is believ'd) by some Religious Conjurer; but whether in the Conclave at Rome, or where else, is not so certain," *General Magazine* 1 (1741): 120–22.

46 *Christian History,* 2:102 and passim. For a later example of the same effort see Samuel Davies, *The State of Religion among the Protestant Dissenters in Virginia; in a Letter to the Rev. Mr. Joseph Bellamy, of Bethlehem, in New-England* (Boston, 1751).

47 Isaac, *Transformation of Virginia,* 5–7, 163–77; William G. McLoughlin, *Revivals, Awakenings, and Reform: An Essay on Religion and Social Change in America, 1607–1977* (Chicago, 1978), 8, 45–97. Also relevant in this context is Christine Leigh Heyrman, *Commerce and Culture: The Maritime Communities of Colonial Massachusetts, 1690–1750* (New York, 1984).

48 Lambert, "Pedlar in Divinity"; idem, *Pedlar in Divinity;* Stout, *Divine Dramatist.*

49 Douglas, *Natural Symbols,* 14; Paul Ricoeur, *The Rule of Metaphor: Multidisciplinary Studies in the Creation of Meaning in Language* (Toronto, 1975), 239–56; idem, *Time and Narrative,* 1:81.

50 Douglas, *Natural Symbols,* 20–21.

51 Ricoeur, "Model of the Text," in *Interpretive Social Science,* ed. Rabinow and Sullivan, 73–101.

52 See Ricoeur, *Rule of Metaphor;* Roger Chartier, *Cultural History: Between Practices and Representations,* trans. Lydia G. Cochrane (Ithaca, N.Y., 1988), 1–16, 95–111.

53 Paul Ricoeur, *Interpretation Theory: Discourse and the Surplus of Meaning* (Fort Worth, 1976), 52–53; Fish, "Normal Circumstances," in *Interpretive Social Science*, ed. by Rabinow and Sullivan, 243–65.

54 John B. Frantz, "The Awakening of Religion among the German Settlers of the Middle Colonies," *William and Mary Quarterly*, 3d ser., 43 (1976): 266–88; Graham Hodges, ed., *Black Itinerants of the Gospel: The Narratives of John Jea and George White* (Madison, Wis., 1993); William De Loss Love, *Samson Occom and the Christian Indians of New England* (Boston, 1899).

1 Itinerancy in Historical Perspective

1 *Pennsylvania Gazette*, Nov. 29, 1739.

2 Frank Lambert, "'Pedlar in Divinity': George Whitefield and the Great Awakening, 1737–1745," *Journal of American History* 77 (1990–91): 818.

3 *Pennsylvania Gazette*, Nov. 15, 1739.

4 Josiah Smith, *A Sermon on the Character, Preaching, &c. of the Rev. Mr. Whitefield*, excerpted in *The Great Awakening: Documents Illustrating the Crisis and Its Consequences*, ed. Alan Heimert and Perry Miller (Indianapolis and New York, 1967), 68.

5 *Postscript to the South Carolina Gazette*, Jan. 22, 1741.

6 *American Weekly Mercury*, Aug. 23, 1740.

7 Thomas Prince to George Whitefield, Dec. 6, 1741, in *The Glasgow Weekly History Relating to the Progress of the Gospel at Home and Abroad. . . . For the Year 1742* (Glasgow, 1743), no. 15; excerpted in the *Proceedings of the Massachusetts Historical Society* 53 (1919–20): 204.

8 *Boston Weekly Post-Boy*, June 23, 1740.

9 "A true and genuine Account of a wonderful Wandering Spirit, raised of late (as is believ'd) by some Religious Conjurer; but whether in the Conclave at Rome, or where else, is not so certain," *General Magazine* 1 (1741): 122.

10 *American Weekly Mercury*, Dec. 9, 1742.

11 Wayne A. Meeks, *The First Urban Christians: The Social World of the Apostle Paul* (New Haven and London, 1983), 17.

12 F. F. Bruce, *New Testament History* (New York, 1971), 291–336; 1 Cor. 9:22.

13 Martin Buber, *Two Types of Faith* (London, 1961), 172–73.

14 1 Cor. 1:2 (New Revised Standard Version [NRSV]). For biblical examples of such practices, see Acts 17–21; Rom. 16; 2 Cor. 8. See also Meeks, *First Urban Christians*, 109.

15 *American Weekly Mercury*, Dec. 9, 1742; the phrase is a verbatim quotation of the Authorized Version of 2 Cor. 10:16, where "line" translates the Greek *kanon*.

16 Titus 2:5; Acts 14:20–23; 20:17–38; Charles Chauncy, *Seasonable Thoughts on the State of Religion in New England, a Treatise in Five Parts* (Boston, 1743), 46–47.

17 G. W. O. Addleshaw, *The Beginnings of the Parochial System* (London, 1954), 4.

18 For an example of rules regulating traveling teachers see *Didache*, xi, xv, in *The Early Christian Fathers: A Selection from the Writings of the Fathers from St. Clement of Rome to St. Athanasius*, ed. and trans. Henry Bettenson (Oxford, 1953), 51. Peter Brown treats the role of celibate monks and hermits in late Roman society in *The Body and Society: Men, Women and Sexual Renunciation in Early Chris-*

tianity (New York, 1988), 42, 190–240; while Robin Lane Fox surveys the spread of Christianity in that era in *Pagans and Christians* (New York, 1989), 265–93. For Old Light appeals to the ancient practice of ordaining "a single bishop to a single flock" and defining itinerant ministries as missionary activity, see Chauncy, *Seasonable Thoughts*, 76.

19 Addleshaw, *Beginnings of the Parochial System*, 8; John Contreni, "From Polis to Parish," in *Religion, Culture and Society in the Early Middle Ages: Studies in Honor of Richard E. Sullivan*, ed. Thomas F. X. Noble and John J. Contreni (Kalamazoo, Mich., 1987), 155–63.

20 J. H. Bettey, *Church and Parish: An Introduction for Local Historians* (London, 1987), 13–14; J. Campbell, "The Church in Anglo-Saxon England," in *The Church in Town and Countryside*, ed. Derek Baker, Studies in Church History no. 16 (Oxford, 1979), 120.

21 Bettey, *Church and Parish*, 14.

22 Contreni, "From Polis to Parish," 159. On construction of the social self in traditional society see Marcel Mauss, "A Category of the Human Mind: The Notion of Person; the Notion of Self," trans. by W. D. Halls, in *The Category of the Person: Anthropology, Philosophy, History*, ed. Michael Carrithers, Steven Collins, and Steven Lukes (Cambridge, 1985), 1–25; Terry Straus, "The Self in Northern Cheyenne Language and Culture," in *Semiotics, Self, and Society*, ed. Benjamin Lee and Greg Urban (Berlin, 1989), 53–68. See also Clifford Geertz, *The Interpretation of Cultures* (New York, 1973), 3–32; Erving Goffman, *Interaction Ritual: Essays on Face-to-Face Behavior* (Chicago, 1967), 47–95.

23 Bettey, *Church and Parish*, 56–66; Benedict Anderson, *Imagined Communities: Reflections on the Origin and Spread of Nationalism* (London, 1983), 20–23.

24 John B. Freed, *The Friars and German Society in the Thirteenth Century* (Cambridge, Mass., 1977), 26, 35–38; Peter Laslett, *The World We Have Lost*, 3d ed. (New York, 1984), 53–80.

25 Freed, *Friars and German Society*, 2–11; Lester K. Little, *Religious Poverty and the Profit Economy in Medieval Europe* (Ithaca, 1978), 82, 163, 187.

26 Frank Hamlin Littell, *The Anabaptist View of the Church: A Study in the Origins of Sectarian Protestantism* (Boston, 1958), 82–100; George Huntston Williams, *The Radical Reformation* (Philadelphia, 1962), 300–319.

27 Ernst Troeltsch, *The Social Teaching of the Christian Churches*, 2 vols., trans. by Olive Wyon (New York, 1960), 2:694–96—compare Troeltsch's extended contrast between the church type and sect type in 1:331–43; Williams, *Radical Reformation*, 137–46, 592–98, and passim.

28 James L. Ainslie, *The Doctrines of Ministerial Order in the Reformed Churches of the Sixteenth and Seventeenth Centuries* (Edinburgh, 1940), 59–61; Roland Bainton, *Here I Stand: A Life of Martin Luther* (New York, 1950), 242–54.

29 John Calvin, *Institutes of the Christian Religion*, trans. Henry Beveridge (Grand Rapids, Mich., 1981), 4. 3. 7.; William Monter, *Calvin's Geneva* (New York, 1967), 125–43; Robert Dean Linder, *The Political Ideas of Pierre Viret* (Geneva, 1964), 21–33, 67–77, 123; Ainslie, *Doctrines of Ministerial Order*, 59–61.

30 Peter Heath, *The English Parish Clergy on the Eve of the Reformation* (London,

1969), 70–73; Claire Cross, *Church and People, 1450–1660: The Triumph of the Laity in the English Church* (Atlantic Highlands, N.J., 1976), 20–25, 53–80.

31 Bettey, *Church and Parish,* 82–84; G. R. Elton, *Policy and Police: The Enforcement of the Reformation in the Age of Thomas Cromwell* (Cambridge, 1972), 68–80; 254–55.

32 Patrick Collinson, *Godly People: Essays on English Protestantism and Puritanism* (London, 1983), 467–98. William Haller, *The Rise of Puritanism: or, the Way to the New Jerusalem as Set Forth in Pulpit and Press from Thomas Cartwright to John Lilburne and John Milton, 1570–1643* (New York, 1957), 173–225; David D. Hall, *The Faithful Shepherd: A History of the New England Ministry in the Seventeenth Century* (New York, 1974), 21–47.

33 Bettey, *Church and Parish,* 88; Christopher Hill, *Society and Puritanism in Pre-Revolutionary England,* (New York, 1964), 420–22. Several English historians have argued that a decline in perambulations during the seventeenth century signaled an erosion of parochial solidarity. The tradition, however, remained strong in many parts of England, and David Underdown points out that the wide variation of local circumstances prohibits making unqualified generalizations concerning the practice. Perambulations, moreover, were not the only means of tracing parish bounds. Villagers also etched them on children's imaginations by offering various rewards for observing their limits and by punishing the children for their transgression by such means as beatings, tripping, or forcing them to sit bare-buttocked on the boundary. See David Underdown, *Revel, Riot and Rebellion: Popular Politics and Culture in England, 1603–1660* (Oxford, 1985), 81; Barry Reay, "Popular Culture in Early Modern England," in *Popular Culture in Seventeenth-Century England,* ed. Barry Reay (New York, 1985), 8.

34 Reay, "Popular Culture in Early Modern England," 7–10; David Grayson Allen, *In English Ways: The Movement of Societies and the Transferral of English Local Law and Custom to Massachusetts Bay in the Seventeenth Century* (New York, 1982), 8–18 and passim; T. H. Breen, *Puritans and Adventurers: Change and Persistence in Early America* (New York, 1980), 6–10.

35 Edmund S. Morgan, *Visible Saints: The History of a Puritan Idea* (New York, 1963), 64–112, 139–52; Breen, *Puritans and Adventurers,* 16–24; Allen, *In English Ways,* 163–204; Sumner Chilton Powell, *Puritan Village: The Formation of a New England Town* (New York, 1965), 92–116.

36 Jon Butler, *Awash in a Sea of Faith: Christianizing the American People* (Cambridge, Mass., 1990), 105.

37 Hall, *The Faithful Shepherd,* 102; Kenneth A. Lockridge, *A New England Town: The First Hundred Years* (New York, 1970), 93–118.

38 David D. Hall, *Worlds of Wonder, Days of Judgment: Popular Religious Belief in Early New England* (New York, 1989), 120–39.

39 See Walter J. Ong, *The Presence of the Word: Some Prolegomena for Cultural and Religious History* (Minneapolis, 1981), 22–35; Geertz, *The Interpretation of Cultures,* 3–32; Goffman, *Interaction Ritual.* For the dramaturgical significance of community gatherings throughout the colonies, see Harry S. Stout, "Religion, Communications and the Ideological Origins of the American Revolution," *William and Mary Quarterly,* 3d ser., 34 (1977): 526; Rhys Isaac, "Dramatizing

the Ideology of Revolution: Popular Mobilization in Virginia, 1774 to 1776," *William and Mary Quarterly*, 3d ser., 33 (1976): 364–67; A. G. Roeber, "Authority, Law, and Custom: The Rituals of Court Day in Tidewater Virginia, 1720 to 1750," *William and Mary Quarterly*, 3d ser., 44 (1987): 29–38.

40 Hall, *The Faithful Shepherd*, 270–74; Harry S. Stout, *The New England Soul: Preaching and Religious Culture in Colonial New England* (New York, 1986), 108–110.

41 Stout, "Religion, Communications and the Revolution," 526. One explicit pre-Awakening example of such a defense was Nathaniel Mather, *A Discussion of the Lawfulness of a Pastor's Acting as an Officer in other Churches besides His own* (London, 1698; reprint, Boston, 1730), reprinted in the context of early-eighteenth-century debates over church polity. In ordination sermons before the Awakening the sanctity of local bonds between minister and people was regularly upheld. See, for example, Eliphalet Adams, *The Gracious Presence of Christ with the Ministers of the Gospel, a ground of great Consolation to them* (New London, 1730), 11–14, 31–33, 43; Azariah Mather, *A Gospel Star, or Faithful Minister* (New London, 1733), 9; John Hancock, *The Lord's Ministers are the People's Helpers* (Boston, 1735), ii, 3–7, 14. After 1740 these exhortations became transformed in Old Light ordination sermons into fierce defenses of the parish boundaries. See, for example, William Balch, *The Duty of Ministers to aim at Promoting and being Partakers of the Gospel* (Boston, 1744).

42 Kevin P. Kelly, "'In dispers'd Country Plantations': Settlement Patterns in Seventeenth-Century Surry County, Virginia," in *The Chesapeake in the Seventeenth Century: Essays on Anglo-American Society*, ed. Thad W. Tate and David L. Ammerman, (New York, 1979); Darret B. Rutman and Anita H. Rutman, *A Place in Time: Middlesex County, Virginia 1650–1750* (New York, 1984), 36–60; Butler, *Awash in a Sea of Faith*, 38–46.

43 Dell Upton, *Holy Things and Profane: Anglican Parish Churches in Colonial Virginia* (Cambridge, Mass., 1986), xiv–xvii, 8–10; Rhys Isaac, *The Transformation of Virginia, 1740–1790* (Chapel Hill, 1982), 50–68.

44 Butler, *Awash in a Sea of Faith*, 46–50. Virginia commissaries complained to the Bishop of London about this practice throughout the colonial period. See William Stevens Perry, ed., *Historical Collections Relating to the American Colonial Church*, 4 vols. (Hartford, Conn., 1870), 1:11, 257–59, and passim.

45 Butler, *Awash in a Sea of Faith*, 50; Perry, *Historical Collections*, 1:328, 365–445 passim.

46 Anthony Gavin to the Bishop of London, August 15, 1738, in Perry, *Historical Collections* 1:360.

47 Butler, *Awash in a Sea of Faith*, 51–55, 63–66; idem, *Power, Authority and the Origins of the American Denominational Order: The English Churches of the Delaware Valley, 1680–1730* (Philadelphia, 1978); Patricia Bonomi, *Under the Cope of Heaven: Religion, Society and Politics in Colonial America* (New York, 1986), 39–127; Ned Landsman, *Scotland and Its First American Colony, 1683–1765* (Princeton, 1985); Douglas G. Jacobsen, *An Unprov'd Experiment: Religious Pluralism in Colonial New Jersey* (Brooklyn, 1991), 53–84; Timothy Smith, "Congregation, State, and De-

nomination: The Forming of the American Religious Structure," *William and Mary Quarterly,* 3d ser., 25 (1968), 155–76.

48 John B. Frantz, "The Awakening of Religion among the German Settlers in the Middle Colonies," *William and Mary Quarterly,* 3d ser., 33 (1976): 266–88, 279–80.

49 Maurice W. Armstrong, Lefferts A. Loetscher, and Charles A. Anderson, eds., *The Presbyterian Enterprise: Sources of American Presbyterian History* (Philadelphia, 1956), 16; Leonard J. Trinterude, *The Forming of an American Tradition: A Reexamination of Colonial Presbyterianism* (Philadelphia, 1949), 32–33.

50 Barry Reay, *The Quakers and the English Revolution* (London, 1985), 8–11, 52–66; Frederik B. Tolles, *Quakers and the Atlantic Culture* (New York, 1960), 21–35, 96–104; Carla Gardina Pestana, *Quakers and Baptists in Colonial Massachusetts* (Cambridge, 1992), 25–43, 65–84, 140–44; Christine Leigh Heyrman, *Commerce and Culture: The Maritime Communities of Colonial Massachusetts, 1690–1750* (New York, 1984), 138–39.

51 Armstrong, Loetscher, and Anderson, eds., *The Presbyterian Enterprise,* 13.

52 John Calan, *Parsons and Pedagogues: The S.P.G. Adventure in American Education* (New York, 1971), 201–2; John Frederick Woolverton, *Colonial Anglicanism in North America* (Detroit, 1984), 81–106; Frantz, "Awakening of Religion among the German Settlers," 270–71; Sydney Ahlstrom, *A Religious History of the American People,* 2 vols. (Garden City, N.Y., 1975), 1:256–323.

53 Trinterude, *Forming of an American Tradition,* 83.

54 Carl Bridenbaugh, *Mitre and Sceptre: Transatlantic Faiths, Ideas, Personalities and Politics, 1689–1775* (New York, 1962), 81.

55 The correspondence of colonial American missionaries for the Society for the Propagation of the Gospel (SPG) is filled with these hopes. Anglicans such as George Keith and Timothy Cutler sought to realize them by urging London to give Harvard College a royal charter and fill its professorships with Anglicans whose students would then carry Anglicanism to the churches of New England. See Perry, *Historical Collections,* 3:66, 89–90, 102–3, and passim; Calan, *Parsons and Pedagogues,* 19; Woolverton, *Colonial Anglicanism,* 126–31.

56 Ian K. Steele, *The English Atlantic, 1675–1740: An Exploration of Communication and Community* (New York and Oxford, 1986), 78–93, 168–88; Bernard Bailyn, *The Peopling of British North America: An Introduction* (New York, 1985), 6–43.

57 Max Schumacher, *The Northern Farmer and His Markets during the Late Colonial Period* (New York, 1975); James A. Henretta, "Families and Farms: *Mentalité* in Pre-Industrial America," *William and Mary Quarterly,* 3d ser., 35 (1978): 16–18. While Henretta attempts to minimize the extent to which New Englanders participated in the market, he nevertheless acknowledges its presence in the localities during the mid-eighteenth century. Studies of consumption in agricultural communities suggest greater involvement in the market than he recognizes. See below, n. 60.

58 Philip J. Greven, *Four Generations: Population, Land, and Family in Colonial Andover, Massachusetts* (Ithaca, N.Y., 1970), 220–58; Georgia C. Villaflor and Kenneth L. Sokoloff, "Migration in Colonial America: Evidence from the Mili-

tia Muster Rolls," *Social Science History* 6 (1982): 539–70; Jonathan Edwards, *A Faithful Narrative of the Surprizing Work of God in the Conversion of Many Hundred Souls in Northampton, and the Neighbouring Towns and Villages of New Hampshire in New England,* in *The Great Awakening,* ed. C. C. Goen (New Haven and London, 1972), 152. Evidence from colonial diaries is suggestive concerning the role played by correspondence and visits of family and acquaintances in linking colonial communities. See, for example, "Extracts from the Interleaved Almanacs of Nathan Bowen, Marblehead," *Essex Institute Historical Collections* 91 (1955): 163–90; Richard Brigham Johnson, ed., "The Diary of Israel Litchfield," *New England Historical and Genealogical Register* 129 (1975): 367–77; Mary Cooper, *Diary of Mary Cooper: Life on a Long Island Farm,* ed. Field Horne (Oyster Bay, N.Y., 1981); Esther Edwards Burr, *The Journal of Esther Edwards Burr, 1754–1757,* ed. Carol F. Karlsen and Laurie Crumpacker (New Haven and London, 1984).

59 Steele, *The English Atlantic,* 113–31.

60 Anderson, *Imagined Communities,* 41–49.

61 Steele, *The English Atlantic,* 145–67.

62 Anderson, *Imagined Communities,* 47.

63 Neil McKendrick, John Brewer, and J. H. Plumb, *The Birth of a Consumer Society: The Commercialization of Eighteenth-Century England* (Bloomington, Ind., 1982), 117–40, 146–94.

64 Gloria L. Main, "The Standard of Living in Colonial Massachusetts," *Journal of Economic History* 43 (1983): 101–8; Carole Shammas, "How Self-Sufficient was Early America?" *Journal of Interdisciplinary History* 13 (1982): 247–72; Lorena S. Walsh, "Urban Amenities and Rural Sufficiency: Living Standards and Consumer Behavior in the Colonial Chesapeake, 1643–1777," *Journal of Economic History* 43 (1983): 109–15; Gregory Nobles, "The Rise of Merchants in Rural Market Towns: A Case Study of Eighteenth-Century Northampton, Massachusetts," *Journal of Social History,* 24 (1990): 5–23.

65 T. H. Breen, "An Empire of Goods: The Anglicization of Colonial America, 1690–1776," *Journal of British Studies* 25 (1986): 467–99; idem, "'Baubles of Britain': The American and Consumer Revolutions of the Eighteenth Century," *Past and Present* 119 (May, 1988): 81–84.

66 Breen, "Baubles of Britain," 80–83, 87–88.

67 Michael Warner, *The Letters of the Republic: Publication and the Public Sphere in Eighteenth-Century America* (Cambridge, Mass., 1990), 13–33; Jürgen Habermas, *The Structural Transformation of the Public Sphere: An Inquiry into a Category of Bourgeois Society,* trans. Thomas Burger with the assistance of Frederick Lawrence (Cambridge, Mass., 1989), 20–26.

68 Compare reports of Whitefield in England from the *Virginia Gazette,* Jan. 18, 1740, and the *South Carolina Gazette,* July 14, 1739, with the report of the evangelist in New England from the *Pennsylvania Gazette,* Oct. 2, 1740.

69 Compare reports from England in the *Pennsylvania Gazette,* July 12, 1739, and the *Virginia Gazette,* Jan. 18, 1740, with reports from America in the *Pennsylvania Gazette,* May 22, 1740, and Oct. 20, 1740.

70 Thomas Prince, Jr., ed., *The Christian History, Containing Accounts of the Revival*

and Propagation of Religion in Great Britain and America, 2 vols. (Boston, 1743–45), 1:282 (hereafter cited as *Christian History*). The *Christian History* was a weekly periodical published by revivalists to chronicle and promote the Awakening. See chapter 3, part IV, of this volume for a fuller description.

71 Ibid., 1:283.

72 *Virginia Gazette,* Oct. 24, 1745.

73 Harry S. Stout, *The Divine Dramatist: George Whitefield and the Rise of Modern Evangelicalism* (Grand Rapids, Mich., 1991), xvii–xviii, 82–83; Lambert, "Pedlar in Divinity," 816–27.

74 See, for example, George Whitefield, *Letters of George Whitefield for the Period 1734–1742,* intro. H. M. Houghton (London, 1771; facsimile reprint, London, 1976), 177, 200. Compare especially the following report sent by Whitefield for publication in London with the ubiquitous notices in colonial newspapers of 1740: "On Thursday last, in the evening, the Rev. Mr. *Whitefield* went on board at *New-Castle,* in order to sail to *Georgia,* after having been on shore thirty-three days, and travelled some hundreds of miles, and preached fifty-eight times. . . . His congregations numbered sometimes of four, sometimes of five, sometimes of eight, twelve, fifteen, and once at *Philadelphia,* of *twenty thousand* people. He had gotten near five hundred pounds sterling . . . for the Orphan-house. . . . Great and visible effects followed his preaching. . . . There was never such a general awakening, and concern for the things of God Known in *America* before" (Whitefield, *Letters,* 179).

75 Colonial newspapers carried such excerpts and endorsements throughout 1740. An excellent example of a Whitefield excerpt appeared in the *American Weekly Mercury,* May 8, 1740; an unsolicited endorsement by Charles Tennent in the *Pennsylvania Gazette,* Oct. 16, 1740.

76 Lambert, "Pedlar in Divinity"; John Gillies, comp., *Historical Collections relating to Remarkable Periods of the Success of the Gospel,* ed. and enlarged by Horatius Bonar (Kelso, Scotland, 1845; facsimile reprint, London, 1981), 429–33.

77 George Whitefield, *George Whitefield's Journals: A New Edition Containing Fuller Material than Any hitherto Published,* ed. by William Wale and others (London, 1960), 339.

78 Whitefield, *Journals,* 341.

79 Quoted in Stuart Clark Henry, *George Whitefield: Wayfaring Witness* (New York, 1957), 152.

80 Benjamin Coleman, *Three Letters to the Reverend Mr. George Whitefield* (Philadelphia, 1739), 3–4.

81 *Christian History,* 1:279–80.

82 Arnold Dallimore, *George Whitefield: The Life and Times of the Great Evangelist of the Eighteenth-Century Revival,* 2 vols. (London, 1970–80), 1:228–29.

83 Ibid., 255; Whitefield, *Journals,* 259. By 1739, parishioners had begun petitioning local bishops to stop this practice because of damage to gravestones. See the *Virginia Gazette,* July 27, 1739.

84 Whitefield, *Journals,* 259; Henry, *George Whitefield,* 49–50.

85 Whitefield, *Journals,* 343.

86 Ibid., 357.

87 Ibid., 348–49.

88 Ibid., 423.

89 Gilbert Tennent, *The Danger of an Unconverted Ministry, The Great Awakening,* ed. Heimert and Miller, 90.

90 *Boston Weekly Post-Boy,* Dec. 3, 1739.

91 James Honyman to the Bishop of London, Sept. 18, 1740; Rev. Charles Brockwell to the Bishop of London, Oct. 21, 1740; Commissary Vessey to the Bishop of London, Dec. 1, 1739; Rev. William Currie to the Bishop of London, July 7, 1740, in *Calendar of Letters from Canada, Newfoundland, Pennsylvania, Barbados and the Bahamas, 1721–1793, Preserved at the United Society for the Propagation of the Gospel* (hereafter *Calendar of SPG Letters*), special series, 5 (London 1972): 17, 49, 71, 199.

92 Commissary Archibald Cummings to the Bishop of London, Aug. 29, 1740, *Calendar of SPG Letters,* 5:171.

93 John Thomson, *The Government of the Church of Christ, and the authority of the Church Judicatories Established on a Scripture Foundation: And the Spirit of rash judging arraigned and condemned* (Philadelphia, 1741), 7–8.

94 See Smith, *Sermon on the Character of Whitefield,* excerpted in *The Great Awakening,* ed. Heimert and Miller, 62–69; Coleman, *Three Letters to Whitefield,* 3–4; and previous discussion in chapter 1, part III, of this volume.

95 Harry S. Stout, *The New England Soul: Preaching and Religious Culture in Colonial New England* (New York, 1986), 38–41, 96–101, 164–65, 185; Heyrman, Commerce and Culture, 183; Marilyn J. Westerkamp, *Triumph of the Laity: Scots-Irish Piety and the Great Awakening, 1625–1760* (New York, 1988), 15–73, 165–94; Leigh Eric Schmidt, *Holy Fairs: Scottish Communions and American Revivals in the Early Modern Period* (Princeton, 1989), 11–68.

96 Smith, *Sermon on the Character of Whitefield,* in *The Great Awakening,* ed. Heimert and Miller, 69.

97 Frantz, "Awakening of Religion among the German Settlers," 272–76. Frantz shows that the aggressive itinerant evangelistic activity of sects such as the Moravians and Seventh-Day Baptists of Ephratha began only a few years before Whitefield's arrival, and midcolonial attacks on Whitefield's approbation of the Moravians reveal how quickly the Anglican evangelist's challenge to local order became identified with that of midcolonial sectarians. The increased scope of sectarian activity after Whitefield's first tour also reveals how readily sectarian itinerants such as the Ephratha evangelist Conrad Beissel exploited the new "fruitful gardens of God containing many converted souls . . . who were commonly called New Lights" (quoted in Frantz, "Awakening of Religion among the German Settlers," 276).

98 *Boston Weekly Post-Boy,* Sept. 28, 1741.

99 *Pennsylvania Gazette,* June 18, 1741.

100 Leigh Eric Schmidt, "'The Grand Prophet,' Hugh Bryan: Evangelicalism's Challenge to the Establishment and Slavery in the Colonial South," *South Carolina Historical Magazine* 87 (1986): 239–50.

101 *South Carolina Gazette,* June 21, 1742.

102 Charles Brockwell to the Secretary for the SPG, Feb. 18, 1742, in Perry, *Historical Collections,* 3:353.

103 *Boston Weekly News-Letter,* April 22, 1742.

2 The Menace of Itinerancy

1 The nineteenth-century historian Joseph Tracy clearly recognized and sought to explain the basic theological agreement among most Old and New Lights. Their shared Calvinism only became obscured in the twentieth century when historians such as Alan Heimert and James Jones identified the entire antirevival movement with the liberal "Enlightenment" views of a few leading figures such as Charles Chauncy and Jonathan Mayhew. Historians of the Awakening have recently begun acknowledging the validity of Tracy's observation—indeed that Chauncy himself espoused a moderate Calvinism in 1740. See Joseph Tracy, *The Great Awakening: A History of the Revival of Religion in the Time of Edwards and Whitefield* (Boston, 1842), 302–72; Alan Heimert, *Religion and the American Mind from the Great Awakening to the Revolution* (Cambridge, Mass., 1966); James Jones, *The Shattered Synthesis: New England Puritanism before the Great Awakening* (New Haven, 1973), 165–97; Conrad Wright, *The Beginnings of Unitarianism in America* (Hamden, Conn., 1976), 9–27; Harry S. Stout, *The New England Soul: Preaching and Religious Culture in Colonial New England* (New York, 1986), 185–216; George W. Harper, "Clericalism and Revival: The Great Awakening in Boston as a Pastoral Phenomenon," *New England Quarterly* 57 (1984): 555–56.

2 George Whitefield, *George Whitefield's Journals: A New Edition Containing Fuller Material Than Any Hitherto Published,* ed. William Wale and others (Edinburgh, 1960), 349.

3 Whitefield was shut out of the Anglican pulpit in New York only two weeks after disembarking at Lewistown in 1739, and his relations with the Anglican clergy remained stormy throughout his first great tour. See Whitefield, *Journals,* 347; Alexander Garden, *Regeneration, and the Testimony of the Spirit. Being the Substance of Two Sermons . . . Occasioned by some erroneous Notions of certain Men who call themselves Methodists* (Charleston, 1740), excerpted in *The Great Awakening: Documents Illustrating the Crisis and its Consequences,* ed. Alan Heimert and Perry Miller (Indianapolis, 1967), 46–61; *Calendar of Letters from Canada, Newfoundland, Pennsylvania, Barbados and the Bahamas, 1721–1793, Preserved at the United Society for the Propagation of the Gospel* (hereafter *Calendar of SPG Letters*), special series, 5 (London, 1972).

4 Archibald Cummings to the SPG secretary, August 29, 1740, *Calendar of SPG Letters,* 17.

5 Leonard J. Trinterude, *The Forming of an American Tradition: A Re-Examination of Colonial Presbyterianism* (Philadelphia, 1948), 86–108; Marilyn J. Westerkamp, *Triumph of the Laity: Scots-Irish Piety and the Great Awakening, 1625–1760* (New York, 1988), 165–94.

6 See, for example, *New-England Weekly Journal,* Sept. 23, 1740; *Invitations to the Rev. Mr. Whitefield from the Eastern Consociation of the County of Fairfield . . . 7 Oct.*

1740 (Boston, 1745), reprinted in *The Great Awakening: Documents on the Revival of Religion, 1740–1745,* ed. Richard L. Bushman (New York, 1969), 23–25; Stout, *New England Soul,* 195.

7 Edwin Scott Gaustad, *The Great Awakening in New England* (New York, 1957), 29–30.

8 George Whitefield to Governor Jonathan Belcher, Nov. 9, 1740, in *Letters of George Whitefield for the Period 1734–1742* (Edinburgh, 1976), 220–21. Tennent arrived in Boston the week of December 16, 1740. By January 12 the *Boston Weekly Post-Boy* was launching an attack on his itinerancy. See *New-England Weekly Journal,* Dec. 16, 1740; *Boston Weekly Post-Boy,* Jan. 12, 1740; Gaustad, *Great Awakening in New England,* 33.

9 Charles Chauncy, *Seasonable Thoughts on the State of Religion in New-England, a Treatise in Five Parts* (Boston, 1743), 50. Others also described the actions of itinerants as a "language" with a social meaning. See *The Testimony of an Association of Ministers convened at Marlborough, January 22, 1744,5. Against the Rev. Mr. George Whitefield and his Conduct* (Boston, 1745), 7.

10 See Paul Ricoeur, "The Model of the Text: Meaningful Action Considered as a Text," in *Interpretive Social Science: A Reader,* ed. Paul Rabinow and William M. Sullivan (Berkeley, 1979), 243–65.

11 See, for example, Harry S. Stout, "Religion, Communications, and the Ideological Origins of the American Revolution," *William and Mary Quarterly,* 3d ser., 34 (1977): 526–67; William T. Youngs, Jr., *God's Messengers: Religious Leadership in Colonial New England* (Baltimore and London, 1976), 40–63; Harper, "Clericalism and Revival," 562.

12 Norman Fiering, *Jonathan Edwards's Moral Thought and Its British Context* (Chapel Hill, 1981), 13–47. For the development of clericalism, see Youngs, *God's Messengers,* 40–63; Frederick Woolverton, *Colonial Anglicanism in North America* (Detroit, 1984). For the role of clergy and lay elites in the mediation of unity through literacy, see Richard D. Brown, *Knowledge is Power: The Diffusion of Information in Early America, 1700–1865* (New York, 1989), 65–81; Michael Warner, *Letters of the Republic: Publication and the Public Sphere in Eighteenth-Century America* (Cambridge, Mass., 1990), 40; Jürgen Habermas, *The Structural Transformation of the Public Sphere: An Inquiry into a Category of Bourgeois Society* (Cambridge, Mass., 1989), 20–26.

13 Isaac Stiles, *A Looking-glass for Changelings, A Seasonable Caveat against Meddling with them that are given to Change* (New London, Conn., 1743), 3.

14 *South Carolina Gazette,* July 12, 1740.

15 Ibid.

16 *South Carolina Gazette,* Aug. 8, 1740.

17 John Hancock, *The Danger of an Unqualified Ministry* (Boston, 1743), 25; Nathaniel Appleton, *Faithful Ministers of Christ, the Salt of the Earth and the Light of the World* (Boston, 1743), 38–39; Stiles, *Looking-glass for Changelings,* 36.

18 W. Hammond Bowden, "Extracts from the Interleaved Almanacs of Nathan Bowen, Marblehead, 1742–1799," *Essex Institute Historical Collections* 91 (1955): 166; *South Carolina Gazette,* July 12, 1740.

19 "A true and genuine Account of a wonderful Wandering Spirit, raised of late (as

is believ'd) by some Religious conjurer; but whether in the Conclave at Rome, or where else, is not so certain," *General Magazine* 1 (1741): 120–22.

20 "Wonderful Wandering Spirit," 120–21.

21 Ibid.

22 Ibid., 122.

23 *Virginia Gazette,* Sept. 28, 1739; *South Carolina Gazette,* Oct. 4, 1740; *Boston Gazette,* Dec. 1, 1741; *Boston Weekly News-Letter,* April 22, 1742; *Pennsylvania Gazette,* June 20, 1743.

24 *South Carolina Gazette,* July 12, 1740.

25 *Boston Weekly Post-Boy,* Jan. 12, 1741.

26 *A Letter from a Gentleman in Boston to Mr. Geo. Wishart, One of the Ministers of Edinburgh, concerning the State of Religion in New-England* (Edinburgh, 1742), 11.

27 John Thomson, *the Government of the Church of Christ, and the authority of Church Judicatories Established on a Scripture Foundation: And the Spirit of rash judging arraigned and condemned* (Philadelphia, 1741), v.

28 Whitefield, *Journals,* 482; compare, for example, "A Lover of Truth and Peace" [Charles Chauncy], *The Late Religious Commotions in New England Considered* (Boston, 1743), 3; John Hancock, *The Danger of an Unqualified Ministry* (Boston, 1743), 15.

29 Gilbert Tennent, *The Danger of an Unconverted Ministry, Considered in a Sermon on Mark VI. 34* (Philadelphia, 1741), reprinted in *The Great Awakening,* ed. Heimert and Miller, 71–99.

30 See Trinterude, *Forming of an American Tradition,* 71–121; Westerkamp, *Triumph of the Laity,* 165–213; Heimert, *Religion and the American Mind,* 93–94.

31 Thomson, *Government of the Church of Christ,* 7.

32 Theophilus Pickering, *The Reverend Mr. Pickering's Letters to the Rev. N. Rogers and Mr. D. Rogers of Ipswich: With their Answer to Mr. Pickering's first Letter* (Boston, 1742), 10.

33 *Boston Weekly Post-Boy,* Sept. 28, 1741.

34 Gaustad, *Great Awakening in New England,* 37–41, 69–70; Harry S. Stout and Peter Onuf, "James Davenport and the Great Awakening in New London," *Journal of American History* 70 (1983–84): 556–78. See also Leigh Eric Schmidt, "'A Second and Glorious Reformation': The New Light Extremism of Andrew Croswell," *William and Mary Quarterly,* 3d ser., 43 (1986): 214–44.

35 *Boston Weekly Post-Boy,* September 28, 1741.

36 *Boston Weekly Post-Boy,* Aug. 10, 1741.

37 Stiles, *Looking-Glass for Changelings,* 15.

38 *Boston Weekly Post-Boy,* October 12, 1741. The quotation is from Judges 19:30.

39 For other examples of marriage as a metaphor for the pastor-parish relationship, see Thomson, *Government of the Church of Christ,* 126; Jonathan Edwards, *The Church's Marriage to her Sons, and to her God* (Boston, 1746), 13–18, 25.

40 *Boston Weekly Post-Boy,* June 23, 1740; Sept. 28, 1741; July 12, 1742; Sept. 6, 1743; *South Carolina Gazette,* Jan. 9, 1742; June 21, 1742.

41 Thomson, *Government of the Church of Christ,* 44.

42 *South Carolina Gazette,* Sept. 19, 1741; Jan. 9, 1742; March 6, 1742; June 21, 1742.

43 Postscript to the *South Carolina Gazette,* Sept. 19, 1742.

44 Ibid.

45 *Boston Weekly Post-Boy,* Sept. 28, 1741.

46 *Boston Weekly Post-Boy,* April 5, 1742; see also ibid., July 5, 1742; *South Carolina Gazette,* June 21, 1742.

47 *Boston Weekly Post-Boy,* Sept. 28, 1741; *South Carolina Gazette,* June 21, 1742.

48 *Boston Weekly Post-Boy,* July 19, 1742; Schmidt, "Second and Glorious Reformation," 221.

49 *South Carolina Gazette,* Postscript, June 18, 1741.

50 Garden, *Two Sermons on Regeneration,* in *The Great Awakening,* ed. Heimert and Miller, 56.

51 The "Arminianism" which New England revivalists attacked was often preparationist theology. Consider Jonathan Parsons' description of an "Opposer" whose preaching provoked outcries when he "set the Nature of *spiritual* convictions and the Danger of grieving the Holy Spirit in an excellent Light." The cries, however, subsided when the opposer "told the awakened that if they did what they could in the Use of the appointed Means, they need not fear, for God had bound himself by Promise, to the endeavours of Men in a natural State." Parsons concluded that the error of the latter portion caused the awakened "to hope that God was not so much of a Sovereign as they had conceived him to be." See Thomas Prince, Jr., ed., *The Christian History, Containing Accounts of the Revival and Propagation of Religion in Great Britain and America,* 2 vols. (Boston, 1743–45), 2:160; Norman Pettit, *The Heart Prepared: Grace and Conversion in Puritan Spiritual Life* (New Haven, 1966), 86–124, 208–10.

52 Garden, *Two Sermons on Regeneration,* in *The Great Awakening,* ed. Heimert and Miller, 61; Thomson, *Government of the Church of Christ,* v, 29; Stiles, *Looking-Glass for Changelings,* 3; Chauncy, *Seasonable Thoughts,* 366–70. For the relationship of social self and community, see Greg Urban and Benjamin Lee, *Semiotics, Self, and Society* (New York, 1989), 1–14; C. Fred Alford, *The Self in Social Theory: A Psychoanalytic Account of Its Construction in Plato, Hobbes, Locke, Rawls, and Rousseau* (New Haven and London, 1991), especially 6–7, 33, 42, 49, 169, 178; Clifford Geertz, "'From the Native's Point of View': On the Nature of Anthropological Understanding," in *Meaning in Anthropology,* ed. Keith H. Basso and Henry A. Selby (Albuquerque, 1976), 2221–37. On the role of conversion in self-construction, see Chana Ullman, *The Transformed Self: The Psychology of Religious Conversion* (New York and London, 1989), 1–26, 191–95. This description of conversion's traditional role in integrating the self into the community is at least indirectly supported in many studies of New England conversion and church admission, for a helpful summary of which see Stephen R. Grossbart, "Seeking the Divine Favor: Conversion and Church Admission in Eastern Connecticut, 1711–1832," *William and Mary Quarterly,* 3d ser., 46 (1989): 698, n. 8. For a suggestive application of anthropological perspectives on the self to early American history, see Michael Zuckerman, "The Fabrication of Identity in Early America," *William and Mary Quarterly,* 3d ser., 34 (1977): 183–214.

53 *Boston Weekly Post-Boy,* Aug. 10, 1741. The biblical quotation is from 1 Cor. 11:16.

54 *Boston Weekly Post-Boy,* Sept. 28, 1741. The Old Light complaint challenges New Light assertions, echoed by historians such as Michael J. Crawford and

Richard L. Bushman, that the "typical" Awakening conversion took place within a matrix of strong communal support. In analyzing Awakening revival accounts it is important to remember that ministers shaped them in a context of heated controversy. For example, the revival narrative of Jonathan Parsons, often cited to support the revivals' communal nature, should not be read as a dispassionate observation of the phenomenon of conversion. Instead, it should be read as a polemic fashioned by Parsons to counter the charge that revivalistic conversion fostered social disorder. Such New Light representations of revival conversions as harmonious, communal events must be weighed against opposing Old Light constructions of these conversions as destructive of the fabric of communal relations. Jonathan Edwards's experience in Northampton during the revivals of 1740–42 indicates that even in revivalistic parishes the bonds of community weakened as people received assurance by the preaching of itinerants. Conversion did constitute an initiation into community, as I will argue in chapter 3, but one of a different scope from the territorially bounded, face-to-face communities the Old Lights defended. See Michael J. Crawford, *Seasons of Grace: Colonial New England's Revival Tradition in Its British Context* (New York and Oxford, 1991), 183–95; Bushman, *The Great Awakening*, 66–67; Patricia J. Tracy, *Jonathan Edwards, Pastor: Religion and Society in Eighteenth-Century Northampton* (New York, 1980), 135–38.

55 *General Magazine*, 1 (1741): 414.

56 *American Weekly Mercury*, Aug. 21, 1741. See also the *Boston Weekly Post-Boy*, June 23, 1740; *Letter to Wishart*, 6–7.

57 *South Carolina Gazette*, Postscript, June 18, 1741.

58 *Letter to Wishart*, 12.

59 *Boston Weekly Post-Boy*, July 12, 1742.

60 *South Carolina Gazette*, June 21, 1742; compare Tracy, *The Great Awakening*, 293.

61 *Letter to Wishart*, 14; compare Tracy, *The Great Awakening*, 354.

62 [Chauncy], *Religious Commotions in New England*, 10.

63 Peter Wood, *Black Majority: Negroes in Colonial South Carolina from 1670 through the Stono Rebellion* (New York, 1974), 308–30.

64 Harvey H. Jackson, "Hugh Bryan and the Evangelical Movement in Colonial South Carolina," *William and Mary Quarterly*, 3d ser., 43 (1986): 594–614; Leigh Eric Schmidt, "'The Grand Prophet,' Hugh Bryan: Early Evangelicalism's Challenge to the Establishment and Slavery in the Colonial South," *South Carolina Historical Magazine* 87 (1986): 238–50.

65 *American Weekly Mercury*, May 27, 1742.

66 *Letter to Wishart*, 8.

67 *American Weekly Mercury*, Sept. 10, 1741.

68 Pickering, *Letters to Rogers*, 15.

69 *American Weekly Mercury*, Postscript, July 31.

70 *South Carolina Gazette*, June 21, 1742.

71 *South Carolina Gazette*, June 21, 1742.

72 *Boston Weekly Post-Boy*, July 19, 1742.

73 *American Weekly Mercury*, Dec. 28, 1744.

74 *Boston Gazette*, Sept. 6, 1743.

75 Tracy, *The Great Awakening*, 293.

76 Tracy, *The Great Awakening*, 322, 345–63 passim.

77 *Records of the Presbyterian Church in the United States of America* (Philadelphia, 1841), 136, 151–52; Trinterude, *Forming of an American Tradition*, 71–85, 95–97; Westerkamp, *Triumph of the Laity*, 182–83; "An Act for regulating Abuses and correcting Disorders in Ecclesiastical Affairs," in *The Public Records of the Colony of Connecticut*, ed. Charles J. Hoadly (Hartford, 1874), 454–57; reprinted in *The Great Awakening*, ed. Bushman, 58–60.

78 William Balch, *The Duty of Ministers to aim at Promoting, and being Partakers of the Gospel. A Sermon Preached at the Ordination of Mr. Benjamin Parker* (Boston, 1744), 17.

79 See, for example, *Boston Gazette*, Nov. 30, 1742; William Hobby, *An Inquiry into the Itinerancy and the Conduct of the Rev. Mr. George Whitefield, An Itinerant Preacher: Vindicating the former against the charge of Unlawfulness and Inexpediency, and the latter against some Aspersions, which have been frequently cast upon him* (Boston, 1745), 5.

80 *American Weekly Mercury*, Dec. 9, 1742; see also William Hooper, *The Apostles Neither Impostors nor Enthusiasts* (Boston, 1742), 14–30 passim.

81 *The Declaration of Ministers in Barnstable County, relating to the late Practice of Itinerant Preaching* (Boston, 1745), 4.

82 Pickering, *Letters to Rogers*, 10; Chauncy, *Seasonable Thoughts*, 47; *Declaration of the Ministers of Barnstable County*, 4.

83 Timothy Walker, *The Way to try All Pretended Apostles: Being the Substance of Two Sermons Preach'd at Rumford in New-Hampshire, January 1742,3* (Boston, 1743), 18, 22.

84 Thomson, *Government of the Church of Christ*, 4, 27, 126–27.

85 Ibid., 27.

86 Ibid.; see also Westerkamp, *Triumph of the Laity*, 43–164.

87 Chauncy, *Seasonable Thoughts*, 53–54.

88 See, for example, Walker, *Pretended Apostles*, 20; Pickering, *Letters to Rogers*, 14–15; *Boston Weekly Post-Boy*, April 19, 1742; *Boston Gazette*, Nov. 30, 1742.

89 *The State of Religion in New-England, since the Reverend Mr. George Whitefield's Arrival there. In a Letter from a Gentleman in New-England to his Friend in Glasgow. To which is subjoined an Appendix, containing Attestations of the principal Facts in the Letter* (Glasgow, 1742), 12; see also Tracy, *The Great Awakening*, 287.

90 Walker, *Pretended Apostles*, 10, 17.

91 Hancock, *Danger of an Unqualified Ministry*, 17–19.

92 Chauncy, *Seasonable Thoughts*, 259.

93 Ibid., 257n.

94 *The Testimony and Advice of a Number of Laymen respecting Religion, and the Teachers of it* (Boston, 1743), 3, 6; compare Henry F. May, *The Enlightenment in America* (New York, 1976), 35–38.

95 Hancock, *Danger of an Unqualified Ministry*, 19; see also *Testimony and Advice*, 2, 4, 6; *American Weekly Mercury*, Dec. 28, 1744.

96 Thomson, *Government of the Church of Christ*, 127.

97 *South Carolina Gazette,* Postscript, Sept. 19, 1741.

98 Charles Chauncy, *Enthusiasm describ'd and caution'd against. A Sermon Preach'd at the Old Brick Meeting-House in Boston on the Lord's Day after the Commencement, 1742* (Boston, 1742), 13; idem, *Seasonable Thoughts,* 418–23.

99 Hobby, *Inquiry into the Itinerancy of Whitefield.*

100 J. F., *A Letter to the Reverend Mr. William Hobby, Pastor of the First Church in Reading* (Boston, 1745), 2, 4–5.

101 *A Twig of Birch for Billy's Breech. A Letter to the Reverend Mr. William Hobby, Pastor of a church in Reading* (Boston, 1745), 5; compare Richard Pateshall, *Pride Humbled, or, Mr. Hobby Chastised: being some remarks on said Hobby's piece, entitled, A Defence of the Itinerancy and the Conduct of the Rev. Mr. Whitefield. In a letter to the Reverend Mr. William Hobby, pastor of the First Church in Reading* (Boston, 1745).

102 Nathaniel Henchman, *A Letter to the Reverend Mr. William Hobby, Occasioned by sundry Passages in his printed Letter, in Vindication of Mr. Whitefield's Itinerancy and Conduct* (Boston, 1745), 4.

103 Ibid., 5.

104 Thomson, *Government of the Church of Christ,* 19.

105 Chauncy, *Religious Commotions in New England,* 24.

106 Chauncy, *Seasonable Thoughts,* 369.

107 Ibid., 369–71.

108 Chauncy, *Religious Commotions in New England,* 14.

109 Chauncy, *Enthusiasm describ'd,* 12, 13; Walker, *Pretended Apostles,* 17–18.

110 See Bernard Bailyn, *The Ideological Origins of the American Revolution* (Cambridge, Mass., 1967), 70; Morton White, *The Philosophy of the American Revolution* (New York, 1978), 269; compare Alford's discussion of the Lockean self in *The Self in Social Theory,* 124, 128.

111 Stiles, *Looking-glass for Changelings,* 3.

112 Ibid., 4.

113 Ibid., 15–16.

114 Ibid., 18.

115 Ibid., 21.

116 Chauncy, *Religious Commotions in New England,* 4; idem., *Seasonable Thoughts,* iv–xv.

117 *Boston Evening Post,* Feb. 4, 1745.

118 *Boston Evening Post,* Dec. 10, 1744. The essay in which this quotation appeared was reprinted in the *American Weekly Mercury,* Jan. 9, 1744, and the *South Carolina Gazette,* Feb. 18, 1745.

119 *Boston Evening Post,* Oct. 27, 1744.

120 *The Testimony of the President, Professors, Tutors, and Hebrew Instructor of Harvard College against the Reverend Mr. George Whitefield, and his Conduct* (Boston, 1744); *The Declaration of the Rector and Tutors of Yale College in New-Haven against the Reverend Mr. George Whitefield, his principles and designs* (Boston, 1745).

121 For complete citations, see Charles Evans, *American Bibliography,* 14 vols., (New York, 1941–67), 2. For summaries and extended excerpts of these testimonies, see Tracy, *The Great Awakening,* 325–72.

122 *American Weekly Mercury,* Dec. 6, 1744.

123 George Gillespie, *Remarks upon Mr. George Whitefield, Proving Him a man under Delusion* (Philadelphia, 1744).

124 *Virginia Gazette,* Oct. 31, 1745; *South Carolina Gazette,* Nov. 12, 1744, Feb. 18, 1745.

125 *Testimony of Harvard Faculty,* reprinted in *The Great Awakening,* ed. Heimert and Miller, 351.

126 *A Twig of Birch for Billy's Breech,* 5.

127 *Testimony of Harvard Faculty,* in *The Great Awakening,* ed. Heimert and Miller, 352.

128 *The Sentiments and Resolutions of an Association of Ministers (convened at Weymouth, Jan. 15th, 1744,5) concerning the Rev. Mr. George Whitefield* (Boston, 1745), 9.

129 *Testimony of Ministers at Marlborough,* 7.

130 *Boston Evening Post,* Feb. 4, 1745.

131 *A Twig of Birch for Billy's Breech,* 5.

132 *American Weekly Mercury,* Dec. 20, 1744.

3 Itinerancy and the Evangelical Imagination

1 *Boston Gazette,* Feb. 2, 1742.

2 See, for example, *Pennsylvania Gazette,* Dec. 24, 1741; *South Carolina Gazette,* Sept. 13, 1742; *Boston Gazette,* May 13, 1742.

3 *Boston Gazette,* Jan. 11, 1743.

4 Joshua Gee, *A Letter to the Reverend Nathaniel Eells, Moderator of the late Convention of Pastors in Boston; containing some Remarks on their Printed testimony Against Several Errors and Disorders in the Land* (Boston, 1743), 9.

5 Paul Ricoeur, *Time and Narrative,* 3 vols., trans. by Kathleen McLaughlin and David Pellauer (Chicago, 1984–88), iii, 155.

6 Josiah Smith, *A Sermon, on the Character, Preaching, &c. of the Rev. Mr. Whitefield* (Boston, 1740), excerpted in *The Great Awakening: Documents Illustrating the Crisis and Its Consequences,* ed. Alan Heimert and Perry Miller (Indianapolis and New York, 1967), 68; compare Gee, *Letter to Nathaniel Eells,* 16; James Robe, *A Short Narrative of the Extraordinary Work of the Spirit of God at Cambuslang, Kilsyth &c.* (Glasgow, 1742; reprint, Philadelphia, 1742), 1–5.

7 George Whitefield, *George Whitefield's Journals: A New Edition Containing Fuller Material than Any hitherto Published,* ed. William Wale and others (London, 1960), 90, 181–83, 387–89, 473.

8 Thomas Foxcroft, *Some Seasonable Thoughts on Evangelic Preaching; its Nature, Usefulness, and Obligation* (Boston, 1740), 5. Complaints about the clergy formed a standard feature of prorevival literature throughout the 1740s. Compare Whitefield, *Journals,* 389, 473, and passim; *New-England Weekly Journal,* March 24, 1741; Thomas Prince, Jr., ed., *The Christian History, Containing Accounts of the Revival and Propagation of Religion in Great Britain and America,* 2 vols. (Boston, 1743–45), passim (hereafter cited as *Christian History*).

9 *General Magazine,* 1 (1741): 101.

10 *New-England Weekly Journal,* March 24, 1741.

11 *A Poem . . . Being a private Christian's Dissent from, and Testimony against that unscriptural and dangerous Opinion . . . That the Minister of each Town or Parish has a*

POWER to license or forbid the preaching of the Gospel by any other than himself in the Parish whereof he is Minister . . . (Boston, 1742).

12 *General Magazine* 1 (1741): 275. I have deliberately chosen to follow the usage of eighteenth-century writers by employing the masculine pronoun in reference to the deity.

13 *Poem against forbidding the preaching of the Gospel;* Elisha Williams, *The Essential Rights and Liberties of Protestants. A Seasonable Plea for the Liberty of Conscience, and the Right of Private Judgment* (Boston, 1744), 64–65.

14 *A Declaration of the Presbyteries of New-Brunswick and New-Castle judicially met together at Philadelphia* (Philadelphia, 1743), 6; William Hobby, *An Inquiry into the Itinerancy and the Conduct of the Rev. Mr. George Whitefield, An Itinerant Preacher: Vindicating the former against the charge of Unlawfulness and Inexpediency, and the latter against some Aspersions, which have been frequently cast upon him* (Boston, 1745), 10–11.

15 On popular support for seventeenth-century Puritan persecution of Quakers see Carla Gardin Pestana, *Quakers and Baptists in Colonial Massachusetts* (Cambridge, 1991), 34.

16 *New-England Weekly Journal,* Jan. 27, 1741; compare *Christian History.*

17 Hobby, *Inquiry into the Itinerancy of Whitefield,* 4.

18 See, for example, *Boston Gazette,* Nov. 30, 1742; *General Magazine* 1 (1741): 272–75, Jonathan Dickinson, *A Display of God's Special Grace* (Philadelphia, 1743), reprinted in *Sermons and Tracts Separately Published at Boston, Philadelphia &c. by Jonathan Dickinson, A.M.* (Edinburgh, 1798), 405.

19 Benjamin Colman, *The Great God has magnified his Word to the Children of Men* (Boston, 1742), 30.

20 William Cooper, preface to *Distinguishing Marks of a Work of the Spirit of God,* by Jonathan Edwards, in *The Great Awakening,* ed. C. C. Goen (New Haven and London, 1972), 217.

21 *South Carolina Gazette,* Aug. 23, 1740.

22 *New-England Weekly Journal,* March 3, 1741.

23 *A Declaration of the Presbyteries of New-Brunswick and New-Castle judicially met together at Philadelphia* (Philadelphia, 1743), 6. See chapter 2 of this volume for a discussion of the Old Light response to itinerancy's erosion of the "bounds of decency."

24 *Christian History,* 2:144; compare Hobby, *Inquiry into the Itinerancy of Whitefield,* 8.

25 See T. H. Breen, "'Baubles of Britain': The American and Consumer Revolutions of the Eighteenth Century," *Past and Present* 119 (1988): 85–86.

26 *Christian History,* 1:404.

27 Compare, for example, the *Virginia Gazette,* Dec. 16, 1737; *Pennsylvania Gazette,* Nov. 29, 1739, and Dec. 13, 1739; *South Carolina Gazette,* Jan. 19, 1740; *General Magazine* 1 (1741): 101–4; *Boston Gazette* May 11, 1742; James Robe, *A Faithful Narrative of the Extraordinary Work of the spirit of god at Kilsyth, and other Congregations in the Neighbourhood near Glasgow,* 2d ed. (London, 1742); Samuel Blair, *A Short and Faithful Narrative of the Late Remarkable Revival of Religion in the congregation of New-Londonderry, and other Parts of Pennsylvania* (Philadelphia, 1744). See also Susan O'Brien, "A Transatlantic Community of Saints: The Great

Awakening and the First Evangelical Network, 1735–1755," *American Historical Review* 91 (1986): 811–32.

28 *Christian History,* 1:384. Compare Porter's sentiment with the ministerial attestations in *Christian History,* 1:168–201, and other revivals described in that work.

29 *Christian History,* 1:243.

30 See Jonathan Edwards, *A Faithful Narrative of the Surprising Work of God in the Conversion of Many Hundred Souls in Northampton, and the Neighbouring Towns and Villages of the county of Hampshire, in the Province of the Massachusetts Bay in New-England,* in *The Great Awakening,* ed. C. C. Goen, 152–53; *Christian History;* John Gillies, *Historical Collections relating to Remarkable Periods of the Success of the Gospel* (Kelso, Scotland, 1845), 429–33; Alexander Webster, *Divine Influence the true Spring of the Extraordinary Work at Cambuslang and other Places in the West of Scotland, illustrated; in a Letter from the Reverend Mr. Alexander Webster, one of the Ministers of this City to a Gentleman in the Country* (Edinburgh, 1742), 10–16.

31 Harry S. Stout, "Religion, Communications, and the Ideological Origins of the American Revolution," *William and Mary Quarterly,* 3d ser., 34 (1977): 519–41; idem, *The New England Soul: Preaching and Religious Culture in Colonial New England* (New York, 1986), 192–202; Rhys Isaac, "Preachers and Patriots: Popular culture and the Revolution in Virginia," in *The American Revolution: Explorations in the History of American Radicalism,* ed. Alfred F. Young, (DeKalb, Ill., 1976), 125–56.

32 Frank Lambert, "A Christian Merchant: George Whitefield and the Great Awakening, 1737–1745," *Journal of American History* 77 (1990–91): 812–37.

33 See the introduction and chapter 1 of this volume for a fuller discussion of this topic.

34 See, for example, J. G. A. Pocock, *The Machiavellian Moment: Florentine Political Thought and the Atlantic Republican Tradition* (Princeton, 1975), 423–505; J. E. Crowley, *This Sheba, Self: The Conceptualization of Economic Life in Eighteenth-Century America* (Baltimore, 1974); T. H. Breen, "'Baubles of Britain': The American and Consumer Revolutions of the Eighteenth Century," *Past and Present* 119 (May, 1988): 79–87.

35 Michael Warner, *The Letters of the Republic: Publication and the Public Sphere in Eighteenth-Century America* (Cambridge, Mass., 1990), 13–33; Richard D. Brown, *Knowledge is Power: The Diffusion of Information in Early America, 1700–1865* (New York, 1989), 65–81, 110–159; Benedict Anderson, *Imagined Communities: Reflections on the Origins and Spread of Nationalism* (London, 1983), 45–49; Jürgen Habermas, *The Structural Transformation of the Public Sphere: An Inquiry into a Category of Bourgeois Society* (Cambridge, Mass., 1989), 20–26.

36 On the local context and itinerancy's disruptions see chapter 2 of this volume; William T. Youngs, Jr., *God's Messengers: Religious Leadership in Colonial New England, 1700–1750* (Baltimore, 1976), 40–63; Christine Leigh Heyrman, *Commerce and Culture: The Maritime Communities of Colonial Massachusetts, 1690–1750* (New York, 1984), 144–81; Stout, "Religion, Communications, and the Revolution," 519–41. On the significance of this behavior see Irving Goffman, *Interaction Ritual: Essays on Face-to-Face Behavior* (New York, 1967), 5–112; Mary

Douglas, *Natural Symbols: Explorations in Cosmology* (New York, 1970), 73, 160–62.

37 See chapter 2 of this volume; Youngs, *God's Messengers*, 40–63.

38 *Poem against forbidding the preaching of the Gospel.*

39 Whitefield, *Journals.*

40 Charles Hartshorn Maxon, *The Great Awakening in the Middle Colonies* (Chicago, 1920), 133.

41 *Christian History*, 2:56.

42 See chapter 2 of this volume; O'Brien, "Transatlantic Community of Saints," 811–32.

43 *Boston Weekly Post-Boy*, Sept. 28, 1741.

44 On the role of local ministers, communities, and families in Puritan conversion, see Gerald F. Moran and Maris A. Vinovskis, *Religion, Family and the Life Course: Explorations in the Social History of Early America* (Ann Arbor, Mich., 1992), 98, 154; Gerald F. Moran, "Religious Renewal, Puritan Tribalism, and the Family in Seventeenth-Century Milford, Connecticut," *William and Mary Quarterly*, 3d ser., 36 (1979): 236–54; idem, "Conditions of Religious Conversion in the First Society of Norwich, Connecticut, 1718–1744," *Journal of Social History* 5 (1971–72): 331–43; James Walsh, "The Great Awakening in the First Congregational Church of Woodbury, Connecticut," *William and Mary Quarterly*, 3d ser., 28 (1971): 543–62; Stephen R. Grossbart, "Seeking the Divine Favor: Conversion and Church Admission in Eastern Connecticut, 1711–1832," *William and Mary Quarterly*, 3d ser., 46 (1989): 696–740.

45 Whitefield, *Journals*, 473.

46 *South Carolina Gazette*, June 21, 1742.

47 *Christian History*, 1:206.

48 Whitefield, *Journals*, 469.

49 James M'Cullough, ed., *The Glasgow Weekly History Relating the late Progress of the Gospel at Home and Abroad; Being a Collection of Letters, partly reprinted from the London Weekly History, and partly printed first here at Glasgow. For the Year 1742* (Glasgow, 1743), excerpted in *Proceedings of the Massachusetts Historical Society* 53 (1919–20): 201.

50 Nathan Cole, *The Spiritual Travels of Nathan Cole*, excerpted in *The Great Awakening*, ed. Heimert and Miller, 184–86.

51 Jonathan Edwards, *The Life of David Brainerd*, in *The Works of Jonathan Edwards*, vol. 7, ed. Norman Pettit (New Haven and London, 1985), 149.

52 Kenneth P. Minkema, "A Great Awakening Conversion: The Relation of Samuel Belcher," *William and Mary Quarterly*, 3d ser., 44 (1987): 121–26. See also Barbara E. Lacey, "The World of Hannah Heaton: The Autobiography of an Eighteenth-Century Connecticut Farm Woman," *William and Mary Quarterly*, 3d ser., 45 (1988): 280–304. For the significance of these conversions in a context of weakening boundaries, see Douglas, *Natural Symbols*, 162.

53 *Christian History*, 1:250–52.

54 *Christian History*, 2:245.

55 *Christian History*, 1:182–84.

56 *Christian History,* 1:243.

57 *Christian History,* 1:182.

58 *Christian History,* 1:106, 2:28; Edwards, *Thoughts Concerning the Revival,* 35–38. Millennial expectations are expressed in the title as well as throughout the text of Samuel Finley's *Christ Triumphing and Satan Raging. A Sermon on Matth. XII. 28. Wherein is Proved, that the Kingdom of God is Come unto Us at This Day* (Philadelphia, 1741). Compare also Josiah Smith, *A Sermon on the Character, Preaching &c. of the Rev. Mr. Whitefield,* in *The Great Awakening,* ed. Heimert and Miller, 68.

59 *Christian History,* 1:404.

60 *Christian History,* 1:197–98.

61 *A Declaration of the Presbyteries of New-Brunswick and New-Castle judicially met together at Philadelphia* (Philadelphia, 1743), 6. Compare also Gee, *Letter to Nathaniel Eells,* 10; and Hobby, *Inquiry into the Itinerancy of Whitefield,* 11.

62 *Boston Gazette,* Nov. 30, 1742.

63 *American Weekly Mercury,* Jan. 27, 1743.

64 *Christian History,* 1:23; O'Brien, "Transatlantic Community of Saints," 828.

65 Gillies, *Historical Collections,* 383.

66 Wesley M. Gewehr, *The Great Awakening in Virginia, 1740–1790* (Durham, N.C., 1930), 47–50.

67 Whitefield, *Journals.*

68 *Christian History.* See also O'Brien, "Transatlantic Community of Saints"; and Susan Durden, "A Study of the First Evangelical Magazines, 1740–1748," *Journal of Ecclesiastical History* 22 (1976): 255–75.

69 Gilbert Tennent, *The Examiner, Examined, or Gilbert Tennent, Harmonious* (Philadelphia, 1743), 25–26.

70 *Boston Gazette,* Nov. 30, 1742; compare *Christian History,* 1:197–98.

71 *Boston Gazette,* July 21, 1744.

72 Charles Chauncy, *Seasonable Thoughts on the State of Religion in New-England, A Treatise in Five Parts* (Boston, 1743), 298.

73 On the well-known eighteenth-century fondness for classical literature and ideas, see Bernard Bailyn, *The Ideological Origins of the American Revolution* (Cambridge, Mass., 1967), 23–24. On the implications of revivalists' interpretive practices, see Anthony C. Thiseleton, *The Two Horizons: New Testament Hermeneutics and Philosophical Description with Special Reference to Heidegger, Bultmann, Gadamer, and Wittgenstein,* foreword by J. B. Torrance (Grand Rapids, 1980), 10–23.

74 Foxcroft, *Seasonable Thoughts on Evangelic Preaching,* 5–6.

75 Josiah Smith, *Whitefield's Character and Preaching,* in *The Great Awakening,* ed. Heimert and Miller, 68; Samuel Blair, "Reflections on a Paper . . . under the title of 'a true and genuine account of a wonderful wandring Spirit' . . ." *General Magazine* 1 (1741): 274–75; Jonathan Edwards, *Some Thoughts Concerning the present Revival of Religion in New-England, and the Way in which it ought to be acknowledged and promoted, Humbly offered to the Publick, in a Treatise on that Subject,* in *The Works of Jonathan Edwards,* gen. ed. John E. Smith, vol. 5, *The Great Awakening,* ed. C. C. Goen (New Haven and London, 1972), 357–58.

76 *American Weekly Mercury,* Dec. 9, 1742.

77 *American Weekly Mercury,* Feb. 19, 1740.
78 Blair, "Reflections on 'a wandring Spirit,'" 273–74.
79 Ibid., 274–76.
80 *Boston Gazette,* Nov. 30, 1742.
81 *Poem against forbidding the preaching of the Gospel.*
82 I use the term "men" intentionally here; defenders of itinerancy generally excluded women from the practice.
83 Samuel Finley, *A Letter to a Friend* (Boston, 1745), 2.
84 *Christian History,* 1:1–2.
85 *Christian History,* 1:58, 63, 71–72.
86 *Christian History,* 1:76.
87 *Christian History,* 1:65; 101–3.
88 *Christian History,* 1:99–100.
89 *Christian History,* 1:107–12.
90 *Christian History,* 1:93–124.
91 *Christian History,* 1:155–210. Ninety ministers gathered in convention on July 7, 1743 and signed a common attestation supplemented by written testimonials of forty-nine others who had been absent from the proceedings. The whole was also published separately as *The Testimony and Advice of an Assembly of Pastors of Churches in New England at a Meeting in Boston July 7, 1743. Occasion'd by the Late Happy Revival of Religion in Parts of the Land. To which are added Attestations contain'd in Letters from a Number of Their Brethren Who Were Providentially Hinder'd from Giving Their Presence* (Boston, 1743).
92 *Christian History,* 2:318–19.
93 *Christian History,* 1:212–13.
94 *Christian History,* 1:232–35.
95 *Christian History,* 2:1–12; 65–76; 220–26.
96 *Christian History,* 1:8.
97 *Christian History,* 1:287.
98 *Christian History,* 2:267.
99 See, for example, Jonathan Edwards, *The Church's Marriage to her Sons, and to her God; A Sermon Preached at the Installment of the Reverend Mr. Samuel Buell as Pastor of the Church and Congregation at East-Hampton on Long Island* (Boston, 1746); Gilbert Tennent, *Love to Christ a necessary Qualification in Order to feed His Sheep. A Sermon Preached at Neshaminie, December 14, 1743 Before the Ordination of the Reverend Mr. Charles Beatty* (Philadelphia, 1744).
100 Colman, *The Great God has magnified his Word,* 31.
101 C. C. Goen, *Revivalism and Separatism in New England, 1740–1800: Strict Congregationalists and Separate Baptists in the Great Awakening* (New Haven and London, 1962), 36. See chapter 4 of this volume for further treatment of the Separates.
102 *Boston Weekly Post-Boy,* Jan. 12, 1741.
103 *New-England Weekly Journal,* Jan. 27, 1741.
104 Ibid.; Hobby, *Inquiry into the Itinerancy of Whitefield,* 4.
105 *New-England Weekly Journal,* Jan. 27, 1741.
106 Ibid.
107 See, for example, *Boston Weekly Post-Boy,* Sept. 28, 1741.

108 See, for example, Gilbert Tennent's comments in the *Pennsylvania Gazette,* Aug. 19, 1742; and the testimony of revivalist ministers against Davenport's book burning, *Boston Gazette,* April 12, 1743.

109 Dickinson, *A Display of God's Special Grace,* 403–20; Edwards, *Distinguishing Marks.*

110 *Christian History,* 1:30.

111 *Christian History,* 1:38, 41.

112 *Christian History,* 1:36.

113 *Christian History,* 1:46.

114 *Christian History,* 1:162–63.

115 *Christian History,* 1:198.

116 *Christian History,* 2:131.

117 Examples of publication include the following: James Davenport, *The Reverend Mr. James Davenport's Confession & Retractions* (Boston, 1744); *Boston Gazette,* Aug. 14, 1744; *American Weekly Mercury,* Aug. 30, 1744; *Pensylvania Gazette,* Oct. 18, 1744; *Christian History,* 2:236–40.

118 Davenport, *Confessions and Retractions,* in *The Great Awakening,* ed. Heimert and Miller, 259.

119 Ibid., 260–61.

120 *Boston Gazette,* Nov. 22, 1744; compare *South Carolina Gazette,* March 11, 1745; *Boston Gazette,* Jan. 8, 1745.

121 *Boston Gazette,* Jan. 8, 1745; *South Carolina Gazette,* Feb. 11, 1745.

122 *Christian History,* 2:335; compare *South Carolina Gazette,* Feb. 11, 1745.

123 *An Invitation from the Eastern Consociation of Ministers of Fairfield County, Connecticut to the Reverend Mr. Whitefield* (Boston, 1745).

124 *The Testimony of a number of Ministers conven'd at Taunton in the County of Bristol, March 5, 1744,5 in favor of the Reverend Mr. Whitefield, &c. giving the reasons of their inviting him into their pulpits* (Boston, 1745).

125 I have based this assertion on a comparison of colonial newspapers published during the two periods. See also Whitefield, *Journals,* 451–83. For an example of scruples relating to Whitefield's ordination, see Theophilus Pickering, *Mr. Pickering's Letter to Mr. Whitefield: Touching his Relation to the Church of England; his Impulses and Impressions; and the Present unhappy state of Things, &c.* (Boston, 1745), 3.

126 *Boston Gazette,* July 2, 1745.

127 *Pennsylvania Gazette,* March 26, 1745; *Boston Gazette,* Aug. 20, 1745.

128 *Virginia Gazette,* Oct. 31, 1745; Patrick Henry to William Dawson, October 14, 1745, Papers of William Dawson, Manuscript Division, Library of Congress, Washington, D.C.

129 *South Carolina Gazette,* Feb. 11, 1745.

130 *South Carolina Gazette,* Dec. 8, 1746.

131 *American Weekly Mercury,* Dec. 20, 1744.

4 The Proliferation of Itinerancy

1 Mary Douglas, *Natural Symbols: Explorations in Cosmology* (New York, 1970), 14.

2 For examples of this line of interpretation, see Jack P. Greene, "Search for

Identity: An Interpretation of the Meaning of Selected Patterns of Social Response in Eighteenth-Century America," *Journal of Social History* 3 (1970): 199–201; Gary B. Nash, *The Urban Crucible: Social Change, Political Consciousness, and the Origins of the American Revolution* (Cambridge, Mass., 1979), 161–263; Christopher M. Jedry, *The World of John Cleaveland: Family and Community in Eighteenth-Century New England* (New York, 1979), 58–135; J. Stephen Kroll-Smith, "Transmitting a Revival Culture: The Organizational Dynamic of the Baptist Movement in Colonial Virginia, 1760–1777," *Journal of Southern History* 50 (1984): 551–68; Stephen A. Marini, *Radical Sects of Revolutionary New England* (Cambridge, Mass., 1982).

3 *Boston Evening Post,* Sept. 23, 1754; see also *Boston Weekly News Letter,* Sept. 26, 1754; *Boston Gazette,* Oct. 22, 1754 and Nov. 19, 1754.

4 *The Querists: Or an Extract of Mr. Whitefield's Sermons &c. with Scruples by Presbyterians* (Philadelphia, 1740; reprint, Boston, 1754).

5 Edward Wigglesworth, *Some distinguishing Characteristics of the Extraordinary and Ordinary Ministers of the Church of Christ, Briefly considered, in Two Discourses delivered at the Publick Lectures, in Harvard-College, Nov. 12th and 19th, 1754* (Boston, 1754), 11, 14.

6 *Boston Gazette,* Oct. 22, 1754.

7 James Davenport, *The Faithful Minister Encouraged* (Philadelphia, 1756), 17.

8 William Henry Foote, *Sketches of Virginia: Historical and Biographical,* 1st ser. (Philadelphia, 1850), 199.

9 Gilbert Tennent, *Irenicum Ecclesiasticum: or a Humble Impartial Essay upon the Peace of Jerusalem . . .* (Philadelphia, 1749), excerpted in *The Great Awakening: Documents Illustrating the Crisis and Its Consequences,* ed. Alan Heimert and Perry Miller (Indianapolis and New York, 1967), 373.

10 Samuel Buell, *A Copy of a Letter from the Rev. Mr. Buell, of East-Hampton, on Long-Island, to the Rev. Mr. Barber, of Groton in Connecticut* (New London, 1764), 5.

11 Foote, *Sketches of Virginia,* 1st ser., 422.

12 C. C. Goen, *Revivalism and Separatism in New England, 1740–1800: Strict Congregationalists and Separate Baptists in the Great Awakening* (New York, 1969), 68–114, 208–57; William G. McLoughlin, *Isaac Backus and the American Pietistic Tradition* (Boston, 1967), 57–88; idem, *New England Dissent, 1630–1833: The Baptists and the Separation of Church and State,* 2 vols. (Cambridge, Mass., 1971), 2:420–39.

13 Goen, *Revivalism and Separatism,* 106, 179–80; McLoughlin, *Isaac Backus,* 28–29.

14 Morgan Edwards, *Material towards a History of the Baptists,* ed. Eve B. Weeks and Mary B. Warren, 2 vols. (Danielsville, Ga., 1984), 2:90.

15 Foote, *Sketches of Virginia,* 2d ser., 46.

16 Henry Melchior Muhlenberg, *The Journals of Henry Melchior Muhlenberg in Three Volumes,* trans. Theodore G. Tappert and John W. Doberstein, 3 vols. (Philadelphia, 1958), 1:320, 680, 683, 696, 716, 721; 2:538, 545.

17 Edwards, *Materials,* 2:62–63. The New Light Mary Cooper provides another example of this identification of Whitefield with the revival community when she complains about a minister who "spoke against Mr. Whitefield as much and something more than we could bear to." See Mary Cooper, *The Diary of Mary*

Cooper: Life on a Long Island Farm, 1768–1773, ed. Field Horne (Oyster Bay, N.Y., 1981), 18.

18 Jonathan Edwards, *An Humble Attempt to Promote Explicit Agreement and Visible Union of God's People in Extraordinary Prayer for the Revival of Religion and the Advancement of Christ's Kingdom on Earth, pursuant to Scripture-Promises and Prophecies concerning the Last Time,* in *The Works of Jonathan Edwards,* gen. ed. John E. Smith, vol. 5, *Apocalyptic Writings,* ed. Stephen J. Stein (New Haven and London, 1977), 321. On the concert for prayer see also Susan O'Brien, "A Transatlantic Community of Saints: The Great Awakening and the First Evangelical Network, 1735–1755," *American Historical Review* 91 (1986): 829–31.

19 Edwards, *Humble Attempt,* 324.

20 Ibid., 317–18.

21 Ibid., 323.

22 Benedict Anderson, *Imagined Communities: Reflections on the Origin and Spread of Nationalism* (London, 1983), 30.

23 Edwards, *Humble Attempt,* 309–11.

24 Stephen J. Stein, introduction to Edwards, *Apocalyptic Writings,* vol. 5 of *Works of Jonathan Edwards,* 48, n. 4.

25 John Gillies, comp., *Historical Collections relating to Remarkable Periods of the Success of the Gospel* (London, 1754; reprint, Kelso, Scotland, 1845), 464.

26 Stein, introduction to Edwards, *Apocalyptic Writings,* 48, n. 4.

27 See Foote, *Sketches of Virginia,* 2d ser., 55.

28 John Cleaveland, *A Short and Plain Narrative of the Late Work of God's Spirit at Chebacco in Ipswich, in the Years 1763 and 1764: together with some Account of the conduct of the fourth Church of Christ in Ipswich in admitting Members—and the Defense of said Conduct* (Boston, 1767), 4.

29 Samuel Davies, *The State of Religion among the Protestant Dissenters in Virginia; in a Letter to the Reverend Mr. Joseph Bellamy, at Bethlehem, in New-England* (Boston, 1751), 3.

30 *Good News from the Netherlands. Extracts of Letters from two Ministers in Holland, confirming and giving further Accounts of the Revival of Religion in Gelderland* (Boston, 1751), 1.

31 Buell, *Copy of a Letter,* 5.

32 Samuel Buell, *A Faithful Narrative of the Remarkable Revival of Religion in the Congregation of East-Hampton on Long-Island, in the Year of our Lord 1764, with Some Reflections* (New York, 1766), xv.

33 Goen, *Revivalism and Separatism,* 184–85.

34 Buell, *Faithful Narrative,* 2.

35 Ibid., 21.

36 Ibid., 24.

37 Douglas, *Natural Symbols,* 14, 33–36.

38 Andrew Croswell, *A Narrative of the New-Gathered Congregational Church in Boston* (Boston, 1749), 13.

39 Ibid., 16. For other examples of Separates who cited the desire to keep the parish open to itinerant preaching see Richard L. Bushman, *The Great Awaken-*

ing: Documents on the Revival of Religion, 1740–45 (New York, 1970), 102–3; Goen, *Revivalism and Separatism,* 54–114 passim.

40 *The Pretended Plain Narrative Convicted of Fraud and Partiality* (Boston, 1748), 26.

41 *A Letter from the Associated Ministers of the County of Windham, To the People in the Several Societies in said County . . .* (Boston, 1745), 6, excerpted in *The Great Awakening,* ed. Heimert and Miller, 402.

42 See, for example, Theophilus Pickering, *A Supplement to a Piece lately printed, intitled A Bad Omen to the Churches &c.* (Boston, 1747), 3.

43 Solomon Paine, *A Short View of the Difference between the Church of Christ, and the Established Churches in the Colony of Connecticut, in Their Foundation and Practice, with Their Ends: Being Discovered by the Word of God and Certain Laws of Said Colony, Called Ecclesiastical* (Newport, 1752), reprinted in *The Great Awakening,* ed. Heimert and Miller, 413.

44 Goen, *Revivalism and Separatism,* 130.

45 Ebenezer Frothingham, *The Articles of Faith and Practice, with the Covenant, that is confessed by the Separate Churches of Christ in General in This Land* (Newport, 1750), 374–80; Paine, *Short View of the Church of Christ,* in *The Great Awakening,* ed. Heimert and Miller, 415–16.

46 Paine, *Short View of the Church of Christ,* in *The Great Awakening,* ed. Heimert and Miller, 417; Ebenezer Frothingham, *A Key to Unlock the Door, That Leads in, to Take a Fair View of the Religious constitution, Established by Law, in the Colony of Connecticut* (n.p., 1767), 204ff.

47 Frothingham, *A Key to Unlock the Door,* 153–55.

48 Besides the pamphlets discussed below, Pickering's attacks on itinerancy include *The Rev. Mr. Pickering's Letters to the Rev. N. Rogers and Mr. D. Rogers of Ipswich: with their Answer to Mr. Pickering's First Letter. As also His Letter to the Rev. Mr. Davenport of Long Island* (Boston, 1742); *Mr. Pickering's Letter to Mr. Whitefield: Touching his Relation to the Church of England; his Impulses and Impressions; and the present unhappy state of Things, &c. Offered in Excuse of Mr. Pickering's Disinclination to open his Pulpit to him in his late Visit to Ipswich, &c.* (Boston, 1745); and a letter "To the Person suppos'd to be Mr. *Ebenezer Cleaveland;* now in Ipswich," *Boston Gazette,* March 18, 1746.

49 Theophilus Pickering, *A Bad Omen to the Churches of New-England: In the Instance of Mr. John Cleaveland's Ordination so termed, over a Separation in Chebacco-Parish in Ipswich; which was essayed by the Reverend Messieurs John Rogers Pastor of the Second Church in Kittery, and Nathaniel Rogers Pastor of the first Church in Ipswich, on the 25th of February, 1746,7* (Boston, 1747), 2, 4, 12.

50 John Cleaveland, *A Plain Narrative of the Proceedings which caused the Separation of a Number of aggrieved Brethren from the Second Church in Ipswich: or A Relation of the Cause which produced the Effects that are exhibited in the Reverend Mr. Pickering's late Print, Intitled, A bad Omen to the Churches* (Boston, 1747), 3.

51 Ibid., 4, and passim.

52 *The Pretended Plain Narrative Convicted of Fraud and Partiality* (Boston, 1748), 5, 26.

53 Cleaveland, *Short and Plain Narrative of the Late Work,* 38. Cleaveland's congre-

gation accepted members from other parishes from the outset and formulated this defense of their practice in 1748.

54 Isaac Stiles, *A Looking-Glass for Changelings: A Seasonable Caveat against Meddling with them that are given to Change* (New London, Conn., 1743), 15; see also chapter 2, parts I and II, of this volume.

55 See chapter 3, part III, of this volume.

56 Cleaveland, *Short and Plain Narrative of the Late Work*, 4.

57 Frothingham, *Articles of Faith and Practice*, 204–64.

58 Quoted in Goen, *Revivalism and Separatism*, 165.

59 Frothingham, *Articles of Faith and Practice*, 153–55, 185–86.

60 John Brunskill to William Dawson, Jan. 30, 1744, Papers of William Dawson, Manuscript Division, Library of Congress, Washington, D.C.; compare with Patrick Henry to William Dawson, Feb. 13, 1745, Dawson papers, reprinted in the *William and Mary Quarterly*, 2d ser., 1 (1921): 26–29.

61 *Virginia Gazette*, March 5, 1752; compare J. C. D. Clark, *English Society, 1688–1832* (Cambridge, 1985), 93–141, 216–35. Historians of colonial Virginia generally recognized that the Church and its clergy were expected to play a significant role in the maintenance of social and moral order. See Richard R. Beeman, "Social Change and Cultural Conflict in Virginia: Lunenburg County, 1746 to 1774," *William and Mary Quarterly*, 3d ser., 35 (1978): 455–76; Lee A. Gladwin, "Tobacco and Sex: Some Factors Affecting Non-Marital Sexual Behavior in Colonial Virginia," *Journal of Social History* 12 (1978): 57–75; James P. Walsh, "'Black Cotted Raskolls': Anti-Anglican Criticism in Colonial Virginia," *Virginia Magazine of History and Biography* 88 (1980): 21–36; Jack P. Greene, *Pursuits of Happiness: The Social Development of Early Modern British Colonies and the Formation of American Culture* (Chapel Hill and London, 1988), 97–100.

62 Rhys Isaac, *The Transformation of Virginia, 1740–1790* (Chapel Hill, 1982), 58–64, 115–54; John Frederick Woolverton, *Colonial Anglicanism in North America* (Detroit, 1984), 136–72; A. G. Roeber, "Authority, Law, and Custom: The Rituals of Court Day in Tidewater Virginia, 1720 to 1750," *William and Mary Quarterly*, 3d ser., 44 (1987): 27–52.

63 Foote, *Sketches of Virginia*, 1st ser., 136–37. The issue of the *Virginia Gazette* that carried this address has been lost.

64 Patrick Henry to William Dawson, April 29, 1747, Dawson papers.

65 For example, Patrick Henry to William Dawson, Dec. 3, 1747 and Aug. 22, 1751; James Maury to Thomas Dawson, Oct. 6, 1755; David Currie and John Leland to Thomas Dawson, April 12, 1758—Dawson papers.

66 Foote, *Sketches of Virginia*, 1st ser., 177; William Dawson to the Bishop of London, June 17, 1752, Dawson papers.

67 *Virginia Gazette*, Oct. 31, 1745. While indirect evidence suggests that the *Gazette* carried on a lively controversy over itinerancy, few issues containing controversial pieces have survived. See Isaac, *Transformation of Virginia*, 149–50; George William Pilcher, *Samuel Davies: Apostle of Dissent in Colonial Virginia* (Knoxville, Tenn., 1971), 27–34.

68 Davies, *State of Religion in Virginia*, 19, 31.

69 Davies, *State of Religion in Virginia*, 6–7.

70 Foote, *Sketches of Virginia,* 1st ser., 183–88, 209.

71 Samuel Davies to John Brunskill, Jan. 4, 1750, Dawson papers.

72 Foote, *Sketches of Virginia,* 1st ser., 160–61, 169; compare with Patrick Henry to William Dawson, June 8, 1747; Samuel Davies to William Dawson, Feb. 3, 1750; James Maury to Thomas Dawson, Oct. 6, 1755—Dawson papers.

73 Foote, *Sketches of Virginia,* 1st ser., 372–88; idem, 2d ser., 40–89, passim.

74 "The Representation of the corporation for ye Relief of poor & distressed Presbyterian Ministers & their Widows & children in the Province of Pensilvania, & of the Counties of New Castle Kent & Sussex upon Delaware," in *The Presbyterian Enterprise: Sources of American Presbyterian History,* ed. Maurice W. Armstrong, Lefferts A. Loetcher, and Charles A. Anderson (Philadelphia, 1956), 71.

75 *Virginia Gazette,* March 5, 1752.

76 *Virginia Gazette,* March 20, 1754.

77 *Virginia Gazette,* April 3, 1752.

78 *Virginia Gazette,* April 10, 1752.

79 See J. G. A. Pocock, *The Machiavellian Moment: Florentine Political Thought and the Atlantic Republican Tradition* (Princeton, 1975), 423–552; Bernard Bailyn, *The Ideological Origins of the American Revolution,* (Cambridge, Mass., 1967), 55–93.

80 Goen, *Revivalism and Separatism,* 107–11; Edwards, *Materials,* 2:114.

81 Robert B. Semple, *A History of the Rise and Progress of the Baptists in Virginia,* revised and extended by G. W. Beale (Richmond, 1894), 13.

82 Isaac, *Transformation of Virginia,* 194–205; idem, "Evangelical Revolt: The Nature of the Baptists' Challenge to the Traditional Order in Virginia, 1765 to 1775," *William and Mary Quarterly,* 3d ser., 31 (1974): 345–68; J. Stephen Kroll-Smith, "Transmitting a Revival Culture: The Organizational Dynamic of the Baptist Movement in Colonial Virginia, 1760–1777," *Journal of Southern History* 50 (1984): 551–68.

83 Edwards, *Materials,* 2:33–117 passim; Kroll-Smith, "Transmitting a Revival Culture," 551–68.

84 Edwards, *Materials,* 2:92.

85 Edwards, *Materials,* 2:35, 42, and passim; see also Beeman, "Social Change in Virginia," 455–76; Kroll-Smith, "Transmitting a Revival Culture," 559–66; D. W. Meinig, *The Shaping of America: A Geographical Perspective on 500 Years of History,* vol. 1, *Atlantic America, 1492–1800* (New Haven, 1986), 147, 159–60; Georgia C. Villaflor and Kenneth L. Sokoloff, "Migration in Colonial America: Evidence from the Militia Muster Roles," *Social Science History* 6 (1982): 544–52.

86 Edwards, *Materials,* 2:91.

87 Isaac, *Transformation of Virginia,* 161–77; idem, "Evangelical Revolt," 359–63.

88 Douglas, *Natural Symbols,* 14.

89 David Thomas, *Virginian Baptist: or, A View and Defense of the Christian Religion as it is Professed by the Baptists of Virginia* (Baltimore, 1774), 24–25.

90 James Craig to Thomas Dawson, Sept. 8, 1759, Dawson papers.

91 *Virginia Gazette* (Purdie & Dixon), July 4, 1771.

92 *Virginia Gazette* (Purdie & Dixon), May 30, 1771.

93 *Virginia Gazette* (Purdie & Dixon), October 4, 1770.

94 *Virginia Gazette* (Purdie & Dixon), Feb. 20, 1772.

95 *Virginia Gazette* (Purdie & Dixon), Feb. 20, 1772.

96 *Virginia Gazette* (Purdie & Dixon), Dec. 19, 1771; May 30, 1771.

Conclusion

1 Richard J. Hooker, ed., *The Carolina Backcountry on the Eve of the Revolution: The Journal and Other Writings of Charles Woodmason, Anglican Itinerant* (Chapel Hill, 1953), 13, 20.

2 Thomas Jefferson, *Notes on the State of Virginia,* ed. William Peden (New York, 1972), 108.

3 Quoted in Nathan O. Hatch, *The Democratization of American Christianity* (New Haven, 1989), 86.

4 "Remarks on the Maryland Government," *The American Magazine* 1 (Jan. 1741): 30. For similar metaphors, see David S. Shields, *Oracles of Empire: Poetry, Politics and Commerce in British America, 1690–1750* (Chicago, 1990), 21–36.

5 Bernard Bailyn, *The Peopling of British North America: An Introduction* (New York, 1986), 1–43.

6 Frank Lambert, "Subscribing for Profits and Piety: The Friendship of Benjamin Franklin and George Whitefield," *William and Mary Quarterly* 3d ser., 50 (1993): 529–54.

7 George Whitefield, *George Whitefield's Journals: A New Edition Containing Fuller Material Than Any Hitherto Published,* ed. William Wale and others (Edinburgh, 1960), 473; compare his comments on Charleston society, p. 384.

8 For the role of women in early American religious life, see Catherine A. Brekus, "'Let Your Women Keep Silence in the Churches': Female Preaching and Evangelical Religion in America, 1740–1845," Ph.D. diss. (Yale University, 1993).

9 Ebenezer Frothingham, *The Articles of Faith and Practice, with the Covenant, that is confessed by the Separate Churches of Christ in General in This Land* (Newport, R.I., 1750), 357–58.

10 Mary Cooper, *The Diary of Mary Cooper: Life on a Long Island Farm, 1768–1773,* ed. Field Horne (Oyster Bay, N.Y., 1981), x, xi, and passim.

11 James B. Taylor, *Virginia Baptist Ministers,* intro. J. B. Jeter, 1st ser. (New York, 1860), 1:23.

12 Samuel Hopkins, *Memoirs of the Life of Mrs. Sarah Osborn, who Died at Newport, Rhode Island, on the Second Day of August, 1796* (Worcester, Mass., 1799), 71–77; Mary Beth Norton, "'My Resting Reaping Times': Sarah Osborn's Defense of her 'Unfeminine' Activities," *Signs* 2 (1976): 515–29.

13 *Virginia Gazette* (Rind), October 27, 1768; February 16, 1769; *Virginia Gazette* (Purdie & Dixon), October 1, 1767; April 18, 1771; September 8, 1775; Billy G. Smith and Richard Wostowicz, *Blacks Who Stole Themselves: Advertisements for Runaways in the "Pennsylvania Gazette," 1728–1790* (Philadelphia, 1989), 97, 110, 208, 221, 230.

14 Richard Allen, *The Life Experience and Gospel Labors of the Rt. Rev. Richard Allen, to which is Annexed the Rise and Progress of the African Methodist Episcopal Church in the United States of America,* ed. George A. Singleton (Nashville, 1960), 18–20; John W. Davies, "George Liele and Andrew Bryan, Pioneer Negro Baptist Preachers," *Journal of Negro History* 3 (1918): 69–71. For another example of

early African-American itinerancy, see Graham R. Hodges, ed., *Black Itinerants of the Gospel: The Narratives of John Jea and George White* (Madison, Wis., 1992).

15 Albert J. Raboteau, *Slave Religion: The 'Invisible Institution' in the Antebellum South* (New York, 1978), 134–43.

16 Solomon Paine, *A Short View of the Difference between the church of Christ, and the Established churches in the Colony of Connecticut, in the Foundation and Practice, with Their Ends: Being Discovered by the Word of God and Certain Laws of Said Colony, Called Ecclesiastical* (Newport, R.I., 1752), reprinted in *The Great Awakening: Documents Illustrating the Crisis and Its Consequences,* ed. Alan Heimert and Perry Miller (Indianapolis and New York, 1967), 413.

17 Elisha Williams, *The essential Rights and Liberties of Protestants. A seasonable Plea for The Liberty of conscience, and the Right of Private Judgment* (Boston, 1744), 64–65.

18 Samuel Davies, *The State of Religion among the Protestant Dissenters in Virginia; in a Letter to the Rev. Mr. Joseph Bellamy, of Bethlehem, in New-England* (Boston, 1751), 21.

19 Solomon Paine, *A Short View of the Difference between the Church of Christ, and the established Churches of the colony of Connecticut*... (Newport, R.I., 1752), excerpted in *The Great Awakening,* ed. Heimert and Miller, 420; Ebenezer Frothingham, *A Key to Unlock the Door, That Leads in, to Take a Fair View of the Religious constitution, Established by Law, in the colony of Connecticut* (n.p., 1767), 204ff.

20 Morgan Edwards, *Materials Toward a History of the Baptists,* ed. Eve B. Weeks and Mary B. Warren, 2 vols. (Danielsville, Ga., 1984), 2:67–71.

21 Hatch, *Democratization of American Christianity,* 3–5.

22 Michael Warner, *The Letters of the Republic: Publication and the Public Sphere in Eighteenth-Century America* (Cambridge, Mass., 1990), 34.

23 T. H. Breen, "Narrative of Commercial Life: Consumption, Ideology and Community on the Eve of the American Revolution," *William and Mary Quarterly,* 3d ser., 50 (1993): 487.

24 John Butler, *Awash in a Sea of Faith: Christianizing the American People* (Cambridge, Mass., 1990), 165; idem, "Enthusiasm Described and Decried: The Great Awakening as Interpretative Fiction," *Journal of American History* 69 (1982): 305–25. See also Benedict Anderson, *Imagined Communities: Reflections on the Origins and Spread of Nationalism* (London, 1982), 28–49.

25 Leigh Eric Schmidt, *Holy Fairs: Scottish Communions and American Revivals in the Early Modern Period* (Princeton, 1989).

26 See Hatch, *Democratization of American Christianity,* 139; Jon Butler, *Awash in A Sea of Faith,* 181–82.

27 See chapter 4 of this volume; Hatch, *Democratization of American Christianity,* 49–122.

Index

Timothy D. Hall is Assistant Professor of
Early American History at Central Michigan University.

Library of Congress Cataloging-in-Publication Data
Hall, Timothy D., 1955–
Contested boundaries : itinerancy and the reshaping of the Colonial American religious world / Timothy D. Hall.
Includes index.
ISBN 0-8223-1511-4 (alk. paper).—ISBN 0-8223-1522-X (pbk. : alk. paper)
1. Great Awakening. 2. Itinerancy (Church polity)—History of doctrines—18th century. 3. Circuit riders—United States—History—18th century. I. Title.
BR520.H323 1994
277.3′07—dc20 94-17145CIP